Learning Perl/Tk

Learning Perl/Tk

Nancy Walsh

O'REILLY®

Beijing · Cambridge · Köln · Paris · Sebastopol · Taipei · Tokyo

Learning Perl/Tk
by Nancy Walsh

Copyright © 1999 O'Reilly & Associates, Inc. All rights reserved.
Printed in the United States of America.

Published by O'Reilly & Associates, Inc., 101 Morris Street, Sebastopol, CA 95472.

Editor: Linda Mui

Editorial and Production Services: TIPS—Technical Publishing, Inc.

Production Editor: Ellie Fountain Maden

Printing History:

January 1999:	First Edition.
March 1999:	Minor corrections.

This book is printed on acid-free paper with 85% recycled content, 15% post-consumer waste. O'Reilly & Associates is committed to using paper with the highest recycled content available consistent with high quality.

ISBN: 1-56592-314-6

Table of Contents

Preface

Perl is a great language for file processing, connecting to databases, and many other tasks that are too tedious to do manually. For many years, however, Perl programs were limited to a command-line interface. The Tk interface changed all that.

The Tk extension to Perl allows you to create graphical interfaces for your programs. Using the modules included with the distribution of Tk, you can create windows with buttons, lists, text, and other types of widgets to help your user navigate within your application.

What You Should Already Know

To get the most out of this book, you should already know the basics of Perl (specifically, Perl version 5). You should be familiar enough with Perl to be able to at least read some code and know what the code is doing. You don't have to be a Perl guru or Perl hacker to learn Perl/Tk, but it will help if you feel comfortable with the language. Here's the laundry list of things you should at least recognize: hashes, arrays, subroutines, and their anonymous versions, $_ and @_.

Perl/Tk utilizes the object-oriented features available in Perl 5, so even if you don't completely understand them, you should be able to recognize them when you see them. The only other thing you'll need is your prior knowledge of other graphical user interfaces (GUIs) and what you did and did not like about them. This helps when deciding what features to include in your own applications. Take a look at the word processor you use on your PC, your web browser, or any program that has buttons and scrollbars and accepts both mouse and keyboard input.

Those applications are pretty major ones; we'll start with much simpler examples and build up from there. We'll be covering each basic widget and all its associated options in detail. You'll learn how to make a window look the way you want it to look. You'll also learn how to make a window user-friendly and attractive.

If you want to know more about Perl in general, you should read *Learning Perl*, *Programming Perl, Advanced Perl Programming,* and *Perl Cookbook,* which are also published by O'Reilly & Associates, Inc. There are also numerous FAQs and documents available on the Web. This book's focus is the Tk extension to Perl, which is a fairly specific portion of Perl.

What's in This Book

Chapter 1, *Introduction to Perl/Tk*

> The first chapter contains some interesting history about Perl and the Tk module. It starts you out with a simple Hello World program and gives a short introduction to event-driven programs.

Chapter 2, *Geometry Management*

> Geometry management is probably the most important concept in using Perl/Tk. It determines how your widgets are to be drawn on the screen (or, in some cases, how not to be drawn on the screen). The three geometry managers—pack, grid, and place—are covered here. Most examples in the book use pack.

Chapter 3, *The Basic Button*

> The button is the first widget we cover and there are lots of details here. There are also tons of code snippets and screen shots showing different ways to manipulate and mutilate the button widget. Many of the options discussed here are common among the other standard widgets.

Chapter 4, *Checkbuttons and Radiobuttons*

> Checkbuttons and radiobuttons are similar to the standard button, but they look different and are usually programmed differently.

Chapter 5, *Label and Entry Widgets*

> The label is the simplest widget of all. It is usually used with an entry widget, which is why they are included in the same chapter. The entry widget will let you get input from your user.

Chapter 6, *Scrollbars*

> Certain widgets in Perl/Tk can be scrolled, which means they can contain more information than you can see on the screen. Scrollbars are used to navigate the data inside these widgets. Chapter 6 tells you how scrollbars communicate with each widget and what you need to do to create and use them.

Chapter 7, *The Listbox Widget*

A listbox can contain any sort of data, but it usually contains a list of options from which the user can select. In Chapter 7, you'll learn how to create the listbox, fill it with some items, and change the way the user selects the items from the list.

Chapter 8, *The Text Widget*

The text widget is a versatile widget you can use for many purposes besides just displaying text. Chapter 8 covers the different things you can put inside a text widget (such as text or other widgets) and how to get the best use out of them.

Chapter 9, *The Canvas Widget*

A canvas can display objects such as circles, rectangles, text, and even other widgets. Chapter 9 covers all the options and methods available and how to use them.

Chapter 10, *The Scale Widget*

The scale widget is great for giving the user a range of numbers from which to select so there is no possibility of a user typing in a number out of range or accidentally typing in letters. Chapter 10 includes examples of the scale widget and covers all the methods available for setting it up and using it.

Chapter 11, *Menus*

Once an application gets complex enough, you will need to put a menu in it. Chapter 11 shows different ways to create menus and how they can best be used in an application.

Chapter 12, *Frames*

The frame widget is used for organizing your other widgets on the screen to get the look you want. Chapter 12 shows how you can use frames in coordination with a geometry manager (covered in Chapter 2) to make your windows look the way you want them to.

Chapter 13, *Toplevel Widgets*

An application often needs more than one window in it. You can use a toplevel widget to create a second window. In Chapter 13 you'll learn how to create one and display it. We also cover the numerous methods available for manipulating toplevel widgets.

Chapter 14, *Binding Events*

One of the best ways to add functionality to your application is to add additional bindings to the widgets. This chapter tells you what a binding is and how to create one and use it.

Chapter 15, *Composite Widgets*
> You can combine widgets to make a much more useful, reusable widget. Many of the additional widgets you can use with Perl/Tk are created this way. Chapter 15 includes an example of a composite widget and gives you some ideas for creating your own.

Chapter 16, *Methods for Any Widget*
> There are several methods available for all widgets in Perl/Tk. We cover them in Chapter 16 and show you how to use them.

Appendix A, *Configuring Widgets with configure and cget*
> Appendix A explains the `configure` and `cget` methods, which are used with every widget. It also includes a table that shows the options and defaults for each widget option.

Appendix B, *Operating System Differences*
> Appendix B covers the differences you'll encounter when you use Perl/Tk on different operating systems, specifically, Unix and Win32.

Appendix C, *Fonts*
> Appendix C covers font usage for Tk, for both Unix and Win32 systems. It also covers the new font syntax in Tk8.

Reading Order

This book was designed and written with two major audiences in mind: people new to Perl/Tk and those who have experience with it.

Perl/Tk Novices

If you have no idea where to start, start at the beginning. This book is designed to lead you into topics by building a foundation of knowledge. We'll start simple with the button widget in Chapter 3, *The Basic Button*, and move up to more complicated widgets. Using Perl/Tk is not really that hard once you understand the basic fundamentals of how it works.

Somewhat Experienced to Gurus

Okay, so you've written a ton of programs with Perl/Tk and think you know how to do things. Chances are you have found a "way that works," and have stuck with it. I recommend reading through Chapter 2, *Geometry Management*, so you have a complete understanding of how the geometry managers work. Then skip around to the widget sections you are interested in. I have included useful snippets of code (and sometimes full programs) that will give you ideas on how to use widgets in different ways. The list of options for each widget are helpful reminders of all those pesky options and how they affect each widget.

Typographical Conventions

The following typographical conventions are used in this book:

Italic

> is used for filenames, command names, URLs, and emphasis. In syntax lines, it is used to identify replaceable values.

`Constant Width`

> is used for function and method names and their arguments, and to show literal code in text.

Bold

> is used to show default values in syntax lines.

We'd Like to Hear from You

We have tested and verified the information in this book to the best of our ability, but you may find that features have changed (which may in fact resemble bugs). Please let us know about any errors you find, as well as your suggestions for future editions, by writing to:

> O'Reilly & Associates, Inc.
> 101 Morris Street
> Sebastopol, CA 95472
> 1-800-998-9938 (in U.S. or Canada)
> 1-707-829-0515 (international/local)
> 1-707-829-0104 (fax)

You can also send us messages electronically. To be put on our mailing list or request a catalog, send email to:

> *info@oreilly.com*

To ask technical questions or comment on the book, send email to:

> *bookquestions@oreilly.com*

We have a web site for the book, where we'll list errata and plans for future editions. Here you'll also find all the source code from the book available for download so you don't have to type it all in.

> *http://www.oreilly.com/catalog/lperltk*

Acknowledgments

This book has taken quite a bit of time out of my life, and I would like to thank the people who helped make it possible and put up with me while I was off writing it: first, my husband Mike, who helped out in so many little ways it is impossible to list them all; our dogs, Brandy and Theo, for keeping my feet warm; our cats, Thumper and Sasha, for keeping the monitor and keyboard anchored to the desk (any typos are completely their fault); my co-worker, Kreg Webb, who suggested this whole crazy idea; and my editor, Linda Mui, for always coming up with positive things to say in addition to the not-so-good things.

I'd also like to thank all the reviewers of the book. They include: Stephen Lidie, Achim Bohnet, Peter Prymmer, Nick Ing-Simmons, and Phivu Nguyen.

1

Introduction to Perl/Tk

There are many different modules available that extend the functionality of Perl. This book will concentrate on the Tk module. The Tk module allows us to easily add a graphical interface to our Perl scripts and still use all the features that make Perl great. Instead of requiring a typed command with some options or user input on the command line, your program is invoked with an icon or a simple command and the interface handles everything from there.

The Tk extension to Perl doesn't come with the standard distribution of Perl.* You'll need to get it separately from a CPAN site and install it. After you install the Tk module, you simply add use Tk; to the top of your Perl scripts.

A Bit of History About Perl (and Tk)

Originally, Perl was written as a "quick-fix" to a problem Larry Wall was having with his job. Typical of all self-admittedly lazy people, he found a better and easier way to do it, and thus Perl was born. It has since evolved into a widespread and well-used language. Perl has been made available for numerous different platforms, has been well documented, and best of all, is license-fee free. Hopefully the reason you're looking at this book is because you're already converted to the way-of-Perl and want to know how to utilize it to the fullest.

The Tk extension to Perl handles all the widgets, whodads, and whatsits that combine to make a graphical interface. It was ported by Nick Ing-Simmons from Tcl/Tk for use with Perl. A common misconception is that you need Tcl/Tk installed in addition to Perl and Tk for the whole thing to work, but all you really need is Perl

---

* Unless you get the Win32 binary from CPAN, or another pre-built distribution such as ActiveState Perl.

and its Tk extension. Thanks to a lot of work by a lot of other people, self-admittedly lazy people like me can download the binary for the machine they have and install it in less than 10 minutes (download time not included). You can also compile it from source for your machine.

Perl/Tk for Both Unix and Windows 95/NT

As I was writing this book and cursing the fact that I didn't have enough machines at home to write this book with MS Word and test code examples on my Linux machine without booting back and forth from OS to OS, a miracle was happening. The Tk extension for Perl was ported to Windows. By Windows, I mean the overly-large, overly-influencing OS that is the default on most PCs nowadays, Microsoft Windows. Most people don't have C compilers for their Windows machines, but thanks to the work of Gurasamy Sarathy, there's a great binary distribution that has Perl and a good selection of the Perl extensions, including Tk. You simply download the binary, run the install, and you're ready to go.

There are no differences between the way you write Perl/Tk applications on a Unix machine and the way you write them on a Windows machine. You can use any simple text editor on either system. There is a small difference in the way you run them; see Appendix B, *Operating System Differences*, for details. For now, I'll just say that I prefer to run my Perl applications on Windows NT 4.0 (Service Pack 3) rather than Windows 95.

Versions

When I started writing this book, the latest and greatest versions of Perl and Tk were 5.003 and 400.202. Since then, a Win32 version of the Tk module has been developed and released. Perl has also had some changes. Right before the book was going to print, the port of Tk800.007 was in beta and Perl was up to 5.004_68 (also beta). I have made every effort to include information that is relevant to the new version of Tk and Perl and to test the examples with the new versions. There are certain instances (fonts, for example) where some significant functionality has been added in the new version of Tk. I have tried to note all the changes where they apply, but for the most part, you don't have to worry about which version you have.

Why Use a Graphical Interface?

Hopefully, you bought this book (or are considering it in the bookstore) because you have some idea of why you might want to use a graphical interface for one or more of your scripts. Just in case you don't, read on....

Because you are familiar with writing Perl scripts, you understand the ways you can get information in and out of one. It usually involves a combination of reading/writing files, command-line options, and possibly, data in or out at application runtime (STDIN/STDOUT, using pipes (|) or <>. Certain applications can run with no input, and others, such as an installation script, require constant information fed to it from the user: Do you want to install this file? Can I overwrite this DLL? Do you want to create this directory? Do you want the help files? Sometimes you can set up a bunch of defaults so the user just has to press return to say yes, but then they are stuck sitting at the keyboard and waiting for the next question to come up. Wouldn't it be nice to gather all that information up front and then have the user press a Go button to execute all the steps after the decisions were made?

A GUI interface adds a little flair and professionalism to an application. However, there are times when it would be overkill to add a GUI to a script. If all you are doing is reading in one file, munging a bit with no user input, and spitting out another, a GUI would be silly and unnecessary. GUI interfaces work best where you require a lot of decisions and input from the user, such as our installation example in the preceding paragraph.

Here are some examples of good uses for a graphical user interface:

- A mini web client that connects to a dictionary server and lets you look up words.

- An application that takes a regular expression as input and displays the state map graphically in a scrollable window.

- An application that interfaces with a database and displays query results in several widgets, with labels to indicate what the data is.

- A mail reader that interfaces with your inbox and can also send out mail messages.

- Sometimes your boss says "make it easy to use!" and that usually means either a wrapper around a script or an interface that makes it easy for users to understand the decisions they have to make. Your users also might be used to a graphical interface rather than a command-line interface.

Why Use Perl/Tk?

Have you ever tried to draw a window using so-called "native" facilities? If you do it in C, you'll end up with about 100 lines of code just to create a Hello World program, whether you use MS Windows or X Windows. This doesn't even include an Exit button that would allow you to quit the application nicely.

I have used several different methods to draw windows and create GUI applications throughout my programming life. Using the basic X Windows routines (such as X_Create_Line_from_x_to_y) is basically a drag. True, you have total control over every little detail, but then again, you have to control every little detail. Sometimes I like not knowing exactly how the button got drawn; it is enough for me to know that it did. (I drive a car, and don't exactly understand the intricate details of the combustion engine. I like that I can turn the key and succeed in my mission of driving to work.)

You have probably seen several books on Tcl/Tk. The problem with Tcl is that you have to program within the constraints of the Tcl language. I much prefer using a language that I already know really well and adding on to it.

Perl/Tk provides you with all the annoying little details. It handles the event loop. It handles drawing the 3D edges on your buttons (if you're not quite sure what I'm talking about, hang in there; I'll explain it all in due time). You can simply use the Perl language to "place a button here," which translates to real Perl as:

```
$mw->Button(-text =>  "Something")->pack();
```

In addition, because of the wonderful community Perl has, there are multitudes of different complex widget types available for use. If you can't find the perfect widget (such as a multi-listbox-selection-thingy with associated canvas), it is fairly simple to create your own by using a combination of some basic and/or not so basic widgets and constructs.

From a programmer's view the bottom line is that using Perl/Tk to write a GUI is fun! It is the best instant-gratification programming high. With just a few lines of code, you can instantly display a button and several other widgets that look like a full-blown application. Of course, it takes a bit more time to code the guts behind it, but it's almost as much fun.

As you go through this book, the best way to understand what is going on is to try lots of different examples. There are tons of working code snippets included for this very reason. Start with the basic Hello World program and change the options to the button as you go through Chapters 2 and 3. See what the results are on your very own screen.

Also, you might want to check out these tools (which we don't cover in this book, but they are fun to use): *tkpsh* and *ptksh* (new in Tk800.007, the latest version of Tk for Perl). You can download them from *http://www.monmouth.com/~beller*. Both programs allow you to type in code on STDIN and have it evaluate each statement (similar to *wish*).

Installing the Tk Module

Before we go into more details on using Perl/Tk, we should cover how to install it. There are many different ways to get Perl and Tk and install them on your machine. You can get the source and compile it (easy in Unix;, not so easy in MS Windows), or you can get a binary distribution and install that. Some of the binary distributions may not have all the components you want in it though, so make sure you read any README files included with the package.

The two major binary distributions for Perl on Win32 are available from ActiveState (*http://www.activestate.com*) and CPAN (*http://www.perl.com*). The binary distribution on CPAN includes the Tk module, so that's the one I'll cover here.

First you need to get Perl installed:

You can test to see if you already have the Tk module installed by using this command (both Unix and Win32):

```
perl -e 'use Tk'
```

If you don't get an error, you're ready to go. If you do get one, the error will look like this:

```
Can't locate Tk.pm in @INC (@INC contains: C:\PERL\lib\site C:\PERL\lib c:\
perl\lib c:\perl\lib\site c:\perl\lib\site .) at myscript line 1.
```

You'll need to find the Tk module on a CPAN site. Try starting with *http://www.perl.com/CPAN/modules/by-module/Tk/*. From that directory, find the following files: *Tk*readme* and *Tk*tar.gz* (always try to grab the latest versions; the * is for the version number). Be careful when you download the *.gz* file because some systems try to rename the file to *.tar.tar*. Simply rename the file back so that is has a *.tar.gz* extension and it will unzip properly. Follow the instructions in the README file to make sure that you have the right version of Perl already. After downloading *Tk*tar.gz*, you need to uncompress it using WinZip for MS Windows or *gunzip* and *tar -xvf* for Unix. Follow the instructions in the Install file once you have it unpacked. It is very similar to installing Perl itself.

Run the test

```
perl -e 'use Tk'
```

again to make sure it all worked correctly. For both MS Windows and Unix, make sure your *perl/bin* directory is in your PATH environment variable. You can then use the *widget* demo to see what types of widgets are available.

Creating Widgets

All widgets are created in the same basic fashion, with only a few exceptions. Each widget must have a parent widget to watch over it as it is created and keep track of it while it exists in the application. When you create an application, you'll have a central window that will contain other widgets. Usually, that window will be the parent of all the widgets inside it and any other windows you create in your application. You are creating an order to the widgets so the communication between child and parent widgets can happen automatically without any intervention from you once you set it all up.

Assuming that the `$parent` widget already exists, the generic usage when you create widget `Widgettype` is as follows:

```
$child = $parent->Widgettype( [ -option => value, . . . ] );
```

Note that the variables that store the widgets are scalars. Actually, they are references to widget objects, but you don't need to know that right now. If you aren't familiar with the object-oriented programming in Perl, using the `->` between the `$parent` and `Widgettype` invokes the method `Widgettype`, from the `$parent` object. It makes the `$parent` related to the child `$child`. As you might guess, the `$parent` becomes the parent of the widget being created. A parent can have many children, but a child can only have one parent. That's pretty much all there is to assigning children to their parents.

When you invoke the `Widgettype` method, there are usually configuration parameters that you send to set up the widget and interactions within the application. The configuration parameters will occur in pairs: an option and associated value. You will see options similar to `-text`, `-state`, or `-variable`. Notice that the options all start with a dash. Even with the dash, they are really just strings that are labels to indicate the next value to come in the list. Usually, it is not necessary to put quotation marks around the options because Perl is smart enough to recognize them as strings. However, if you are using the *-w* switch, Perl may complain about an option that it thinks is not text. You can stick quotes around all your options all the time to avoid this, but it shouldn't be necessary. The option names are always all lowercase (except in a few very rare cases, which are noted as we cover them).

Options are specified in list form like this:

```
(-option => value, -option => value, -option => value)
```

Don't be fooled by the funny-looking `=>`; it is just a different way of saying "comma." In fact, you could use just the commas and not the `=>` notation, that is:

```
(-option, value, -option, value, -option, value)
```

However, it's much harder to tell which are the option/value pairs. Consider the following syntactically equal statements (which each create a button widget that is 10 pixels by 10 pixels, displays the word "Exit," and performs the action of quitting the application when pressed):

```
$bttn = $parent->Button(-text, "Exit", -command, sub { exit }, -width, 10,
-height, 10);

$bttn = $parent->Button(-text => "Exit", -command => sub { exit }, -width =>
10, -height => 10);
```

In the second line, it is much more obvious which arguments are paired together. The option must be directly before the value associated with it: -text is paired with "Exit," -command has the value sub { exit }, and -width and -height both have values of 10.

Congratulations, we're not even done with the first chapter yet, and you already know how to read a typical line of Perl/Tk code!

Quick Definitions of Toplevel, MainWindow, and Frame Widgets

The next chapter covers geometry management, and several of the examples use widgets you don't know anything about yet. Most of the widgets are easy to figure out, but a few require a short introduction.

A MainWindow widget is a special version of a toplevel widget. Both MainWindow and toplevel are the windows that contains other widgets. The only difference between a toplevel and a MainWindow is that the MainWindow is the first window you create in your application. Both of these widgets are covered in greater detail in a later chapter (Chapter 13, *Toplevel Widgets*).

The other type of widget you need to know about is a frame widget. A frame is a container that can also contain other widgets. It is usually invisible and just used to arrange the widgets as desired. The frame widget is also discussed in its own chapter (Chapter 12, *Frames*).

Here is what each widget's creation code looks like:

```
$mw = new MainWindow; # or $mw = MainWindow->new();
$top = $mw->Toplevel();
$frame = $mw->Frame(-borderwidth => 2, -relief => "groove");
```

For now, just keep in mind the general meanings of MainWindow, toplevel, and frame widgets.

Coding Style

The code lines in a Perl/Tk script can get quite cumbersome and clunky because of all the option/value pairs used in defining and configuring each widget. There are several ways to format the code to deal with readability (and in some cases, "edit-ability"). Most just involve adding extra spaces or tabs to line up different portions of code. Once you get used to seeing the code, it won't appear to be quite so mysterious and unwieldy.

One coding style places each option/value pair on separate lines (this is my personal favorite, and I use it all the time):

```
$bttn = $parent->Button(-text => "my text",
                        -command => sub { exit },
                        -width => 10,
                        -height => 10);
```

With this type of coding style, it is extremely obvious what the pairs are and what value is associated with which option. (You could also go to the extreme of aligning each => to make nice columns, depending on how much time you have to press the space bar.) Some people like to start the option/value pairs on the next line and put the ending); on its own separate line, after the last option/value pair, which retains the comma for formatting ease:

```
$bttn = $parent->Button(
    -text => "Exit",
    -command => sub { exit },
    -width => 10,
    -height => 10,
    );
```

This makes the code easier to edit; an option/value pair can be added or deleted on each line without having to mess with parentheses, semicolons or commas. It also keeps the next lines closer to the left side of the page so if you have several indentation levels, you don't end up with code quite so deep to the right.

Sometimes, if there are only one or two option/value pairs, it just makes sense to leave them all on the same line and conserve a little bit of space:

```
$bttn = $parent->Button(-text => "my text", -command => sub { exit });
```

Eventually you'll come up with a style that works for the way you read the code and the way you edit it. Whichever way you choose, just try to be consistent throughout your scripts in case someone else takes over the maintenance of your code (it could even be you a year or more down the road).

Displaying a Widget

You use two separate commands to create a widget and display it, although sometimes they are squished into the same line, which makes them look like the same command. In the examples so far, we've used the `Button` method to create the button, but nothing is displayed by using that method alone. Instead you have to use a geometry manager to cause the widget to be displayed in its parent widget or in another widget. The most commonly used geometry manager is `pack`, and to use it, you simply call the `pack()` method on the widget object like this:

```
$widget->pack();
```

For example:

```
$button->pack();
```

There are arguments that can be sent to the `pack` method, but we'll cover those in Chapter 2, *Geometry Management*.

It is not necessary to invoke the `pack` method on a separate line. The `->pack` can be added to the creation of the widget:

```
$parent->Button(-text => "Bye!", -command => sub { exit })->pack();
```

The other geometry managers available are `grid` and `place`. All three behave differently, and which one you use often depends on the look you are trying to get in your application. Again, look for information on the geometry managers in Chapter 2.

The Anatomy of an Event Loop

When you are programming an application that uses a graphical interface rather than a textual interface, there are a lot of different things to consider. In a text-based application, you can read from standard input (STDIN), use command-line options, read files, or prompt the user for specific information. The keyboard is your only avenue of input from the user. In a GUI, input can not only come from those places, but it can also come from the mouse and the window manager (such as a "close" directive from a window manager like *mwm* or MS Windows). Although this extra input allows more flexibility in our applications, it also makes our job more difficult. As long as we tell it what to do, Perl/Tk helps us handle all that extra input gracefully.

Input in a GUI is defined by events. Events are typically different combinations of using the keyboard and mouse at the same or different times. If the user pushes the left mouse button on button "B", that is one type of event. Pushing the right mouse button on button "C" would be another event. Typing the letter "a" would be another event. Yet another event would be holding down the Control key and clicking with the middle mouse button. You get the idea.

Events are processed during an event loop. This event loop does just what its name says—it handles events during a loop. It determines what subroutines to call based on what type of event happened. Here is a pseudo-code event loop:

```
while (1) {
   get_event_info

   if event is left-mouse-click call process_left_mouse_click
   else if event is right-mouse-click call process_right_mouse_click
   else if event is keyboard-input call type_it
   else handle events for redrawing, resizing etc
}
```

Obviously, this is a very simplistic approach to an event loop, yet it still shows the basic idea. The event loop is a weeding-out process to determine what type of input was given to the application. For example, the subroutine `process_left_mouse_click` might determine where the pointer was when the mouse click occurred and then call other subroutines based on that information.

In Perl/Tk, the event loop is initiated by calling a routine called `MainLoop`. Anything prior to this statement is just setting up the interface. Any code after this call will not happen until after the GUI has been exited by using `$mw->destroy`.[*]

If we forget to include the `MainLoop` statement, the program will think about things for a while and then go right back to the command prompt. None of the windows, buttons, or widgets will be drawn at all. One of the first things that occurs after calling `MainLoop` is that the interface is drawn and the event loop is started.

Before we get too much further into the event loop and what it does (and what you need to do so it works right), let's look at a real, live, working program, Hello World. (You were expecting something else?)

Hello World Example

Every programming language goes through the Hello World example. It is a good example because it shows how to do something very simple but useful. In our

---

[*] Throughout the book, I will use $mw to indicate the variable that refers to the main window created at the beginning of the application.

Hello World example, we'll have the title of our window say "Hello World" and create a button that will dismiss the application:

```
#!/usr/bin/perl
use Tk;
my $mw = MainWindow->new;
$mw->title("Hello World");
$mw->Button(-text => "Done", -command => sub { exit })->pack;
MainLoop;
```

Despite only being six lines long, there is quite a bit going on in our little program. The first line, as any Perl programmer knows, invokes Perl (only on Unix; in Win32 you have to type *perl hello.pl* to invoke the program). The second line tells Perl that we would like to use the Tk module.

The third line

```
my $mw = MainWindow->new;
```

is how we create a window. The window will have the same basic window manager decorations as all your other windows. In a Unix environment, it will look like all your other windows, and if it were in MS Windows, it would look like those windows.

The title of our window is changed by using the `title` method. If we hadn't used this method, the text across the top of the window would be the same as the name of the file containing the code. For instance, if my code were stored in a file named *hello_world*, the string "Hello_world" would appear across the title bar of my application (Tk automatically capitalizes the first character for you). Using the `title` method is not required, but it makes the application look more polished.

Any string we put as an argument becomes the title. If I wanted the title to be "Hey! Look at my great program!" this would be the place. This is akin to using the *-title* option when starting up any standard X Windows application. There are more methods for a MainWindow object, which will be covered later in Chapters 12 and 13.

The next line creates a Button widget, sets basic properties, and packs it. (See Chapter 3, *The Basic Button*, for all available configuration options.)

The button is set up to display the text "Done" and to perform the Perl command `exit` when pushed. Finally, the last item of concern is the `MainLoop` command. This starts the event handler in motion, and from then on the application will do only what we have told it to do: If the user clicks on the button, the application will exit. Anything else the user does—minimizing, resizing, changing to other applications—will all be processed by the window manager and ignored by our application. See Figure 1-1 for a picture of the Hello World window.

Figure 1-1. Hello World window

Using exit Versus Using destroy

In all of the examples in this book you will see sub { exit; } used to quit the Perl/Tk application. This works fine as long as you have done a use Tk; in the same file that contains the sub { exit }. Perl/Tk defines its own exit routine which does some cleanup and various other things that are important to Tk. Another way to quit the Tk portion of the application is to call $mw->destroy(), which destroys the main window and returns to the code listed after MainLoop. The code after MainLoop will not be executed even if you use sub { exit }. Keep this in mind if you are going to be doing anything after the GUI portion is done.

Naming Conventions for Widget Types

Naming conventions? How boring! Well, sometimes our programs get so large and unwieldy that we can't remember what that stupid $button variable was pointing to. If there are over 10 buttons in our program, we would be hard-pressed to figure out which button was $button3 without digging through a bunch of code.

I'm merely going to suggest a naming convention, and if you like it, please use it! If not, either come up with your own, or hope you have a really good memory.

For buttons, I like to use _b, _bttn, or Button as a type of qualifier to the variable name. For instance, I would name my button in the Hello World example $done_b, $done_bttn, or $doneButton.

A specialized widget type is the very first window we create with the MainWindow method. I always use $mw as the variable name for this. You will see other programs use $main or $mainwindow as well.

Table 1-1 contains a list of widget types and my suggested naming conventions for them. Replace "blah" with a sensible description of the widget's purpose (e.g., exit). If you use this convention, you'll always know what type of widget you're working with.

Table 1-1. Naming conventions by widget type

Widget Type	Suggested Name	Examples
Button	$blah_b (or $blah_bttn, $blah-Button)	$exit_b, $apply_b, $newButton
Canvas	$blah_canvas or $blahCanvas	$main_canvas, $tinyCanvas
Checkbutton	$blah_cb or $blahCheckbutton	$uppercase_cb, $lowercaseCheckbutton
Entry	$blah_e or $blahEntry	$name_e, $addressEntry
Frame	$blah_f or $blahFrame	$main_f, $left_f, $canvasFrame
Label	$blah_l or $blahLabel	$name_l, $addressLabel
Listbox	$blah_lb or $blahListbox	$teams_lb, $teamsListbox
Menu	$blah_m or $blahMenu	$file_m, $edit_m, $helpMenu
Radiobutton	$blah_rb or $blahRadiobutton	$blue_rb, $grey_rb, $redRadiobutton
Scale	$blah_scale or $blahScale	$age_scale, $incomeScale
Scrollbar	$blah_scroll (or $blah_sbar) or $blahScroll	$x_scroll, $yScroll
Text	$blah_t (or $blahText)	$file_txt, $commentText
Toplevel	$blah_w or $blahWindow	$main_w, $fileopenWindow

I admit I don't follow my own rules all the time. Throughout this book, you'll see me use just $button in example code. I'll use $button1 and $button2 if there are two in the example. Anything larger than just a few lines, I will try (scout's honor?) to use my own convention. I will always use a name that indicates what type of widget I'm referring to.

Using print for Diagnostic/Debugging Purposes

Normally, you'll run your Perl/Tk program by typing the program name at the command prompt:

```
% hello_world
```

or

```
C:\>perl hello_world
```

When you invoke the program this way, any output created by using a print (or printf) is to that terminal window. Sometimes, you won't see the information actually printed until you quit the program. This is probably because you didn't put a \n on the end of the string to be printed, which causes an automatic flushing of output. During your application processing, if you think you aren't seeing a print statement when you should be, make sure a \n is on the print statement.

Designing Your Windows (A Short Lecture)

Before you decide what events to handle, it is worthwhile to spend some time sketching out a few windows on paper and deciding what should happen (from the user's perspective) when you click a button or invoke a menu item.

One of the most important things to keep in mind when you design your application's windows is that nothing happens until that event loop starts up. Everything prior to the call to `MainLoop` is just preparation for the event loop.

A GUI often makes the application look much more polished and purposeful than a command-line interface does. Also, it is often much easier to manipulate many different kinds of user input through a GUI.

Here are some things to consider when you are deciding what the GUI should look like:

- Every widget should have a purpose. It should be intuitive and informative.

- Think about the way a user will use an application and design it accordingly.

- Don't try to cram everything your application is doing into one window.

- Don't always try to separate everything into different windows. Sometimes the application is so simple that one window is all you need.

- Colors are great, but there are a lot of color-blind people out there. If you insist on using color, allow it to be customized via a file or through the application itself.

- Some widgets do their job better than others do. Use the right widget for the right job.

That's it for the lecture. Now, get ready to learn the ropes.

2

Geometry Management

To display widgets on the screen, they must be passed to a geometry manager. The geometry manager controls the position and size of the widgets in the display window. There are several geometry managers available with Perl/Tk: pack, place, and grid.

All three geometry managers are invoked as methods on the widget, but they all have their own methodologies and arguments to change where and how the widgets are put on the screen:

```
$widget1->pack(); $widget2->place(); $widget3->grid();
```

When you organize the widgets in your window, it is often necessary to separate groups of widgets to get a certain look and feel. For instance, when you use pack(), it is difficult to have widgets stacked both horizontally and vertically without grouping them in some fashion. We group widgets by using a frame widget inside a window or by using another window (a toplevel widget).

We create our first window by calling MainWindow. The MainWindow is a special form of a toplevel widget. For more detailed information on how to create/configure frames and toplevel widgets, see Chapter 12, *Frames*, and Chapter 13, *Toplevel Widgets*.

Because of the differences between the three geometry managers, it is difficult (not entirely impossible, but definitely not recommended) to use more than one geometry manager within the same area. In our $mw, I can display many types of widgets, but if I start using pack(), I should continue to use pack() on all of the widgets contained directly in $mw. I wouldn't want to switch in the middle to using grid(). Because a window can contain a frame, which in turn contains other widgets, we use pack() to pack the frame inside the main window and then we could use grid() to manage the widgets inside the frame. See Figure 2-1.

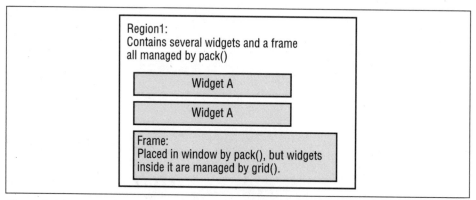

Figure 2-1. Frame within a window that uses a different geometry manager

Although the different geometry managers have their own strengths and weaknesses, the most commonly used is `pack()`, so I'll discuss it first and in the most detail. The `grid()` geometry manager was under development as I was writing this book. `grid` has been improved greatly with the release of Tk 8.0 and subsequent porting to Perl. The `place()` geometry manager is the most tedious to use because you have to determine exact coordinates for every single widget.

Pack

Remember when you were a small child and you had those wooden puzzles to put together? They often had cute little pictures of animals on them. Each piece in the puzzle had exactly one place where it could go, and there weren't any overlaps allowed between pieces.

With the **pack** geometry manager, our windows are similar to the wooden puzzle because widgets cannot overlap or cover each other (partially or completely). See Figure 2-2. If a button is packed in a certain space on the window, the next button (or any widget) will have to move around the already packed button. Luckily, our windows will only be dealing with rectangular shapes instead of funny-shaped puzzle pieces.

The order in which you pack your widgets is very important because it directly affects what you see on the screen. Each frame or toplevel maintains a list of items that are displayed within it. This list has an order to it; if widget A is packed before widget B, then widget A will get preference. This will become clear as we go through some examples. You will often get a very different look to your window just by packing the widgets in a different order.

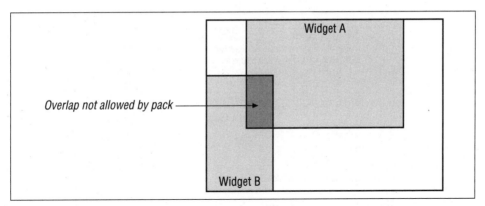

Figure 2-2. Overlap error

If you don't care what the window looks like and how the widgets are put in it, you can use **pack()** with no arguments and skip the rest of this chapter. Here it is again:

```
$widget->pack();
```

To make your window look nicer and more manageable (and user friendly), there are arguments that can be sent to the **pack** method that will change the way the widgets and the window looks. As with anything in Perl/Tk, the arguments are arranged in pairs. So the more sophisticated usage would be:

```
$widget->pack( [ option => value, ... ] );
```

Here is the code to create a window that doesn't use any options to **pack()**. Figure 2-3 shows the resulting window (I know we haven't covered all the widgets used in this example, but hang in there, it's pretty simple).

```
#!/usr/bin/perl -w
use Tk;

my $mw = MainWindow->new;
$mw->title("Bad Window");
$mw->Label(-text => "This is an example of a window that looks bad\nwhen you
don't send any options to pack")->pack;

$mw->Checkbutton(-text => "I like it!")->pack;
$mw->Checkbutton(-text => "I hate it!")->pack;
$mw->Checkbutton(-text => "I don't care")->pack;
$mw->Button(-text => "Exit",
            -command => sub { exit })->pack;
MainLoop;
```

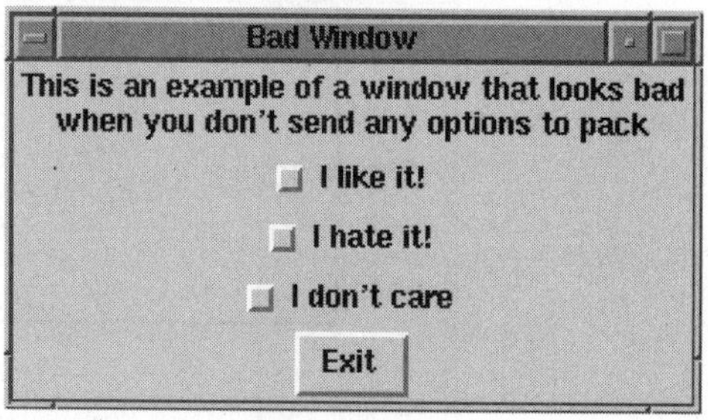

Figure 2-3. Window with widgets managed by pack

We can alter the preceding code and add some options to the `pack()` calls that will make our window look much nicer:

```
#!/usr/bin/perl -w
use Tk;

my $mw = MainWindow->new;
$mw->title("Good Window");
$mw->Label(-text => "This window looks much more organized, and less
haphazard\nbecause we used some options to make it look nice")->pack;

$mw->Button(-text => "Exit",
            -command => sub { exit })->pack(-side => 'bottom',
                                             -expand => 1,
                                             -fill => 'x');
$mw->Checkbutton(-text => "I like it!")->pack(-side => 'left',
                                              -expand => 1);
$mw->Checkbutton(-text => "I hate it!")->pack(-side => 'left',
                                              -expand => 1);
$mw->Checkbutton(-text => "I don't care")->pack(-side => 'left',
                                                -expand => 1);
MainLoop;
```

Figure 2-4 shows the much more organized window.

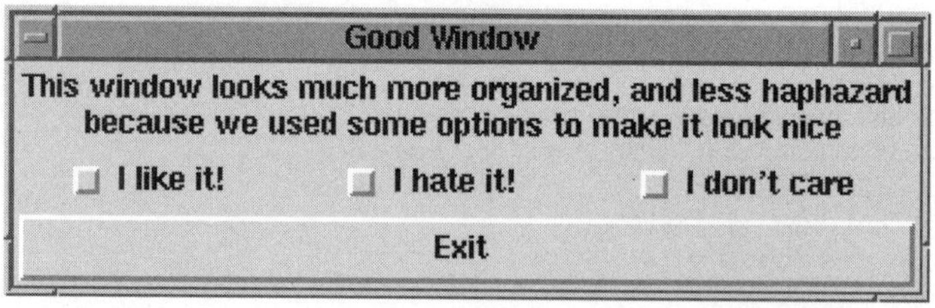

Figure 2-4. Window with widgets managed by pack using some options

Using `pack()` allows you to control:

- Position in the window relative to the window or frame edges
- Size of widgets, relative to other widgets or absolute
- Spacing between widgets
- Position in the window's or frame's widget list

The options, values, and defaults are listed and discussed in the following section.

Pack Options

This list shows all the options available when you call `pack()`. The default values are shown in bold (which indicates if you don't use that option, you'll get the effects of that value for that option).

`-side => 'left' | 'right' | 'top' | 'bottom'`
Puts the widget against the specified side of the window or frame

`-fill => 'none' | 'x' | 'y' | 'both'`
Causes the widget to fill the allocation rectangle in the specified direction

`-expand => 1 | 0`
Causes the allocation rectangle to fill the remaining space available in the window or frame

`-anchor => 'n' | 'ne' | 'e' | 'se' | 's' | 'sw' | 'w' | 'nw' | 'center'`
Anchors the widget inside the allocation rectangle

`-after => $otherwidget`
Puts `$widget` after `$otherwidget` in packing order

`-before => $otherwidget`
Puts `$widget` before `$otherwidget` in packing order

`-in => $otherwindow`
Packs `$widget` inside of `$otherwindow` rather than the parent of `$widget`, which is the default

`-ipadx => `*amount*
Increases the size of the widget horizontally by *amount* × 2

`-ipady => `*amount*
Increases the size of the widget vertically by *amount* × 2

`-padx => `*amount*
Places padding on the left and right of the widget

`-pady => `*amount*
Places padding on the top and bottom of the widget

Positioning Widgets

Each window (or frame) has four sides to it: top, bottom, left, and right. The packer uses these sides as points of reference for widgets. By default, `pack()` places the widgets against the top of the toplevel or frame.

You can control what side a widget is placed against by using the `-side` option:

```
-side => 'left' | 'right' | 'top' | 'bottom'
```

For example, if we would like our button against the left edge of the window, we can specify `-side => 'left'`.

Using our Hello World example as a base, let's look at what happens when we pack our button against the different sides. The only line we will change is the `->pack` part of the Button creation line. We'll also change the "Hello World" string in the `$mw->title` command to easily show the new options to pack.

```perl
$mw->Button(-text => 'Done',
    -command => sub { exit })
->pack(-side => 'top');
```

OR

```perl
$mw->Button(-text => 'Done',
    -command => sub { exit })
->pack;
```

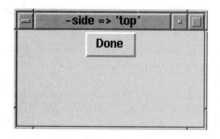

```perl
$mw->Button(-text => 'Done',
    -command => sub { exit })
->pack(-side => 'bottom');
```

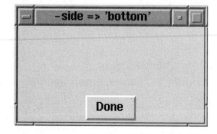

```perl
$mw->Button(-text => 'Done',
    -command => sub { exit })
->pack(-side => 'left');
```

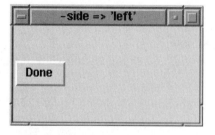

```
$mw->Button(-text => 'Done',
    -command => sub { exit })
->pack(-side => 'right');
```

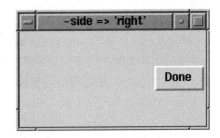

The windows shown here have been made a bit larger to emphasize the difference that using alternative values for -side makes. Normally, the window will be only as large as required to show the button. When you are deciding which way to place widgets in a window, it is always a good idea to see what happens when you make the window both larger and smaller. Make sure the behavior you get is what you want.

So far, pack() seems pretty simple, but what if you want to put more than one button in your application? What happens when we simply add more buttons?

```
$mw->Button(-text => 'Done1', -command => sub { exit })->pack;
$mw->Button(-text => 'Done2', -command => sub { exit })->pack;
$mw->Button(-text => 'Done3', -command => sub { exit })->pack;
$mw->Button(-text => 'Done4', -command => sub { exit })->pack;
```

Since the default -side is top, we would expect them to all be mushed up against the top of the window, right? Sort of. The packer allocates space for each widget and then manipulates the widget inside that space and the space inside the window.

Figure 2-5 shows what the window with the four Done buttons looks like; the next section explains why.

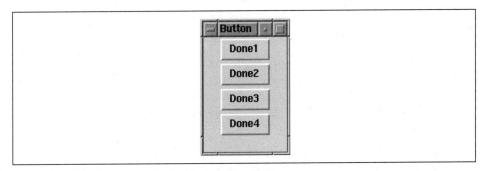

Figure 2-5. Four buttons packed with default settings

Allocation Rectangles

When given an item to pack, the packer first looks to see which side (top, bottom, right, or left) to use. It then sets aside an invisible rectangular area across the length of that side for use only by that widget.

In Figure 2-6, the solid-line rectangle represents our empty window (or frame), and the dotted-line rectangle is the rectangular area that the packer sets aside for the first button. It actually does go all the way across the width or height of the window, but to make it easier to see, it's shown a little indented.

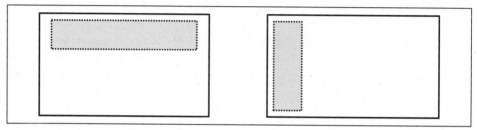

Figure 2-6. Rectangular areas set aside by packer when using -side => 'top' and -side => 'left'

The dimensions for the dotted-line box, which we'll call the allocation rectangle, are calculated based on the size of the requesting widget. For both the top and bottom sides, the allocation rectangle is as wide as the window and only as tall as the widget to be placed in it. For the right and left sides, the allocation rectangle is as tall as the window but only as wide as required to fit the widget.

Our examples so far have used buttons in which the text of the button determines the width of the button. If we create a button with the text "Done" on it and one with the text "Done, Finished, That's it," the second button is going to be much wider than the first. When these two buttons are placed up against either the right or left side of the window, the second button would have a wider allocation rectangle than the first. If we placed those same two buttons against the top and the bottom, the allocation rectangles would be the same height and width because the width is determined by the window, not the widget.

After the size of the allocation rectangle is determined, the widget is placed within the allocation rectangle according to other options passed and/or the default values of those options. I will go over those options and how they can affect the allocation rectangle later.

Once the first widget has been placed in the window, the amount of area available for subsequent allocation rectangles is smaller because the first allocation rectangle has used some of the space (see Figure 2-7).

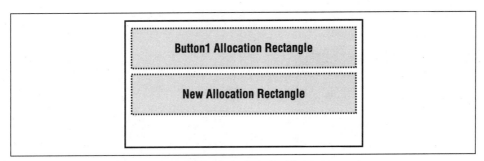

Figure 2-7. Second allocation rectangle when default side 'top' is used

When more than one button is placed against different sides in the same window, the results will vary depending on the order used.

We'll start by placing one button along the top, one along the bottom, and then buttons right and left:

```
$mw->Button(-text => "TOP", -command => sub { exit })
    ->pack(-side => 'top');

$mw->Button(-text => "BOTTOM", -command => sub { exit })
    ->pack(-side => 'bottom');

$mw->Button(-text => "RIGHT", -command => sub { exit })
    ->pack(-side => 'right');

$mw->Button(-text => "LEFT", -command => sub { exit })
    ->pack(-side => 'left');
```

The allocation rectangles for this window would look like the diagram in Figure 2-8.

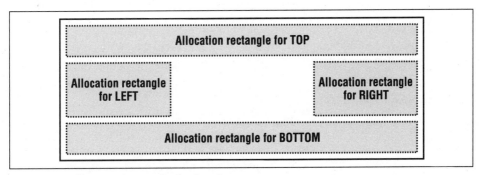

Figure 2-8. Allocation rectangles for four buttons

Figure 2-9 shows what the actual window looks like, both normal size and resized so it's a bit larger.

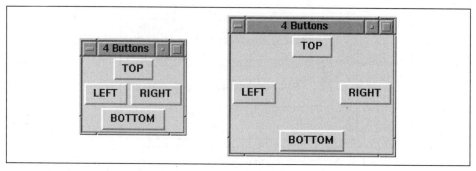

Figure 2-9. Four buttons placed around the sides of the window

Filling the Allocation Rectangle

Normally, the widget is left at the default size, which is usually smaller than the allocation rectangle created for it. If the -fill option is used, the widget will resize itself to fill the allocation rectangle according to the value given. The possible values are:

```
-fill => 'none' | 'x' | 'y' | 'both';
```

Using the value 'x' will resize the widget in the x direction. Likewise, 'y' will cause the widget to resize in the y direction. Using -fill => 'both' is a good way to see exactly what size and placement was given to the allocation rectangle because 'both' resizes the widget in both x and y directions. Using our four-button example again, we'll specify -fill => 'both'.

```
$mw->Button(-text => "TOP", -command => sub { exit })
  ->pack(-side => 'top', -fill => 'both');

$mw->Button(-text => "BOTTOM", -command => sub { exit })
  ->pack(-side => 'bottom', -fill => 'both');

$mw->Button(-text => "RIGHT", -command => sub { exit })
  ->pack(-side => 'right', -fill => 'both');

$mw->Button(-text => "LEFT", -command => sub { exit })
  ->pack(-side => 'left', -fill => 'both');
```

Figure 2-10 shows the resulting window.

If we switch the button we create first, we get a different result. The window in Figure 2-11 was created by packing the widgets in this order: left, right, top, bottom.

Figure 2-12 demonstrates yet another order, which really shows that the allocation rectangles change size depending on what gets packed first.

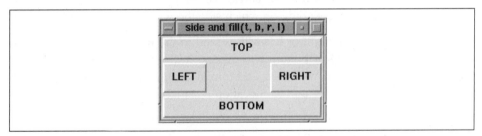

Figure 2-10. Four buttons packed to each side using -fill => 'both'

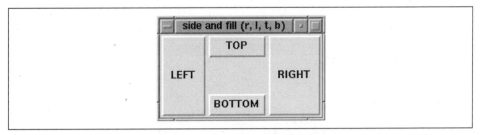

Figure 2-11. Four buttons packed to each side in a different order using -fill => 'both'

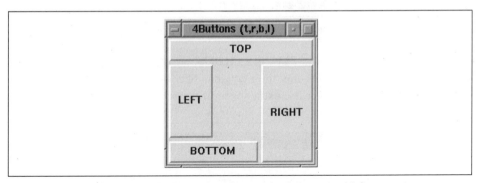

Figure 2-12. Four buttons packed in order of top, right, bottom, and left

A common use of **-fill** is on widgets with scrollbars: listbox, canvas, and text. Usually, the scrollbars are along the edge of the window, and you want the listbox to fill the remaining area. See Chapter 6, *Scrollbars*, and Chapter 7, *The Listbox Widget*, for more information.

Expanding the Allocation Rectangle

The **-expand** option manipulates the allocation rectangle and not the widget inside it. The value associated with **-expand** is a boolean value.

```
-expand => 1 | 0
```

Given a true value, the allocation rectangle will expand into any available space left over in the window depending on which side the widget was packed.

Widgets packed with side right or left will expand in the horizontal direction. Widgets packed with side top or bottom will expand in the vertical direction. If more than one widget is packed with -expand turned on, the extra space in the window is divided evenly among all the allocation rectangles that want it.

In Figure 2-9 or 2-10, you saw that there was some space left in the center of the window that wasn't occupied by any widget. If we change the code and add -expand => 1 to the list of pack options for each button, the result is the window in Figure 2-13.

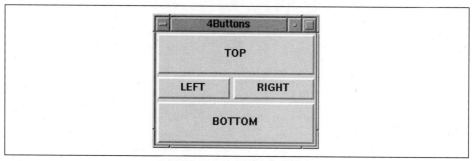

Figure 2-13. Four buttons using the -expand => 1 and -fill => 'both' options

Note that Figure 2-13 left the -fill => 'both' option in the code. If we omit the -fill option, the buttons stay their original size, but the allocation rectangles (which are invisible) take over the extra space in the window (see Figure 2-14).

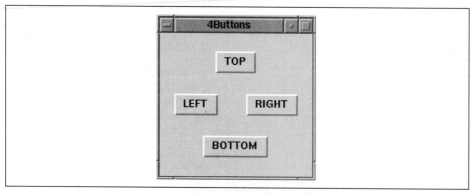

Figure 2-14. Four buttons using -expand => 1 and -fill => 'none'

In Figure 2-14, the buttons are centered in their allocation rectangles because of the default value of the -anchor option, which is 'center'.

Anchoring a Widget in Its Allocation Rectangle

The anchor option manipulates the widget inside the allocation rectangle by anchoring it to the place indicated by the value passed in. It uses the points of a compass as a reference.

```
-anchor => 'e' | 'w' | 'n' | 's' | 'ne' | 'nw' | 'se' | 'sw' | 'center'
```

Figure 2-15 shows those locations in an example allocation rectangle.

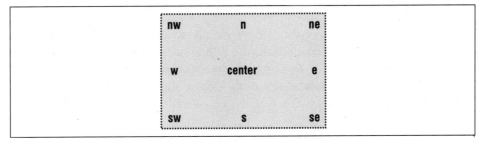

Figure 2-15. Allocation rectangle with -anchor points labeled

The default for -anchor is 'center', which keeps the widget in the center of its allocation rectangle. Unless the -expand option is set to a true value, this won't seem to change much of anything in the window. As seen in Figure 2-16, which shows the result of using the -expand => 1 option, it is obvious that the widget sticks to that center position when the window is resized.

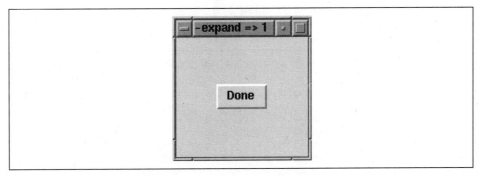

Figure 2-16. Default behavior of -anchor with -expand set to 1

If all other defaults are used to pack the widget, Figure 2-17 shows what -anchor => 'e' and -anchor => 'w' does.

Remember that the allocation rectangle is created based on which side the widget is packed against, so certain combinations will appear to have not had any effect. For example:

```
$mw->Button(-text => "Done", -command => sub { exit })
   ->pack(-side => 'top', -anchor -> 'n');
```

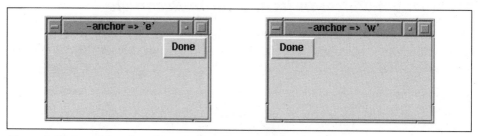

Figure 2-17. Examples of -anchor => 'e' and -anchor => 'w'

This code fragment will leave the widget exactly where it was if the −anchor option had not been specified because the allocation rectangle does not change size at all. If the −expand option is also specified, then when the window is resized, the widget would stick to the north side of the window. If −anchor => 's' had been specified, when the window is resized, the widget would stick to the south side of the window.

The −anchor option is more often used to line up several widgets in a row. Figure 2-18 and Figure 2-19 show two common examples.

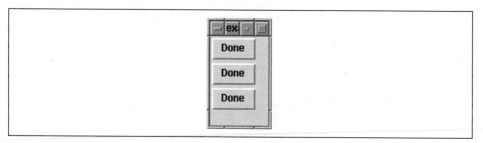

Figure 2-18. Window with three buttons all packed with -side => 'top', -anchor => 'w'

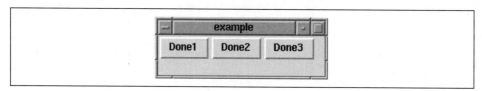

Figure 2-19. Windows with three buttons all packed with -side => 'left', -anchor => 'n'

Sometimes, when −side and −anchor are used together, the results don't seem to be what you would expect at first glance. Always keep in mind that invisible allocation rectangle and how it affects what you see on the screen.

Widget Order in the Window

Each window that has widgets packed into it keeps track of those widgets in an ordered list. The order of this list is normally determined by the order in which the widgets were packed. The last item packed is the last item in the list. Using the -after option, you can change the default order by specifying which widget should be placed after your new widget. On the opposite end, if you use the -before option, you can put the new widget before a previously packed widget:

```
-after => $otherwidget
-before => $otherwidget
```

As an example, let's create four buttons ($widget1, $widget2, $widget3, $widget4) and only pack three to begin with. The **pack** command for $widget4 might then be:

```
$widget4->pack(-after => $widget1);
```

Figure 2-20 shows two windows: one before $widget4 is packed and one after $widget4 is packed.

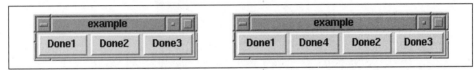

Figure 2-20. On left: the window with three buttons packed in order. On right: the button with Done4 label was packed using -after => $widget1

If we want to put $widget4 in front of $widget1, we use this command, and see the results in Figure 2-21.

```
$widget4->pack(-before => $widget1);
```

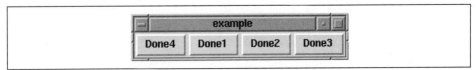

Figure 2-21. Button with Done4 label was packed using -before => $done1

Padding the Size of the Widget

The final way to force pack to size the widget is to use the padding options. The first set of padding options affects the widget itself by adding to its default size. Different amounts can be added in the x and y direction, or they can be the same. To specify how much padding should occur in the x direction, use the `-ipadx` option:

```
-ipadx => amount
```

Specify padding for the y direction like this:

```
-ipady => amount
```

The *amount* is a number that is a valid screen distance. I'll discuss the definition of a valid screen distance in the next section.

Both the `-ipadx` and `-ipady` options change the size of the widget before the allocation rectangle is calculated. `-ipadx` adds the amount specified to both the right and left sides of the widget. The overall width of the widget would increase by (2 x *amount*). `-ipady` adds to the top and bottom of the widget, causing the overall height of the widget to increase by (2 x *amount*). Figure 2-22 shows how the `-ipadx` and `-ipady` options affect a button.

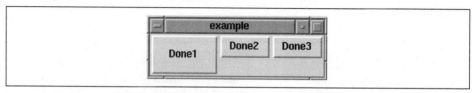

Figure 2-22. The Done1 button was created with options: -ipadx => 10, -ipady => 10

The other kind of padding is inserted between the edge of the widget and the edge of the allocation rectangle and is done with the `-padx` and `-pady` options:

```
-padx => amount
-pady => amount
```

Using `-padx` and `-pady` does not affect the size of the widget, but it does affect the size of the allocation rectangle. It acts as a buffer around the widget, protecting it from having to touch other widgets. Figure 2-23 shows the effects of using `-padx` and `-pady`.

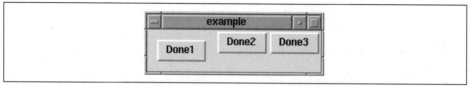

Figure 2-23. The Done1 button was created with options -padx => 10, -pady => 10

A good way to remember the difference between `-ipadx/y` and `-padx/y` is that the "i" stands for "inside the widget" or "internal padding."

Valid screen distances

Many times you'll see options that require values specified in screen units (or what is called a valid screen distance). The options -ipadx and -ipady are examples of this type of option. Always check to see what value the option actually requires.

A screen unit is a number followed by a designation for the unit to use. If there is no designation, the units are in pixels. Table 2-1 shows all the possibilities.

Table 2-1. Valid screen units

Designator	Meaning	Examples
(none)	Pixels (default)	20, 30, "20", "40"
c	Centimeters	'3c', '4c', "3c"
i	Inches	'2i', "3i"
m	Millimeters	'4m', "4m"
p	Printer points (1/72 inch)	"72p", '40p'

To use these designators, it is necessary to use quotes (either single or double) around the value. Here are some examples:

```
$button->pack(-ipadx => 20);      # 20 pixels
$button->pack(-ipadx => '20');    # Also 20 pixels
$button->pack(-ipadx => "1i");    # 1 inch
$button->pack(-ipadx => '1m');    # 1 millimeter
$button->pack(-ipadx => 1);       # 1 pixel
$button->pack(-ipadx => "20p");   # 20 printer points
```

Remember that a "p" designator does not stand for pixels, but printer points. I recommend always using pixels as your unit of measure. Different screens display different resolutions; one screen might display an actual inch and another might display something else.

Displaying in a Parent Other Than Your Own

By default, when a widget is packed, it is packed inside the region that created it. Sometimes it is necessary to display a widget inside a different region. Use the -in option to do so:

```
-in => $otherwindow
```

It puts the new widget at the end of the packing order for the $otherwindow and displays it accordingly. All other options specified in the pack() call still apply.

Methods Associated with Pack

There are a few methods that are used in conjunction with the pack geometry manager. They allow the programmer to get information about either the widget that has been packed or the parent widget in which other widgets are packed.

Unpacking a widget

To unpack a widget from a window or frame, use the `packForget` method:

```
$widget->packForget();
```

`packForget` makes it look like the widget disappears. The widget is not destroyed, but it is no longer managed by pack. The widget is removed from the packing order, so if it were repacked later, it would appear at the end of the packing order.

Retrieving pack information

To return a list containing all the pack-configuration information about a widget, use `packInfo`:

```
@list = $widget->packInfo();
```

The format of the list is in option/value pairs. The first pair in the list is `-in` and the current window that contains `$widget` (usually also the parent). This is an example of the information returned from `packInfo`:

```
-in MainWindow=HASH(0x818dcf4) -anchor n -expand 0 -fill none -ipadx 0 -ipady
0 -padx 10 -pady 10 -side left
```

From this, we can tell that we packed our `$widget` into the main window rather than a frame. Since the list has a "paired" quality to it, we could easily store the result from `packInfo` in a hash and reference the different option values by using a key to the hash:

```
%packinfo = $widget->packInfo;
print "Side used: ", $packinfo{-side}, "\n";
```

Disabling and enabling automatic resizing

When you put a widget inside a window, the window (or frame) will resize itself to accommodate the widget. If you are dynamically placing widgets inside your window while the program is running, the window will seem to bounce from size to size. You can turn off this behavior by using `packPropagate` on the frame or toplevel widget:

```
$widget->packPropagate(0);
```

If set to 0 or `'off'`, `packPropagate` changes the behavior of the widget so that it doesn't resize to accommodate items packed inside of it. When a false value is sent to `packPropagate` before widgets are placed inside it, this automatic resizing doesn't happen, so you can't see any of the widgets placed inside the parent until it is manually resized. If you call `packPropogate` after the widgets have been placed inside it, the widget will ignore any size changes from its child widgets.

Listing widgets

You can determine the widgets your frame or toplevel holds with the `packSlaves` method:

```
@list = $parentwidget->packSlaves();
```

`packSlaves` returns an ordered list of all the widgets that were packed into the `$parentwidget`. An empty string (or empty list) is returned if no widgets were packed into `$parentwidget`.

The list returned from `packSlaves` looks like this:

```
Tk::Button=HASH(0x81b2970) Tk::Button=HASH(0x8116ccc)
Tk::Button=HASH(0x81bcdd4)
```

Each item is a reference to a packed widget and can be used to configure it. For example, you can increase the size of each widget by 20 in both the x and y directions by looping through it and "packing" it with new information. Using our good window example in Figure 2-4, we can add a button that will contain a subroutine that uses `packSlaves`:

```
$mw->Button(-text => "Enlarge",
            -command => \&repack_kids)->pack(-side => 'bottom',
                                             -anchor => 'center');
sub repack_kids {
  my @kids = $mw->packSlaves;
  foreach (@kids) {
    $_->pack(-ipadx => 20, -ipady => 20);
  }
}
```

Figure 2-24 shows the resulting window.

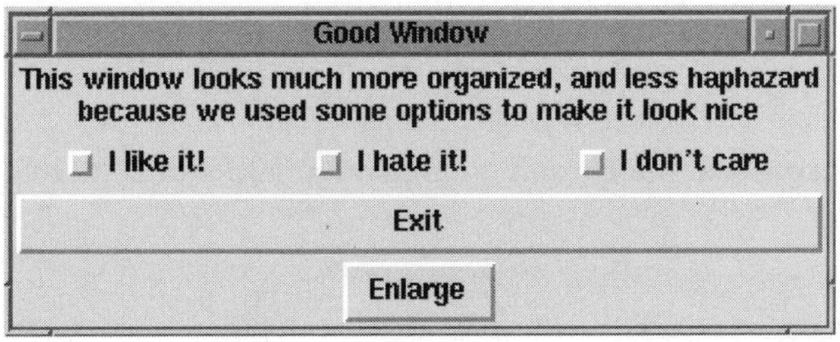

Figure 2-24. Window before pressing Enlarge button

Let's look at what happens when we press the Enlarge button. As shown in Figure 2-25, all the widgets are now repacked with additional parameters of `-ipadx => 20, -ipady => 20`. These new options are in addition to any other parameters the widgets were packed with before. If an option is repeated, the last one specified overrides the previous ones.

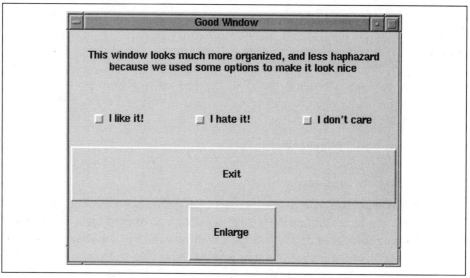

Figure 2-25. Window after pressing Enlarge button

The window is suddenly huge! Subsequent presses of the Enlarge button will do
nothing more to the window because all the widgets already have an **-ipadx** and
-ipady of 20. If we wanted to always add 20 to the values of **-ipadx** and
-ipady, we would have to request the current values and add 20 to them. Here's
the code for that:

```
sub repack_kids {
  my @kids = $mw->packSlaves;
  foreach (@kids) {
    %packinfo = $_->packInfo();
    $_->pack(-ipadx => 20 + $packinfo{"-ipadx"},
             -ipady => 20 + $packinfo{"-ipady"});
  }
}
```

We use **packInfo** to get the current configuration and add 20 to that value.

Grid

The **grid** geometry manager divides the window into a grid composed of columns and rows starting at 0,0 in the upper left-hand corner. Figure 2-26 shows a
sample grid.

Rather than using the sides of a window as reference points, **grid()** divides the
screen into columns and rows. It looks a lot like a spreadsheet doesn't it? Each
widget is assigned a grid cell using the options available to **grid()**.

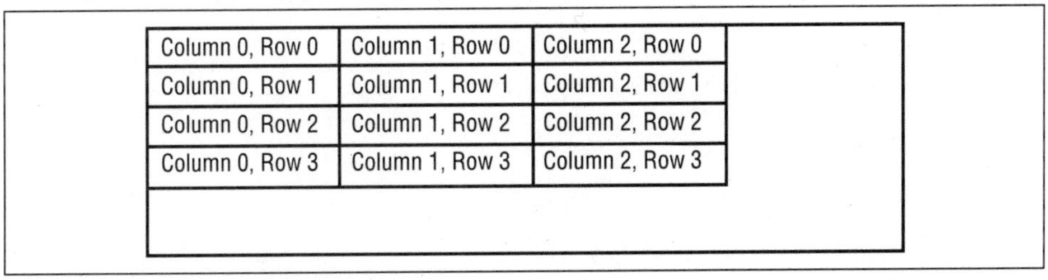

Column 0, Row 0	Column 1, Row 0	Column 2, Row 0
Column 0, Row 1	Column 1, Row 1	Column 2, Row 1
Column 0, Row 2	Column 1, Row 2	Column 2, Row 2
Column 0, Row 3	Column 1, Row 3	Column 2, Row 3

Figure 2-26. Diagram showing window divided into grid

The `grid()` method takes a list of widgets instead of operating on only one widget at a time.* Here is the generic usage:

```
$widget1->grid( [ $widget2, ... , ] [ option => value, ... ] );
```

A specific example:

```
$widget1->grid($widget2, $widget3);
```

Instead of using three separate calls, you can use one `grid()` call to display all three widgets. You can also invoke `grid()` on each widget independently just as you can `pack()`. Each call to `grid()` will create another row in the window. So in our example, `$widget1`, `$widget2`, and `$widget3` will be placed in the first row. Another call to grid would create a second row. This is what happens when you do not specify any additional options to the `grid()` call.

For greater control, you can specify explicit `-row` and `-column` options for each widget in the window. I will cover these options later.

These assumptions are made when additional options are not specified:

- The first widget in the row (for example, `$widget1` in the preceding example) invokes the `grid()` command.

- All remaining widgets for that row will be specified as arguments to the `grid()` command.

- Each additional call to `grid()` will add another row to the display.

- Special characters can be used to change the `-columnspan` and `-rowspan` of the widget without using `-columnspan` or `-rowspan` explicitly.

A few examples will help demonstrate. Each call to `grid()` will create another row, so we know we have two rows in the following example:

```
# Create two rows, each with four widgets
$widget1->grid($widget2, $widget3, $widget4);
$widget5->grid($widget6, $widget7, $widget8);
```

---

* Several people have told me that `pack` can also take a list of widgets. I didn't cover this because it is not how `pack` is normally used.

In this example, we have created four rows and there is only one widget in each row:

```
# Create four rows, each with one widget
$widget1->grid();
$widget2->grid();
$widget3->grid();
$widget4->grid();
```

We can also create widgets as we go:

```
$mw->Button(-text => 'Button1', -command => \&call1)->grid(
        $mw->Button(-text => 'Button2', -command => \&call2),
        $mw->Button(-text => 'Button3', -command => \&call3),
        $mw->Button(-text => 'Button4', -command => \&call4));
```

Pay careful attention because the second, third, and fourth calls to `Button` are inside the call to `grid()`. All four of the buttons will be placed in the first row. If we executed the same exact command again, the new widgets would be placed in the next row.

Special Characters

There are several special characters that can be used to alter the way the widgets are gridded in the window. Each special character serves as a type of placeholder that indicates what to do with that position in the grid:

`"-"` *(a minus sign)*

> Tells grid that the widget specified right before this one in the list should span this column as well. To span more than one column, place a `"-"` in each widget position to span. A `"-"` may not follow a `"^"` or an `"x"`.

`"x"`

> Effectively leaves a blank space where a widget would otherwise be placed.

`"^"`

> A widget in row x will span row x and $x + 1$ when this character is placed in the `grid` command for row $x + 1$ in that row/column position. The number of `"^"` characters must match the number of columns the widget spans in row x. Similar to `"-"`, but goes down, not across.[*]

The following sections include some examples that illustrate what the special characters do.

---

[*] When I used the special character `"^"` with Tk4.002, I got a nasty core dump. This is fixed in Tk8.0, so if you get this error also, check which version you have.

Spanning columns

The following bit of code creates three rows of buttons. The first two rows are normal, and in the third, the second button spans three columns. Each `"-"` character adds one to the number of columns the button uses, and the default is 1. So the original column and two hyphens (`"-"`,`"-"`) indicate that there are three columns to span. The `-sticky` option is necessary for the widgets to stick to the sides of the cells it spans. If the `-sticky` option had been left out, the button would be centered across the three cells it spans.

```
$mw->Button(-text => "Button1", -command => sub { exit })->grid
  ($mw->Button(-text => "Button2", -command => sub { exit }),
   $mw->Button(-text => "Button3", -command => sub { exit }),
   $mw->Button(-text => "Button4", -command => sub { exit }));

$mw->Button(-text => "Button5", -command => sub { exit })->grid
  ($mw->Button(-text => "Button6", -command => sub { exit }),
   $mw->Button(-text => "Button7", -command => sub { exit }),
   $mw->Button(-text => "Button8", -command => sub { exit }));


$mw->Button(-text => "Button9", -command => sub { exit })->grid
  ($mw->Button(-text => "Button10", -command => sub { exit }),
   "-", "-",  -sticky => "nsew");
```

The resulting window is shown in Figure 2-27.

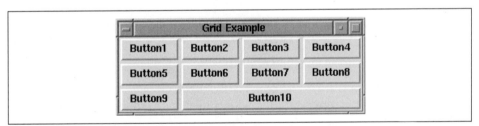

Figure 2-27. Example of column spanning using the "-" character

Empty cells

The `"x"` character translates to "skip this space" and leaves a hole in the grid. I removed the line that created Button6 and replaced it with an "x" in the following code. The cell for it is still there, it just doesn't contain a widget.

```
$mw->Button(-text => "Button1", -command => sub { exit })->grid
  ($mw->Button(-text => "Button2", -command => sub { exit }),
   $mw->Button(-text => "Button3", -command => sub { exit }),
   $mw->Button(-text => "Button4", -command => sub { exit }));

$mw->Button(-text => "Button5", -command => sub { exit })->grid
  ("x",
   $mw->Button(-text => "Button7", -command => sub { exit }),
   $mw->Button(-text => "Button8", -command => sub { exit }));
```

The resulting window is shown in Figure 2-28.

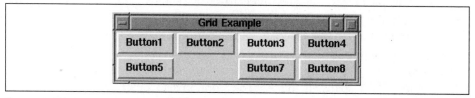

Figure 2-28. Leaving an empty cell between widgets

Grid Options

The rest of the options are similar to those used with `pack()`:

"-"

> Special character used in `grid` widget list. Increases `columnspan` of widget prior to it in widget list.

"x"

> Special character used in `grid` widget list. Leaves a blank space in the grid.

"^"

> Special character used in `grid` widget list. Increases `rowspan` of the widget in the grid directly above it.

-column => *n*

> Sets the column to place widget in ($n >= 0$).

-row => *m*

> Sets the row to place widget in ($m >= 0$).

-columnspan => *n*

> Sets the number of columns for the widget to span beginning with -column.

-rowspan => *m*

> Sets the number of rows for the widget to span beginning with -row.

-sticky => *string*

> String contains characters n, s, e, or w. Widget will stick to those sides.

-in => $otherwindow

> Indicates that widget is gridded inside $otherwindow instead of parent of $widget.

-ipadx => *amount*

> $widget becomes larger in x direction by 2 × *amount.*

-ipady => *amount*

> $widget becomes larger in y direction by 2 × *amount.*

-padx => *amount*

> Buffer space equal to *amount* is placed to left and right of widget.

-pady => *amount*

> Buffer space equal to *amount* is placed on top and bottom of widget.

Explicitly Specifying Rows and Columns

Rather than letting grid() make assumptions, it is sometimes necessary to explicitly state the row and column in which the widget should be placed. This is done by using the -row and -column options. Each option takes a nonnegative integer as an argument:

```
-column => n, -row => m
```

When you use -row and -column, it is not necessary to build or grid() the widgets in any sort of logical order (except for your own sanity when you are debugging). You could place your first widget in column 10 and row 5 if you like. All of the other cells with lower row and column values will remain empty.

Explicitly Spanning Rows and Columns

It is also possible to explicitly indicate that a widget (or widgets) should span some columns or rows. The option to use to span columns is -columnspan. For spanning rows, the option is -rowspan. Both options take an integer that is 1 or greater. The value indicates how many rows or columns should be spanned, including the row or column in which the widget is placed.

For this example, I have used the easy way to place widgets in columns and rows by not explicitly specifying the -row and -column options. Note that the second grid command applies to two button widgets, so the single -columnspan option applies to *both* buttons created there.

```
$mw->Button(-text => "Button1", -command => sub { exit })->grid
  ($mw->Button(-text => "Button2", -command => sub { exit }),
   $mw->Button(-text => "Button3", -command => sub { exit }),
   $mw->Button(-text => "Button4", -command => sub { exit }),
   -sticky => "nsew");

# Button5 will span Columns 0-1 and Button6 will span 2-3
$mw->Button(-text => "Button5", -command => sub { exit })->grid
  ($mw->Button(-text => "Button6", -command => sub { exit }),
   -sticky => "nsew", -columnspan => 2);
```

The resulting window is shown in Figure 2-29.

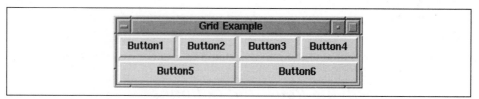

Figure 2-29. -columnspan example

This window could also have been created using the "`-`" special character to indicate column spanning, like this:

```
$mw->Button(-text => "Button1", -command => sub { exit })->grid
  ($mw->Button(-text => "Button2", -command => sub { exit }),
   $mw->Button(-text => "Button3", -command => sub { exit }),
   $mw->Button(-text => "Button4", -command => sub { exit }),
   -sticky => "nsew");

# Button5 will span Columns 0-1 and Button6 will span 2-3
$mw->Button(-text => "Button5", -command => sub { exit })->grid
  ("-", $mw->Button(-text => "Button6", -command => sub { exit }), "-"
   -sticky => "nsew");
```

This example illustrates how to explicitly use the **-row** and **-column** options in addition to the **-rowspan** option:

```
$mw->Button(-text => "Button1", -command => sub { exit })->
  grid(-row => 0, -column => 0, -rowspan => 2, -sticky => 'nsew');
$mw->Button(-text => "Button2", -command => sub { exit })->
  grid(-row => 0, -column => 1);
$mw->Button(-text => "Button3", -command => sub { exit })->
  grid(-row => 0, -column => 2);
$mw->Button(-text => "Button4", -command => sub { exit })->
  grid(-row => 0, -column => 3);

$mw->Button(-text => "Button5", -command => sub { exit })->
  grid(-row => 1, -column => 1);
$mw->Button(-text => "Button6", -command => sub { exit })->
  grid(-row => 1, -column => 2);
$mw->Button(-text => "Button7", -command => sub { exit })->
  grid(-row => 1, -column => 3);
```

See Figure 2-30 for the resulting window.

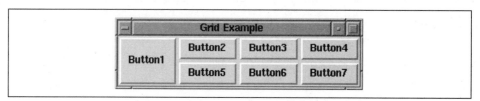

Figure 2-30. Explicit -rowspan example

Forcing a Widget to Fill the Cell

When you use the pack() command, it is necessary to indicate both -fill and -expand options to get the widget to resize inside its allocation rectangle. The grid() command doesn't have an allocation rectangle to fill, but it does have the cell within the grid. Using the -sticky option with grid() is similar to using -fill and -expand with pack().

The value associated with -sticky is a string containing the compass points to which the widget should "stick." If the widget should always "stick" to the top of the cell, you would use -sticky => "n". To force the widget to fill the cell completely, use -sticky => "nsew". To make the widget as tall as the cell but only as wide as it needs to be, use -sticky => "ns". The string value can contain commas and whitespace, but they will be ignored. These two statements are equivalent:

```
-sticky => "nsew"
-sticky => "n, s, e, w"  # Same thing
```

If you use -sticky with your widgets and then resize the window, you'll notice that the widgets don't resize as you think they should. They don't because resizing of the cells and the widgets in them is taken care of with the gridColumn-configure and gridRowconfigure methods, which are discussed later in this chapter.

Padding the Widget

grid() also accepts these four options: -ipadx, -ipady, -padx, -pady. They work exactly the same as they do in pack(), but instead of affecting the size of the allocation rectangle, they affect the size of the cell in which the widget is placed.

In this example, the -ipady and -ipadx options are applied to the top row of buttons and not the bottom row. Notice in Figure 2-31 how Buttons 5 through 8 are also wider than they really need to be. This is because we used the -sticky => "nsew" option.

```
$mw->Button(-text => "Button1", -command => sub { exit })->grid
  ($mw->Button(-text => "Button2", -command => sub { exit }),
   $mw->Button(-text => "Button3", -command => sub { exit }),
   $mw->Button(-text => "Button4", -command => sub { exit }),
   -sticky => "nsew", -ipadx => 10, -ipady => 10);

$mw->Button(-text => "Button5", -command => sub { exit })->grid
  ($mw->Button(-text => "Button6", -command => sub { exit }),
   $mw->Button(-text => "Button7", -command => sub { exit }),
   $mw->Button(-text => "Button8", -command => sub { exit }),
   -sticky => "nsew");
```

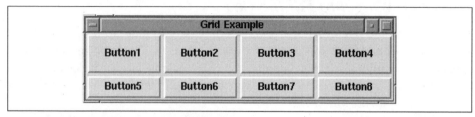

Figure 2-31. grid -ipadx and -ipady example

In this example, the –pady and –padx options are applied to the top row of buttons and not the bottom row. Figure 2-32 shows the results.

```
$mw->Button(-text => "Button1", -command => sub { exit })->grid
   ($mw->Button(-text => "Button2", -command => sub { exit }),
    $mw->Button(-text => "Button3", -command => sub { exit }),
    $mw->Button(-text => "Button4", -command => sub { exit }),
    -sticky => "nsew", -padx => 10, -pady => 10);

$mw->Button(-text => "Button5", -command => sub { exit })->grid
   ($mw->Button(-text => "Button6", -command => sub { exit }),
    $mw->Button(-text => "Button7", -command => sub { exit }),
    $mw->Button(-text => "Button8", -command => sub { exit }),
    -sticky => "nsew");
```

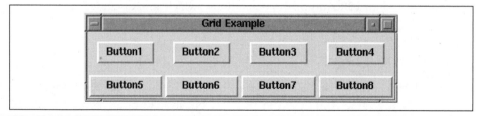

Figure 2-32. grid -padx and -pady example

Specifying a Different Parent

The –in option works the same way it does in pack(). The $widget will be placed in $otherwindow and not in the default parent of $widget. Here is the usage:

```
-in => $otherwindow
```

Configuring Columns and Rows

As with any of the geometry managers, grid has a few methods that are associated with it. Each method is invoked via a widget that has been placed on the screen by using grid(). Sometimes it is necessary to change the options of the group of cells that makes up your grid.

You can control resizing and the minimum size of a cell with the gridColumn-configure and gridRowconfigure methods. Each takes a column or a row number as its first argument and then takes some optional arguments that will change the configuration of that column or row.

Both gridColumnconfigure and gridRowconfigure work very similar to the configure method used with widgets. Unlike the configure method used with widgets, however, the options you can specify with gridColumnconfigure and gridRowconfigure cannot be used with the grid() command. The options you can use with gridColumnconfigure and gridRowconfigure are -weight, -minsize, and -pad.

If you send only a row or column number, an array is returned with the current options and their values for that method:

```
@column_configs = $mw->gridColumnconfigure(0);
@row_configs = $mw->gridRowconfigure(0);
```

In this example, we are getting the options and their values for the first column and the first row. The results of using the default values would look like this:

```
-minsize 0 -pad 0 -weight 0
-minsize 0 -pad 0 -weight 0
```

You can get the value of only one of the options by sending that option as the second argument:

```
print $mw->gridColumnconfigure(0, -weight), "\n";
print $mw->gridRowconfigure(0, -weight), "\n";
```

The results would be:

```
0
0
```

To change the value of the options, use the option and then the value you want associated with it immediately after the option; for example:

```
$mw->gridColumnconfigure(0, -weight => 1);
$mw->gridRowconfigure(0, -weight => 1);
```

You can also specify multiple options in one call:

```
$mw->gridColumnconfigure(0, -weight => 1, -pad => 10);
$mw->gridRowconfigure(0, -weight => 1, -pad => 10);
```

Now that we know how to call gridColumnconfigure and gridRowconfigure, we need to know what the three different options do.

Weight

The -weight option sets how much space is to be allocated to that column or row when the window is divided into cells. Remember to use -sticky => "nsew" in

your `grid()` command if you want the widget to resize when the cell does. The default -weight is 0, which causes the column width or row height to be dictated by the largest widget in the column. Each -weight value has a relationship to the other -weights in the rows or columns.

If a column or row has a -weight of 2, it is twice as big as a column or row that has a -weight of 1. Columns or rows of -weight 0 don't get resized at all. If you want all your widgets to resize in proportion to the size of the window, add this to your code before you call MainLoop:

```
($columns, $rows) = $mw->gridSize();
for ($i = 0; $i < $columns; $i++) {
  $mw->gridColumnconfigure($i, -weight => 1);
}
for ($i = 0; $i < $rows; $i++) {
  $mw->gridRowconfigure($i, -weight => 1);
}
```

This code will assign the -weight of 1 to every single row and column in the grid, no matter what size the grid is. Of course, this method only works if you want to assign the same size to each row and each column, but you get the idea.

Here is an example of how the -weight option works (Figure 2-33 shows the result):

```
$mw->Button(-text => "Button1", -command => sub { exit })->grid
  ($mw->Button(-text => "Button2", -command => sub { exit }),
   $mw->Button(-text => "Button3", -command => sub { exit }),
   $mw->Button(-text => "Button4", -command => sub { exit }),
   -sticky => "nsew");

$mw->Button(-text => "Button5", -command => sub { exit })->grid
  ("x",
   $mw->Button(-text => "Button7", -command => sub { exit }),
   $mw->Button(-text => "Button8", -command => sub { exit }),
   -sticky => "nsew");

$mw->gridColumnconfigure(1, -weight => 1);
$mw->gridRowconfigure(1, -weight => 1);
```

By giving row 1 and column 1 a weight of 1 (whereas all other rows and columns have 0 weight), they take over any extra available space when the size of the window is increased. Notice that columns 0, 2, and 3 are only as wide as is necessary to draw the buttons and their text, but column 1 has filled in the extra space. The same effect happens for row 0 with a weight of 0 and row 1 with a new weight of 1. (The window has been resized larger to demonstrate the effects of -weight.)

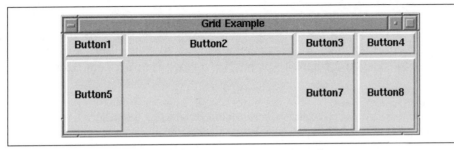

Figure 2-33. gridRowconfigure and gridColumnconfigure example

Minimum cell size

The option **-minsize** sets the smallest width for the column or the smallest height for each row. The **-minsize** option takes a valid screen distance as a value. In this example, the minimum size of the cells in row 0 and column 0 is set to 10 pixels:

```
$mw->gridColumnconfigure(0, -minsize => 10);
$mw->gridRowconfigure(0, -minsize => 10);
```

If the column or row was normally less than 10 pixels wide, then it would be forced to be at least that large.

Padding

You can add padding around the widget and to the widget by using the **-padx/y** and **-ipadx/y** options. You can also add a similar type of padding by using the **-pad** option with the **gridColumnconfigure** and **gridRowconfigure** methods. The padding is added around the widget, not to the widget itself. When you call **gridColumnconfigure**, the **-pad** option will add padding to the left and right of the widget. Calling **gridRowconfigure** with **-pad** will add padding to the top and bottom of the widget. Here are two examples:

```
$mw->gridColumnconfigure(0, -pad => 10);
$mw->gridRowconfigure(0, -pad => 10);
```

Bounding box

To find out how large a cell is, you can use the **gridBbox** method:

```
($xoffset, $yoffset, $width, $height) = $master->gridBbox(0, 2);
```

This example gets the bounding box for column 0 and row 2. All the values returned are in pixels. The bounding box will change as you resize the window. The four values returned represent the x offset, the y offset, the cell width, and the cell height (offsets are relative to the window or frame where the widget is gridded).

Removing a Widget

Like `packForget`, `gridForget` causes the widget(s) to be removed from view on the screen. This may or may not cause the window to resize itself; it depends on the size of $widget and where it was on the window. Here are some examples:

```
$mw->gridForget();              # Nothing happens
$widget->gridForget();          # $widget goes away
$widget->gridForget($widget1);  # $widget and $widget1 go away
$widget->gridForget($w1, $w3);  # $widget, $w1, $w3 go away
```

The widgets are undrawn from the screen, but the cells they occupied remain.

Getting Information

The `gridInfo` method returns information about the $widget in a list format. Just as with `packInfo`, the first two elements indicate where the widget was placed:

```
@list = $widget->gridInfo();
```

Here are some sample results from `gridInfo`:

```
-in Tk::Frame=HASH(0x81abc44) -column 0 -row 0 -columnspan 1 -rowspan 2
-ipadx 0 -ipady 0 -padx 0 -pady 0  -sticky nesw
```

Widget Location

The `gridLocation` method returns the column and row of the widget nearest the given (x, y) coordinates:

```
($column, $row) = $master->gridLocation($x, $y);
```

Both $x and $y are in screen units relative to the master window (in our examples, $mw). For locations above or to the left of the grid, -1 is returned.

When given the arguments (0, 0), our application returned this:

```
0 0
```

which indicates the cell at column 0 and row 0.

Propagation

There is a `gridPropagate` method that is similar to `packPropagate`:

```
$master->gridPropagate( 0 );
```

When given a false value, `gridPropagate` turns off geometry propagation, meaning size information is not sent upward to the parent of $master. By default, propagation is turned on. If `gridPropagate` is not given an argument, the current value is returned.

How Many Columns and Rows?

To find out how large the grid has become after placing numerous widgets in it, you can use `gridSize` to get back the number of columns and the number of rows:

```
($columns, $rows) = $master->gridSize();
```

The list returned contains the number of columns and then the number of rows. In many of the earlier examples, we had a grid size that was four columns by two rows.

```
($c, $r) = $f->gridSize();     #$c = 4, $r = 2
```

It is not necessary for a widget to be placed in a column/row for it to be considered a valid column/row. If you place a widget in column 4 and row 5 using `-row=>5`, `-column=>4` and the only other widget is in row 0 and column 0, then `gridSize` will return 5 and 6.

Grid Slaves

There are two ways to find out which widgets have been put in a window or frame. Use `gridSlaves` without any arguments to get the full list or specify a row and column. Here are examples of both:

```
@slaves = $mw->gridSlaves();
print "@slaves\n";
```

The preceding code would have printed this:

```
Tk::Button=HASH(0x81b6fb8) Tk::Button=HASH(0x81ba454)
Tk::Button=HASH(0x81ba4cc) Tk::Button=HASH(0x81ba538)
Tk::Button=HASH(0x81b6fa0) Tk::Button=HASH(0x81ba5e0)
Tk::Button=HASH(0x81ba6dc) Tk::Button=HASH(0x81ba748)
```

We could have specified the widget in column 0, row 0:

```
$widget = $mw->gridSlaves( -row => 0, -column => 0 );
print "$widget\n";
# Would print this: Tk::Button=HASH(0x81b6fb8)
```

If you specify only the `-row` option, you'll get a list containing only the widgets in that row. The same goes for only specifying a `-column`; your list will contain only the widgets in that column.

Place

The `place()` geometry manager is different than `grid()` or `pack()`. Rather than referencing against a cell location or a window's side, most of the time you'll be

using a relative form of x and y coordinates. You can also use `place()` to overlap portions of widgets, which isn't allowed in either `grid()` or `pack()`.

Invoking `place()` is similar to calling the other geometry managers:

```
$widget->place( [ option => value, . . . ] );
```

The options specified when you call `place()` affect how the widgets are put on
the screen.

Place Options

`-anchor => 'n' | 'ne' | 'e' | 'se' | 's' | 'sw' | 'w' | 'nw' |
    'center'`
   Sets the position in the widget that will be placed at the specified coordinates.

`-bordermode => 'inside' | 'outside' | 'ignore'`
   Determines whether or not the border portion of the widget is included in the
   coordinate system.

`-height => amount`
   Sets the absolute height of the widget.

`-in => $window`
   Indicates that the child widget will be packed inside $window instead of in the
   parent that created it. Any relative coordinates or sizes will still refer to the
   parent.

`-relheight => ratio`
   Indicates that the height of the widget relates to the parent widget's height by
   ratio.

`-relwidth => ratio`
   Indicates that the width of the widget relates to the parent widget's width by
   ratio.

`-relx => xratio`
   Indicates that the widget will be placed relative to its parent by *xratio*.

`-rely => yratio`
   Indicates that the widget will be placed relative to its parent by *yratio*.

`-width => amount`
   Indicates that the width of the widget will be *amount*.

`-x => x`
   Indicates that the widget will be placed at *x*. *x* is any valid screen distance.

`-y => y`
   Indicates that the widget will be placed at *y*. *y* is any valid screen distance.

Absolute Coordinates

The parent window (or frame) has a standard coordinate system where 0,0 is in the upper-left corner. The x values increase to the right, and the y values increase as you go down. See Figure 2-34.

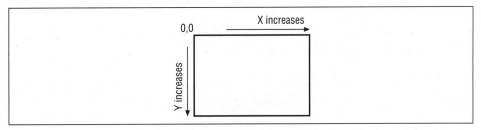

Figure 2-34. Coordinate system of parent window when absolute coordinates are used

To use absolute coordinates to specify where to place the widget, we would use options **-x** and **-y**:

```
-x => x, -y => y
```

Valid values for *x* and *y* are valid screen distances (for example, 5, which is in pixels). The widget will have its anchor position (controlled by **-anchor**) placed at the x and y coordinates. The default anchor is **"nw"**; the upper-left corner of the widget.

Another major difference between **place()** and the other geometry managers is that at least two arguments are required when **place()** is invoked. There are no default values for the **-x** and **-y** options. You will get an error if you try to invoke **place()** with no arguments (for example, **$widget->place()**).

The simplest example of using **-x** and **-y** is to place a widget at 0,0:

```
$mw->Button(-text => "Exit",
            -command => sub { exit })->place(-x => 0, -y => 0);
```

As you would expect, the widget ends up in the upper-left corner of the window as shown in Figure 2-35. No matter what size the window, our widget will remain positioned at (0,0). Even when the window is resized as small as possible, the widget will not move.

Here is an example of using **-x** and **-y** to create some overlapping widgets:

```
$mw->Button(-text => "Exit",
            -command => sub { exit })->place(-x => 10, -y => 10);
$mw->Button(-text => "Exit",
            -command => sub { exit })->place(-x => 20, -y => 20);
```

Figure 2-36 shows the resulting window.

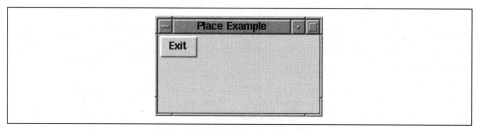

Figure 2-35. Button placed using -x => 0, -y => 0

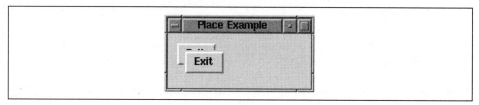

Figure 2-36. Overlapping buttons with place()

Relative Coordinates

In place(), there is an additional coordinate system defined for the parent widget that allows relative placement within it. This coordinate system is shown in Figure 2-37.

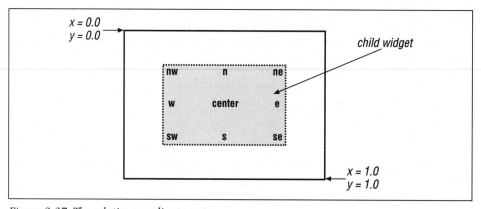

Figure 2-37. The relative coordinate system

The upper-left corner has the coordinates (0.0,0.0). The lower-right corner's coordinates are (1.0, 1.0). The middle of the window would be (0.5, 0.5). The coordinates are specified in floating point form to allow place() to handle any size window. This allows the widget to remain at that position (in the center, for instance) no matter how the window is resized.

It is valid to specify coordinates both smaller than 0.0 and larger than 1.0. However, your widget most likely won't be completely visible in the window when you use out-of-range coordinates.

This code snippet produces the button shown in Figure 2-38:

```
$b = $mw->Button(-text => "Exit", -command => sub { exit });
$b->place(-relx => 0.5, -rely => 0.5);
```

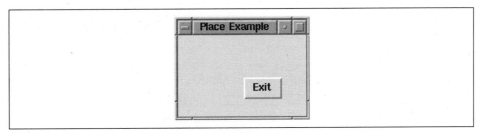

Figure 2-38. Using place with -relx => 0.5, -rely => 0.5

Although the button in Figure 2-38 is placed in the middle of the screen, it looks off-center because the upper-left corner of the widget was placed in the middle of the window instead of the center. You can change this with the -anchor option, which I'll discuss shortly. If we resize this window, the button still stays in the middle of the window (see Figure 2-39).

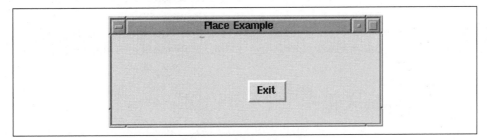

Figure 2-39. -relx => 0.5, -rely => 0.5 window resized larger

This next example creates two buttons, both placed in the window with relative coordinates:

```
$mw->Button(-text => "Exit",
            -command => sub { exit })->place(-relx => 0.2,
                                             -rely => 0.2);
$mw->Button(-text => "Exit",
            -command => sub { exit })->place(-relx => 0.5,
                                             -rely => 0.5);
```

No matter what size the window is or where other widgets are in the screen, the two buttons will stay in those relative locations (see Figure 2-40).

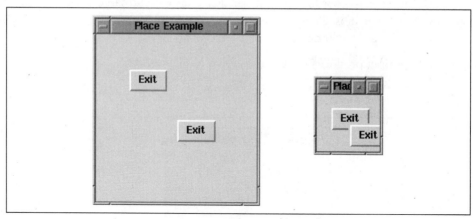

Figure 2-40. Two buttons placed relative to the parent window

The left window in Figure 2-40 is the default size of the window when it was created. The right window is what it looks like after the window was resized to make
it much smaller. Notice that the second button placed in the window remains on
top. It does so because we are still maintaining the ordered list of widgets in the
window; the second Exit button (placed at 0.5,0.5) is drawn last, so it's drawn
above the other button.

You can also combine the absolute and relative coordinate systems simply by
using both in the argument list. The relative coordinate system is considered first,
and then the x or y value is added to that position. The options `-relx => 0.5,`
`-x => -10` means to place the widget 10 pixels to the left of the middle of the
window.

Anchoring the Widget

Think of the child widget as a piece of paper that you want to put on your bulle-
tin board (the board is the parent widget). You have a tack that you are going to
use to keep the paper up on the board. You can put the tack right through the
center of the paper, in the upper-left corner (`"nw"`), or in the lower-right corner
(`"se"`). The point where the tack is going to stick the paper to the board is the
`-anchor` point. The `-anchor` point on the widget is "tacked" to the coordinates
given by `-x`, `-y` or `-relx`, `-rely`. The default `-anchor` is `"nw"`. Figure 2-37 shows
these `-anchor` points within the child widget.

It is important to know where the `-anchor` is because it will affect how we see
the widget within the parent.

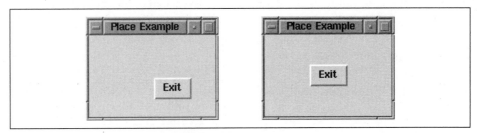

Figure 2-41. Different -anchor values affect where the widget is placed in the window

In Figure 2-41, almost identical place commands were used to put the Exit button in the window, but the -anchor value was changed. The left window's button was created with this command:

```
$mw->Button(-text => "Exit",
            -command => sub { exit })->place(-relx => 0.5,
                                             -rely => 0.5);
```

The window on the right in Figure 2-41 used this command:

```
$mw->Button(-text => "Exit",
            -command => sub { exit })->place(-relx => 0.5,
                                             -anchor => "center",
                                             -rely => 0.5);
```

As with pack() and grid(), the possible values for -anchor are: 'n', 'e', 's', 'w', 'center', 'nw', 'sw', 'ne', and 'se'. However, the value now applies to the child widget instead of the position within the allocation rectangle.

Width and Height

When you use place(), you can specify the width and height of the widget in one of three ways:

* Allow the widget to determine its own size.

* Specify width and/or height in absolute measurements.

* Specify width and/or height in relative measurements (relative to the parent widget).

To let the widgets determine their own size, no options are specified at all. The other ways involve the options -width, -height and -relwidth, -relheight respectively.

The -width and -height options allow you to specify the exact width or height of the widget in a screen distance:

```
-width => amount, -height => amount
```

Each amount is a valid screen distance (discussed earlier in this chapter under `pack`). The widget will be these sizes even if it cuts off edges of the items displayed in it. Our button looks quite silly on the screen when we use a `-width` of 40 pixels (see Figure 2-42).

```
$mw->Button(-text => "This Button Will Cause the Program to Exit",
            -command => sub { exit })->place(-x => 0, -y => 0,
                                              -width => 40);
```

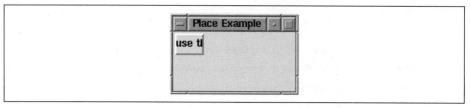

Figure 2-42. Using -width with place()

The other two options, `-relwidth` and `-relheight`, determine the widget in relation to the parent widget.

```
-relwidth => ratio, -relheight => ratio
```

The *ratio* is a floating point number (similar to that specified by `-relx` or `-rely`). A value of 1.0 will make the widget as wide (or as tall) as the parent widget. A value of 0.5 will make the widget half as wide as the parent (see Figure 2-43).

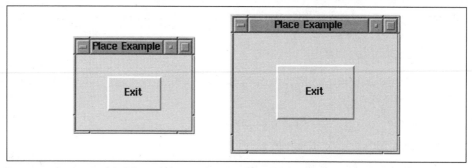

Figure 2-43. Example of the same window resized with -relwidth => 0.5, -relheight => 0.5

The options `-width` and `-relwidth` are additive when used together, and so are `-height` and `-relheight`.

Border Options

Normally, the border of the widget is used as the edge of the possible space in the window, which means any widgets placed with either the absolute or relative coordinate system will be placed inside the border. This can be changed by using the -bordermode option:

```
-bordermode => 'inside' | 'outside' | 'ignore'
```

Using 'outside' will allow the coordinate system to use the space occupied by the border as well. A value of 'ignore' will have the coordinate system use the space designated as the official X area. Overall, this option is pretty useless, as you can see from the difference each makes on our example in Figure 2-44.

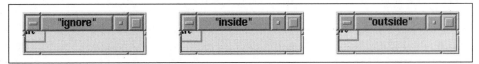

Figure 2-44. -bordermode examples

If you look very closely (get out your magnifying glass), you can see that the 'outside' version is two pixels higher and two pixels to the left than the 'inside' version. This is because on my window manager (*fvwm*), my border is defined as 2 pixels.

Methods Associated with Place

The methods for place() are simple and don't allow much manipulation of the widgets.

Removing the widget

As with pack and grid, there is a place version of the Forget method:

```
$widget->placeForget();
```

If you use this method on the widget, the widget will be removed from view on the screen. It is also removed from the list maintained by the parent widget.

Place information

The placeInfo method returns a list of information related to the widget:

```
@info = $widget->placeInfo();
print "@info";

## Produced these results (there are blanks where there are no values)
-x 0 -relx 0 -y 0 -rely 0 -width   -relwidth  -height  -relheight -anchor nw
```

Place slaves

```
@widgets = $parent->placeSlaves();
```

placeSlaves returns a list of the slave widgets that are within $parent. The list looks the same as it does when it is returned from packSlaves() or grid-Slaves() .*x*

Geometry Management Summary

You now know more about the three different geometry managers than you'll ever need to know to write a successful Perl/Tk application. Here are some helpful hints on deciding which geometry manager to use:

- pack() is good for general purpose use and will be your choice around 95% of the time.

- grid() is perfect for those situations in which you would like to create a columnar layout that is similar to a spreadsheet.

- place() is most useful when you want your widgets to stay in a position or size that is relative to the widget that created them. When it is used correctly, it can be very powerful.

- No matter which manager you use, take the time to get the widgets on your window where they belong (or more likely, where you want them). There's nothing more unsettling than a button that looks like it just doesn't belong in the window.

As you read through this book, you'll notice that some of the option names for the geometry managers are also option names when you are creating or configuring a widget type. For example, you can specify the **-width** of a button without using place(). Always keep in mind the context in which the option is used. Sometimes the functional difference is very subtle.

3

The Basic Button

The Button Widget

Button Widget Of all of the widgets available with Perl/Tk, the button is one of the most commonly used. Just see all the examples in Chapter 2, *Geometry Management*. When the button is pressed, something happens. That something can vary from exiting the program (as in our Hello World example) to beginning a longer series of operations such as opening a file or starting another process. The button typically displays a short text string: Done, Apply, Save, Ok, Exit.

Other widgets are also classified as buttons: radiobuttons, checkbuttons, and menubuttons. This chapter covers the traditional button. Chapter 4, *Checkbuttons and Radiobuttons*, and Chapter 11, *Menus*, will cover the other types because they look different on the screen and behave differently as well.

We cover the button widget first because it is easy to see the way different options affect it on the screen. Many of the other widgets included in Perl/Tk utilize the same options. Usually, if the option name is the same, the change to the widget will also be the same (more or less).

Creating a Button

The basic usage to create a button is as follows:

```
$button = $parentwidget->Button( [ option => value, . . . ] );
```

We have already seen examples of buttons in our Hello World program in Chapter 1, and in all the geometry management examples in Chapter 2. In these examples, a button is created and placed on the screen with a command like this:

```
$mw->Button(-text => "Done",-command => sub { exit })->pack;
```

You can save a reference to the button like this:

```
$button = $mw->Button(-text => "Done",-command => sub { exit })->pack;
```

In Hello World, we didn't need to refer to the button again later, so it wouldn't have made sense to save a reference to it. But most of the examples for this chapter will assume that we've saved a reference to the button widget when we created it.

Button Options

The rest of this chapter covers the options available to change the look of the button and how to make it do what you want.

`-activebackground =>` *color*
> Sets the color the background should be when the mouse cursor is over the button. A color is a text string such as `"red"`.

`-activeforeground =>` *color*
> Sets the color the text should be when the mouse cursor is over the button.

`-anchor =>` `'n'` | `'ne'` | `'e'` | `'se'` | `'s'` | `'sw'` | `'w'` | `'nw'` | `'center'`
> Causes the text to stick to the specified position in the button.

`-background =>` *color*
> Sets the background of the button to *color*.

`-bitmap =>` `'bitmapname'`
> Sets default bitmap or the location of a bitmap file (with @ in front of path).

`-borderwidth =>` *amount*
> Changes the width of the edge drawn around the button. (Emphasizes the `-relief`.)

`-command =>` *callback*
> Indicates a pointer to a function that will be called when the button is pressed.

`-cursor =>` `'cursorname'`
> Indicates that the mouse cursor will change to `'cursorname'` when over the button.

`-disabledforeground =>` *color*
> Sets the color the text should be when the button is disabled.

`-font =>` `'fontname'`
> Changes the font of all the text on the button.

`-foreground =>` *color*
> Changes the text color to *color*.

`-height => ` *amount*

Sets the height of the button in characters if text is displayed, and the screen distance if an image or bitmap is displayed.

`-highlightbackground => ` *color*

Sets the color of the area behind the focus rectangle (shows when widget does not have focus).

`-highlightcolor => ` *color*

Sets the color of the focus rectangle.

`-highlightthickness => ` *amount*

Sets the thickness of the black box around the button; indicates focus.

`-image => $imgptr`

`$imgptr` is a pointer to an Image object that was made with a GIF or PPM/PGM file.

`-justify => 'left' | 'right' | `**`'center'`**

Sets the side of the button against which multiline text will justify itself.

`-padx => ` *amount*

Adds extra space to the left and right side of the button inside the button edge.

`-pady => ` *amount*

Adds extra space to the top and bottom of the button inside the button edge.

`-relief => 'flat'|'groove'|`**`'raised'`**`|'ridge'|'sunken'|'solid'`

Changes the type of edges drawn around the button

`-state => `**`'normal'`**` | 'disabled' | 'active'`

Indicates the button's state of responsiveness. If set to `"disabled"`, the button does not respond.

`-takefocus => 0 | 1 | `**`undef`**

Indicates that the button will never get focus (0), always get focus (1), or let the application decide (`undef`).

`-text => 'text'`

Sets the text string displayed on the button.

`-textvariable => \$variable`

Pointer to a variable containing text to be displayed in button. Button text will change as `$variable` does.

`-underline => ` *n*

Underlines the *n*th character in the text string. Allows keyboard input via that character when button has the focus.

`-width => ` *amount*

> Sets the width of the button in characters if text is displayed and as a screen distance if an image or bitmap is displayed.

`-wraplength => ` *amount*

> Sets the screen distance for the maximum amount of text displayed on one line. Default: 0.

Displaying Text

For the user to know what the button does when it's pressed, you need to indicate the function of the button with its text string. The option that does this is `-text`:

```
-text => 'text'
```

When you are trying to come up with a descriptive text string, short and simple is the key. You don't want your button to take over the whole window with a long text string.

The string can be anything: alphanumeric, newline(s), or variables. Just like any other string in Perl, if it is put in single quotes, it is taken literally, and with double quotes, it is interpolated. The interpolation only happens once (the first time the option is parsed). If the variable changes later in the program, it has no effect on the text in the button. The only way the text in the button can be changed after it has been created is by using the **configure** method to reset it (e.g., **$button->configure(-text => "newtext");**) or by using the **-textvariable** option.

There is no default for the **-text** option; the button will simply have no text if **-text** is not specified.

The other way to display text on the button is by using the **-textvariable** option. The **-textvariable** option allows a scalar variable to be associated with the button; anything in the variable will be displayed on the button. Specify the scalar variable as follows:

```
-textvariable => \$variable
```

This means the text of the button will change as the contents of **$variable** change. When the text within the button changes, the button may become larger or smaller, and the entire window may change size.

This piece of code shows how the **-textvariable** option is used:

```
$count = 0;
$mw->Button(-text => "Add 1",
            -command => sub { $count++ })->pack(-side => 'left');
$mw->Button(-textvariable => \$count)->pack(-side => 'left');
$mw->Button(-text => "Exit",
            -command => sub { exit })->pack(-side => 'left');
```

Figure 3-1 shows two windows. The first window shows how it looks when it is first created, and the second window shows what it looks like after clicking on the "Add 1" button many times.

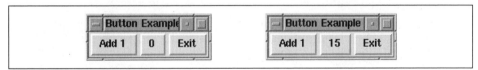

Figure 3-1. Example of using -textvariable

Displaying an Image or Bitmap Instead of Text

Instead of displaying a text string on the button, you can use the **-image** option to display an image:

```
-image => $imgptr
```

GIF and PPM/PGM formats are valid image types. Support is available for JPEG images in a separate module (Tk::JPEG), which is available for download from CPAN. Other types of images are also supported as more modules like Tk::JPEG are being developed. Check CPAN to see what is currently available.

When using an image, only the image will be displayed because the button can display only a text string or an image, not both. To create an **$imgptr** variable, use the **Photo** method (and supply the name and path if the image is not in the current directory) of the image file. The **$imgptr** is passed in as a value to the **-image** option:

```
$arrow = $mw->Photo(-file => "Xcamel.gif");
$mw->Button(-text => 'Exit', -command => sub { exit },
            -image => $arrow)->pack;
```

Figure 3-2 shows an example of a button with a GIF file on it.[*]

Figure 3-2. Button with image instead of text

Use the **-bitmap** option to allow a button to display a bitmap specified in a text string:

```
-bitmap => 'bitmapname'
```

---

[*] When I tried this example under the Windows 95 OS, I didn't get a good colormap of the GIF file. The problem may have been my video card or video driver for Windows 95, so it might look better on your machine.

There are several default bitmaps: `error`, `gray12`, `gray25`, `gray50`, `gray75`, `hourglass`, `info`, `questhead`, `question`, and `warning` (see Figure 3-3). They are specified in the option by placing single quotes around the bitmap name:

```
$mw->Button(-bitmap => 'error', -command => \&handle_error)->pack;
```

To specify a bitmap from a file, you need to put an `@` in front of the path.

```
$mw->Button(-bitmap => '@/usr/nwalsh/mybitmap',
            -command => sub { exit })->pack;
```

Note that, if you use double quotes, you have to escape the `@` with a backslash, (e.g., `"\@/usr/nwalsh/mybitmap"`).

Figure 3-3. Window showing all the default bitmaps

Assigning a Callback

In addition to the `-text` option, the `-command` option is almost always used to create a button. For the button to do something when pressed, we have to associate a callback with the button via the `-command` option. The callback happens when mouse button 1 is released over the button.* If you click down on the button but move the cursor away from the button before releasing, nothing happens because the mouse-click was aborted.

In the Hello World program, we used the `exit` routine as our callback:

```
$mw->Button(-text => "Done", -command => sub { exit })->pack;
```

There are several ways to associate a subroutine or set of commands with the button. This discussion will apply to all widgets that have a `-command` option, so you will see this option referred to often.

Defining a -command Callback

There are several ways the callback can be defined:

- Anonymous subroutine: e.g., `sub { .. do something .. }`
- Reference to a subroutine: e.g., `\&mysub`
- Anonymous list with the first element as a subroutine pointer, and the rest of the list as arguments to the subroutine: `[ \&mysub, $arg0, $arg1, \@arg2...]`

---

* Mouse button 1 is the leftmost mouse button, mouse button 2 is the middle mouse button, and mouse button 3 is the rightmost mouse button.

The button we created in our Hello World program used an anonymous subroutine. Here is the code again:

```
$mw->Button(-text => "Done", -command => sub { exit; })->pack;
```

We also could have created the anonymous subroutine prior to the button creation and sent the reference to it instead:

```
$mysubref = sub { exit };
$mw->Button(-text => "Done", -command => $mysubref)->pack;
```

This is useful when our anonymous subroutine does some fancy things and it would look awkward shoved into the list of arguments.

We could also create a regular subroutine to handle the exit and then just pass a reference to it:

```
sub do_exit {
  &do_something_else;
  exit;
}
$mw->Button(-text => "Done", -command => \&do_exit )->pack;
```

It is a good idea to use a subroutine like this if you have more than one way to exit the application. For instance, you could set up your application to exit via a menu, a button, or the window manager Close command.

If we need to pass arguments to our **do_exit()** routine we would use the anonymous list form:

```
sub do_exit {
  my ($arg1, $arg2) = @_;
  &do_something_else if ($arg1 = 12);
  exit;
}
$mw->Button(-text => "Done",
            -command => [ \&do_exit, $arg1, $arg2 ])->pack;
```

It is important to remember how the different ways to specify a callback affect the scope and which variables you can access.

Anonymous subroutines

Anonymous subroutines merely get "set aside" to be called later from within **MainLoop**. The commands inside the anonymous subroutine are not parsed until then. Any variables you use will not be evaluated until that time.

```
foreach (@names) {
  $mw->Button(-text => $_,
              -command => sub { print "$_ was pressed!\n"; })->pack;
}
```

In the preceding code, we are using the $_ variable in the foreach loop. The button's text string will be set as expected because the $_ is evaluated when the button is created. However, the $_ that is inside the scope of the anonymous sub-routine doesn't get evaluated until the button is actually pressed. At that point, $_ is undefined and errors start printing out every time you click the button.

Subroutine references: arguments or no arguments

The subroutine reference and the anonymous list are very similar except the list allows additional arguments (especially ones from within the current scope) to be sent to the subroutine:

```
foreach (@names) {
  $mw->Button(-text => $_,
              -command => [ \&print_name, $_ ])->pack;
}
sub print_name {
  print "$_[0] was pressed!\n";
}
```

The anonymous list gets created during the call to create the button. This means that $_ in the list is evaluated within the context of the foreach loop and will be set to the same value as the -text option uses.

Those of you who are comfortable with creating anonymous subroutines on the fly can also do it this way:

```
foreach (@names) {
  $mw->Button(-text => $_,
              -command => [ sub { print "$_[0] was pressed!\n"; },
                            $_ ])->pack;
}
```

The anonymous subroutine is the first item in the list to the -command option, and the second item in the list is the argument $_. Keep in mind that sometimes you'll want a lot more than a single print statement in the subroutine, and for readability, it makes sense to put it in a separate subroutine.

If all this anonymous stuff is confusing you, the Camel Book* has all the information you would ever want and more.

Disabling a Button

When a button is created, it shows up on the screen by default, ready for action. The button will change colors when the mouse passes over it and will perform the assigned callback when pushed. You can change this by using the -state option:

```
-state => "normal" | "disabled" | "active"
```

---

* Technically known as *Programming Perl*, also available from O'Reilly & Associates, Inc.

The "normal" state was just described. The "active" state is when the mouse cursor is physically over the button and is used internally. The "disabled" state is when the button appears grayed out (or with whatever colors have been specified by -disabledforeground and -disabledbackground) and will not respond to the mouse at all.

A button should not be available for selecting unless it makes sense in the application; for example, a button that disables another when it is pressed. The code would look like this:

```
my $exit_b = $mw->Button(-text => 'Exit',
                         -command => sub { exit })->pack;
$var = "Disable Exit";
$mw->Button(-textvariable => \$var,
            -command => sub { my $state = $exit_b->configure(-state);
                              if ($state eq "disabled") {
                                  $exit_b->configure(-state => 'normal');
                                  $var = "Disable Exit";
                              } else {
                                  $exit_b->configure(-state => 'disabled');
                                  $var = "Enable Exit";
                              }})->pack;
```

In this example, a reference to the Exit button is saved because it needs to be used later to change the state of the button. Also, note that $exit_b is used inside the scope of the anonymous subroutine. This will only work if $exit_b is left in the global scope of the entire program so that $exit_b will be defined when the anonymous subroutine is executed. Be careful to not set $exit_b to something else; if you do, when the anonymous subroutine is invoked, it will refer to the new value in $exit_b, not the one you wanted.

Figure 3-4 shows the window after we have clicked on the Disable Exit button once.

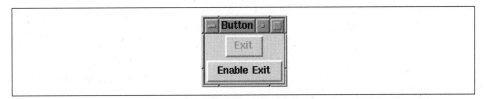

Figure 3-4. Window with disabled button (Exit) and normal button

The configure() method is explained later in this chapter; you don't need to worry about how it works just yet.

By disabling widgets when they can't do anything, you can give users visual hints about what they can and cannot do in the application.

Manipulating the Text

In addition to displaying text in the button, you can alter the appearance and location of the text within the button. The simplest thing you can do is to use the -font option to change the font:

```
-font => 'fontname'
```

There are several ways to specify the font. If you are using Tk4 (which is the current version as the book is being written) you should follow the directions in the following paragraphs. If you are using the newest version of Perl/Tk, which includes Tk8.0,* you should see Appendix C, *Fonts*; it covers the new methods to use with fonts.

The new font is specified as a text string that contains a font name. There is a difference in the way you specify fonts for Win32 systems and Unix systems. Valid fonts for your Unix system can be obtained by using the *xlsfonts* command or by using the Tk::Fonts module. The default font for the button widget on my Unix system is†:

```
"-Adobe-Helvetica-Bold-R-Normal--*-120-*-*-*-*-*-*"
```

Although you'll see this default on a Win32 system, you need to send a different type of string as the value to the -font option. Here's an example:

```
-font => "{Times New Roman} 12 {normal}"
```

You can look in the Control Panel under Fonts to see which fonts are available. Double-clicking on them will bring up a window that shows the font in the different sizes available. Use the name of the font as it's listed in the Fonts directory for the first part of the font name between the curly braces. The number after the font name is the size of the font in points. The third part is the type of the font, usually normal, italic, or bold.

There can only be a single font for each button, so the text string cannot change font in the middle of a word. Each button (or widget) in an application can have a different font. Here is an example of two buttons in a window, one with the default font and the other with **"lucidasans-14"** (a Unix font) as its font:

```
$mw->Button(-text => "Exit",
            -command => sub { exit })->pack(-side => 'left',
                                    -fill => 'both', -expand => 1);
$mw->Button(-text => "Exit",
            -font => "lucidasans-14",
            -command => sub { exit })->pack(-side => 'left',
                                    -fill => 'both', -expand => 1);
```

Figure 3-5 shows the resulting window.

---

* The numbering system for Perl/Tk follows the Tcl/Tk version numbers. I have no idea why they skipped 5, 6, and 7.

† Not all fonts are available on every system, although your system's default should work. Use the following command to get the default font for your system: @config = $button->configure(-font); print "@config\n";

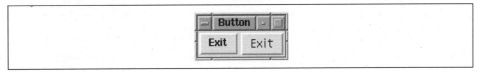

Figure 3-5. Buttons with various fonts

In addition to changing the font, you can also move the text around within the button. As you can in a word processing document, you can change where the text will adjust itself. The option that controls this is -justify:

```
-justify => 'left' | 'right' | 'center'
```

The default for -justify is 'center'. Normally, the text displayed in a button is a quick one- or two-word statement; for example, Exit, Done, Yes, No, or Cancel. The justification of the text isn't too obvious unless multiple lines of text are used. By default, the button will only display multiple lines if a \n is included in the string. You can have the program help decide when to wrap by using the -wraplength option:

```
-wraplength => amount
```

The *amount* indicates the maximum length of the line as a valid screen distance (see Chapter 1). If the length of the text string in the button exceeds this amount, the text will be wrapped around to the next line. The default for -wraplength is 0.

This is an example that uses both the -justify and -wraplength options:

```
foreach (qw(left center right)) {
    $b =  $mw->Button(-text =>"This button will be justified $_",
                      -command => sub { exit },
                      -wraplength => 53,
                      -justify => $_)->pack(-side => 'left',
                                            -fill => 'both',
                                            -expand => 1);

}
```

Figure 3-6 shows the results of the three buttons. Although this example doesn't show it, it is possible for the text to be wrapped in the middle of a word.

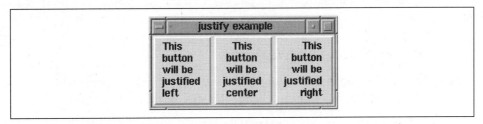

Figure 3-6. Effects of -justify and -wraplength in a button

The final possible adjustment to the text (or bitmap) is its position within the button. This is controlled by the -anchor option, which is similar to the -anchor option used with the different geometry managers:

```
-anchor => 'n' | 'ne' | 'e' | 'se' | 's' | 'sw' | 'w' | 'nw' | 'center'
```

Like the window, the button has compass points that define locations within the button. Figure 3-7 shows where these points are in the button.

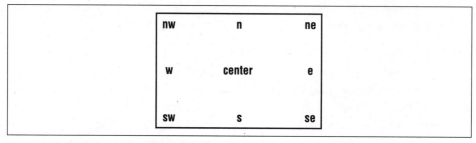

Figure 3-7. Anchor points within a button

The default position for the text is 'center'. When the position is changed, it is not obvious that this option is in effect unless the button is resized larger. In Figure 3-8, the button is the same one that was created in the -justify example (Figure 3-6) except -anchor => 'nw' has been added to the option list.

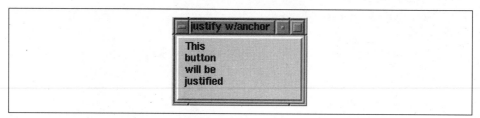

Figure 3-8. Anchor on button set to 'nw'

As mentioned earlier, this option is similar to the -anchor option to the pack command. It is important to note that this option changes the position of the text in the button; the -anchor option to pack() changes the position of the widget in the window.

Altering the Button's Style

By default, a button looks like it's slightly raised off the surface of the window. By using the -relief option, you can change the style of the button edges:

```
-relief => 'flat'|'groove'|'raised'|'ridge'|'sunken'|'solid'
```

Each value changes the look of the button slightly, as you can see in Figure 3-9.

flat

> Makes it look like only text is present in the window. 'flat' is not recommended for a button because the user has no visual information that the button can be pressed (the button looks just like a label).

groove

> Gives a slightly depressed look to the edge (as if there were a ditch around the text).

raised

> The default; gives a 3D look with a shadow on the lower and right sides of the button, which causes it to look higher than the window surface.

ridge

> The opposite of 'groove'; makes it look like a ridge is around the text.

sunken

> The opposite of 'raised'; gives the 3D effect of being below the surface of the window.

No matter which value is specified for the -relief option, when the button is pressed with the mouse, its relief will change to 'sunken'.

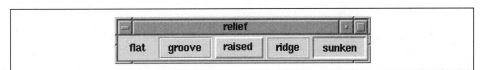

Figure 3-9. Different relief types for a button

In addition to changing the type of edge drawn around a button, you can also change the thickness of the edge by using -borderwidth:

    -borderwidth => *amount*

The default -borderwidth is 2. The wider the -borderwidth, the more dramatic the effects of the -relief option become. Figure 3-10 shows what a borderwidth of 10 does to each relief type.

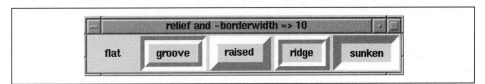

Figure 3-10. Different relief types with -borderwidth set to 10

Borderwidth can also be specified by using -bd as an abbreviation. Although using -bd will obtain the same results, using -borderwidth makes your code easier to follow later on. Also, **-bd** isn't supported with all widgets, so relying on it can be dangerous.

I don't recommend using **-borderwidth** with values greater than 4, because it makes the widgets look extremely odd. In each of the widget chapters you'll find a screenshot showing what happens to the widget with a larger **-borderwidth** value for each of the possible **-relief** values. The best use of **-borderwidth** is making one widget stand out more than the others temporarily during development. (I also use it often with frames to figure out where the frame is. Normally they are invisible. See Chapter 12.)

Changing the Size of a Button

Normally, the size of the button is automatically determined by the application and is dependent on the text string or image displayed in the button. The width and height can be specified explicitly by using the **-width** and/or **-height** options:

```
-width => x, -height => y
```

The values specified for *x* and *y* change depending on whether a bitmap/image or text is displayed in the button. When a bitmap or image is displayed, the values in *x* and *y* represent valid screen distances. If text is displayed on the button, *x* and *y* are character sizes.

This example has one button that is default size and another that is drawn with **-width** of 10 and **-height** of 10. (It is not necessary that the amounts for **-width** and **-height** be the same or that you use both):

```
$mw->Button(-text => "Exit",
            -command => sub { exit })->pack(-side => 'left');
$mw->Button(-text => "Exit",
            -width => 10, -height => 10,
            -command => sub { exit })->pack(-side => 'left');
```

In Figure 3-11, the second button is much taller than it is wide because text characters are taller than they are wide.

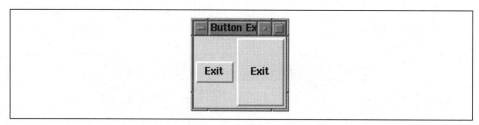

Figure 3-11. Example of button displaying default text and text with -width => 10, -height => 10

The value specified for both **-width** and **-height** are characters because the button is displaying text. When **-width** and **-height** are used with a bitmap, the amount specified is in screen distance. Here is an example of using -width and -height with a bitmap:

```
$mw->Button(-bitmap => 'error',
            -width => 10, -height => 10,
            -command => sub { exit })->pack(-side => 'left');
$mw->Button(-bitmap => 'error',
            -command => sub { exit })->pack(-side => 'left');
$mw->Button(-bitmap => 'error',
            -width => 50, -height => 50,
            -command => sub { exit })->pack(-side => 'left');
```

The first button is created with a restriction on the width and height of 10. The middle button looks like it would normally. The third button is created with a width and height of 50. Figure 3-12 shows the resulting window.

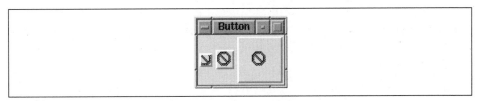

Figure 3-12. A bitmap displayed three times with different values for -width and -height

The default value for both -width and -height is 0. Using 0 allows the program to dynamically decide the height and width of the button.

The total width for buttons with text is calculated by the width the text takes up plus 2 × -padx amount. The height is the text height plus 2 × -pady amount. The width and height for buttons with a bitmap is just the width and height of the bitmap itself. Any -padx or -pady options are ignored when a bitmap is displayed.

As an alternative to specifying an explicit width or height, it is possible to increase the size of the button by using the options -padx and/or -pady to add padding between the text and edge of the button:

```
-padx => amount, -pady => amount
```

The *amount* specified with -padx is added to both the left and right side of the button. The *amount* specified with -pady is added to both the top and bottom of the button. Figure 3-13 shows an example.

By using these options you are telling the button to be sized larger than it normally would, but you don't have to worry that it will be sized too small, as you would if you explicitly set -width and -height.

Remember, -padx and -pady are ignored when a bitmap is displayed.

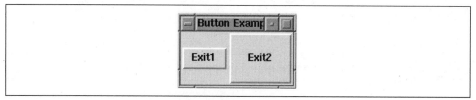

Figure 3-13. Example of -padx => 20, -pady => 20

Adding a Keyboard Mapping

A button is traditionally invoked by clicking mouse button 1 when the mouse cursor is over the button. It can also be invoked by pressing the Tab key until the button has the keyboard focus and then pressing the spacebar. The effects are the same: The callback associated with the button is called, and the button -relief changes momentarily. The keyboard focus is visually indicated by a thin black rectangle drawn around the widget (see Figure 3-20 later in this chapter).

To allow an additional keyboard character to invoke the button, you can use the -underline option in a button displaying text:

```
-underline => N
```

This will underline the Nth character in the text string. The first character of the text string is the 0th character, so with the text string "Exit", -underline => 1 will underline the second character in the string, the "x" (see Figure 3-14).

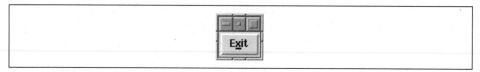

Figure 3-14. Example of -underline => 1

The default value for -underline is -1, which means no characters will be underlined in the text string.

Color Options

The options that can change the button's colors are -background, -foreground, -activebackground, -activeforeground, and -disabledforeground. Each option takes a string that identifies a color. This string could either be a color description such as "blue" or a hex string such as "#d9d9d9", which also describes a color, but is much more cryptic.

For either Win32 or Unix systems you can run the *widget* demo included with the Tk module. If the *perl/bin* directory is in your path, you can simply type "widget" on the DOS or Unix command line. Under the listbox section is an example that displays color names. You can double-click on the names in the list to see them change the application's color.

Valid values for the color string are available on your Unix system in a file called *rgb.txt*. Typically this file is located in the X11 *lib* directory. On my Linux system, it is located in */usr/X11R6/lib/rgb.txt*. You can also use the X application *xcolors* or *showrgb*. Check the manpages for each command to determine the best way to use them.

Another place to look for valid color names (and this applies to Win32 as well) is in your Perl distribution directory. Look for the file *xcolors.h*. It is a text file that contains the RGB values and names for quite a few colors. I found this file in *C:\ Perl\lib\site\Tk\ptk* on my Windows 95 machine.

The color of the button depends on the state the button is in at the time. When the button has a state of 'normal', the colors assigned to -foreground and -background are in effect. The background of the button is the area behind the text string but within the edges of the button.

The background is specified like this:

```
-background => color
```

The default background color is a light gray color ("#d9d9d9" in its hexadecimal RGB representation). Figure 3-15 shows the results of changing the second Exit button's background to blue.*

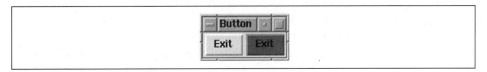

Figure 3-15. Example of -background => 'blue'

The foreground of the button is the text (or bitmap) displayed. The foreground color is specified like this:

```
-foreground => color
```

By default -foreground is 'black'. Make sure that whatever color you pick contrasts enough with the background color to be readable. In the example in Figure 3-15, I left the text the default color, and it doesn't contrast very well with the background color of the button. If we change -foreground to 'white', then

---

* Although we are talking about color, the figures are in black and white. Unfortunately, using color figures would have made the book too expensive to produce. I've tried to make color choices that contrast so the figures look as good as possible. The best way to determine what happens with each color option is to experiment and run the examples.

we will be able to see the text much more easily, as you'll see in Figure 3-16. (The shortcut for `-foreground` is `-fg`, which may or may not work on other types of widgets. I suggest sticking with `-foreground` as the option name.)

Figure 3-16. Example of -background => 'blue' and -foreground => 'white'

When you use the `-foreground` and `-background` options in conjunction with a bitmap, the bitmap foreground and background will change to the specified colors. The effect of the colors depends on the bitmap. See Figure 3-17.

Figure 3-17. 'error' bitmap with -foreground => 'white' and -background => 'black'

The `-foreground` and `-background` options control what color the button is when it is in the `'normal'` state. When the button has the mouse cursor over it, the `-activebackground` and `-activeforeground` colors are used:

    -activebackground => *color*, -activeforeground => *color*

These colors are different because we want users to have some visual clues that they can press the button. By having the colors change slightly when the mouse cursor is over the button, users know that the button can be pressed to do something. The default for `-activebackground` is a slightly darker gray color (`"#ececec"`).

The final color option, `-disabledforeground`, is the color of the text when the button's state is `'disabled'`.

    -disabledforeground => *color*

When the button is in a disabled state, it will not respond when the mouse cursor is over it, or if it is pressed. The default for the color of the text (or bitmap) is `"#a3a3a3"`. Figure 3-18 shows the difference between the text colors with one disabled button and one normal button. (We also saw this example in Figure 3-4. Look there for the code that created this window.)

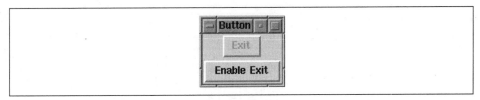

Figure 3-18. -disabledforeground example

Changing the Mouse Cursor

The mouse cursor normally looks like an arrow.* This can be changed on a widget-by-widget basis with the **-cursor** option:

```
-cursor  => cursorname
```

When the mouse is over the button, the cursor will change to the one specified. The cursor change will happen whether the button is disabled or not. There is a large set of available cursors. Following is a list of cursors, and Figure 3-19 shows what they look like.

X_cursor	arrow	based_arrow_down	based_arrow_up
boat	bogosity	bottom_left_corner	bottom_right_corner
bottom_side	bottom_tee	box_spiral	center_ptr
circle	clock	coffee_mug	cross
cross_reverse	crosshair	diamond_cross	dot
dotbox	double_arrow	draft_large	draft_small
draped_box	exchange	fleur	gobbler
gumby	hand1	hand2	heart
icon	iron_cross	left_ptr	left_side
left_tee	leftbutton	ll_angle	lr_angle
man	middlebutton	mouse	pencil
pirate	plus	question_arrow	right_ptr
right_side	right_tee	rightbutton	rtl_logo
sailboat	sb_down_arrow	sb_h_double_arrow	sb_left_arrow
sb_right_arrow	sb_up_arrow	sb_v_double_arrow	shuttle
sizing	spider	spraycan	star
target	tcross	top_left_arrow	top_left_corner
top_right_corner	top_side	top_tee	trek
ul_angle	umbrella	ur_angle	watch
xterm			

---

* What cursor is displayed is dependent on the window manager you are using, but most of the time it is an arrow.

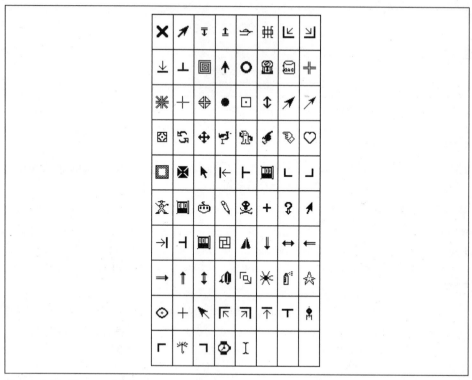

Figure 3-19. The standard cursors

Here's a program to look at the different cursors interactively:

```perl
#!/usr/bin/perl -w
use Tk;

## Create elements of window
$mw = MainWindow->new;
$mw->Button(-text => "Exit",
            -command => sub { exit })->pack(-side => "bottom",
                                            -fill => "x");
$scroll = $mw->Scrollbar;
$lb = $mw->Listbox(-selectmode => 'single',
                   -yscrollcommand => [set => $scroll]);
$scroll->configure(-command => [yview => $lb]);

$scroll->pack(-side => 'right', -fill => 'y');
$lb->pack(-side => 'left', -fill => 'both');

## Open file that contains all available cursors
## Might have to change this if your cursorfont.h is elsewhere
## On Win32 systems look in C:\Perl\lib\site\Tk\X11\cursorfont.h
open (FH, "/usr/X11R6/include/X11/cursorfont.h") ||
  die "Couldn't open cursor file.\n";
```

```
while (<FH>) {
  push(@cursors, $1) if (/\#define XC_(\w+) /);
}

close(FH);

$lb->insert('end', sort @cursors);
$lb->bind('<Button-1>',
    sub { $mw->configure(-cursor => $lb->get($lb->curselection)); });

MainLoop;
```

Although this program might seem a bit complicated at this point in the book, take a look at how it does things. If you don't completely understand it right away, it's okay. Keep reading for a few chapters and then come back and look at it again until it starts to sink in. For reference, listboxes are covered in Chapter 7, *The Listbox Widget*, and bind is covered in Chapter 14, *Binding Events*.

Focus Options

In an application, you can tab between widgets to make them available for input from the keyboard. The application indicates that a widget is available for keyboard input by drawing an outline around it in black (this is called the highlight rectangle; see Figure 3-20). If a widget has this outline around it, it is said to have the focus of the application. (You can force the focus of an application to start with a specific widget by using $widget->focus;.) Once a button has the focus, you can use the spacebar on your keyboard to activate it instead of using the mouse.

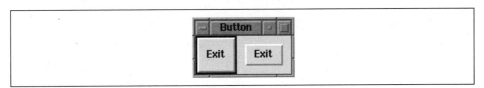

Figure 3-20. The first button has the input focus.

You can force the application to not allow your button to receive the keyboard focus at all by using the -takefocus option:

```
-takefocus => 0 | 1 | undef
```

The -takefocus option is normally set to an empty string (undef), which allows the application to dynamically decide if the widget will accept focus. If a widget has its state set to 'disabled', it will be skipped over when users tab through all the widgets. To have the application always ignore the widget when tabbing through, use -takefocus => 0. To have the application always allow focus to the widget, use -takefocus => 1.

Altering the Highlight Rectangle

The highlight rectangle* is normally displayed with a thickness of 2 pixels. This can be changed by using the `-highlightthickness` option:

```
-highlightthickness => amount
```

The amount specified is any valid screen distance. In Figure 3-21, the Exit button on the right has a `-highlightthickness` of 10 and has the focus.

Figure 3-21. Example of -highlightthickness => 10

When the button doesn't have the keyboard focus, a small space is left around it. If this extra space bothers you, you can set `-highlightthickness` to 0 and the space won't display even if that widget has the focus. It is bad style to set the `-highlightthickness` to 0 if you aren't also setting `-takefocus` to 0.

The color of the highlight rectangle can also be changed. There are two values for this: the color of the highlight rectangle when the button does not have the focus and the color of the highlight rectangle when it does have the focus. The option `-highlightcolor` is the color of the highlight rectangle when the button does have focus:

```
-highlightcolor => color
```

Figure 3-22 shows the right button with the focus and with `-highlightcolor` set to `'yellow'`. Compare it to the picture in Figure 3-21 to see the difference.

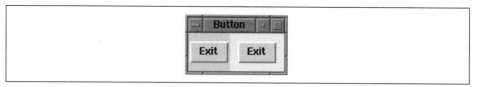

Figure 3-22. Example of button with -highlightcolor => 'yellow'

To change the color of the space left around the button when it doesn't have the focus, use the option `-highlightbackground`:

```
-highlightbackground => color
```

---

* On Win32 systems, the highlight rectangle is drawn as a dashed line within the widget.

Normally, the highlight rectangle is the same color as the background of the window, which allows it to blend in with the background of the window or frame that contains the button.

Figure 3-23 shows an example where both buttons have the following configuration:

```
-highlightcolor => 'blue', -highlightbackground => 'yellow'
```

The right button is the one that has the focus.

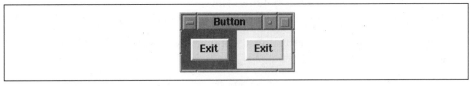

Figure 3-23. Example of button with -highlightcolor => 'blue' and -highlightbackground => 'yellow'

Configuring a Button

After creating the widget and saving a reference to it in a scalar (such as $button), it is possible to use methods on that button.

There are two methods available to configure a button after it is created and to get configuration information back: `configure` and `cget`. They are generic to all widgets and are covered in Appendix A, *Configuring Widgets with configure and cget*. Here are some common examples to get you started:

```
$state = $button->cget(-state);          # Get the current value for -state
$state = $button->configure(-state);     # Get the current value for -state
$button->configure(-text => "New Text"); # Change the text
$text = $button->cget(-text);            # Get the current text value
@all = $button->configure();             # Get info on all options for button
```

Flashing the Button

The `flash` method will cause the button to appear to be "flashing" on the screen. It changes back and forth from the normal state colors to the active state colors:

```
$button->flash();
```

Invoking the Button

The `invoke` method invokes the subroutine to which the `-command` option points. Once you use `-command` to assign the callback, then anytime you need to perform that same task, you can use `invoke()`:

```
$button->invoke();
```

Some Fun Things to Try

One of the best ways to figure out how Perl/Tk works is to try it. Once you understand the basics, you'll spend most of your time tweaking options and callbacks to
do the correct thing. Here are some ways to learn about the button widget:

- Create a window with three buttons in it. Have each button print something
  different when clicked on.

- Create a window with three buttons. Have the first two buttons change each
  other's text when pressed. The last button should allow you to exit the program.

- Make some really big buttons and some really tiny buttons all in the same
  window.

4

Checkbuttons and Radiobuttons

This chapter discusses both checkbutton and radiobutton widgets. Although they are very similar, they are used for different purposes.

Checkbuttons are useful when you want to select as many items as you want, such as a shopping list. Radiobuttons are used in group situations when you must make a choice between items, such as on a multiple-choice exam:

```
Q1: What year did Columbus discover America?
A) 1400
B) 1470
C) 1472
D) 1492
E) none of the above
```

Because radiobuttons are grouped together, you are forced to select one and only one choice in that group. If the default choice is always A and you click on D, A would be automatically unclicked (or unselected).

The two sections in this chapter cover how to use both widget types and ways to set them up and configure them.

The Checkbutton Widget

■ **Checkbutton Widget**
In Chapter 3, *The Basic Button*, you learned the options associated with the button widget. A checkbutton is also considered a type of button (and it uses many of the same options), even though the way it is used in an application is different from the way a standard button is used.

Instead of clicking on a checkbutton and expecting something to happen immediately, you use it to indicate a yes or no answer. If the checkbutton is checked it means yes; unchecked means no. You might use a checkbutton to list options for printing a document. The text on the checkbuttons might say Print Header Page, Even Pages Only, Odd Pages Only, and Number Pages. At the bottom of the window there would be a Print button, and when you clicked on it, the program would find out which checkbuttons were selected and submit the print job accordingly.

A window listing several jobs to run (like a batch job controller) might use checkbuttons to ask the user if each job should be run. If the checkbutton next to the job name is selected, the job will be run. If the checkbutton is unselected, then the job will be skipped this time around.

Each time a checkbutton is used, the application is asking the user to answer a yes or no question. Checkbuttons that make up a group are typically related (as in our print job example), but they don't have to be because the answer to each checkbutton is independent of any other widgets or checkbuttons on the screen.

The checkbutton is similar to a button; it displays a text string, but it also has an indicator on the left side of the widget. By default, the outside edges of the checkbutton don't have 3D relief like a standard button does, but the indicator (that little square on the left) does.

A checkbutton operates in the same way a standard button does; you click on it with the left mouse button. A button will change its own `-relief` (the way the edges of the button are drawn) to look like it has been pushed down whereas a checkbutton will only change the state of the indicator. If the checkbutton is on, the indicator will look as if it has been pushed into the window and filled with a darker color.* If the checkbutton is off, it will look like a tiny gray button.

Sometimes the terminology becomes confusing because there is the indicator's status (or value) and the state of the checkbutton itself. If the checkbutton looks like a tiny raised button without color, then it is off (Figure 4-1; left checkbutton). If it is filled in with color, we say it is on (Figure 4-1; right checkbutton). The state of the entire checkbutton (including the indicator) can be normal, active, or disabled. Both checkbuttons in Figure 4-1 have a state of normal.

Figure 4-1. A checkbutton that is off and one that is on

---

* Some operating systems actually put a checkmark (✔) into the little box. Others use a tiny "x" in the indicator to show the state as on.

As when creating any widget, the checkbutton is created using a method named after the capitalized version of the widget name, `Checkbutton`, invoked from the parent widget. The basic usage looks like this:

```
$cb = $parentwidget->Checkbutton( [ option => value, . . . ] )->pack;
```

In addition to having an indicator with a status, the checkbutton also can have a callback that uses the `-command` option associated with it. When the checkbutton is clicked (regardless of the indicator's status), the callback is invoked. However, it isn't always necessary to associate a callback for radiobuttons and checkbuttons since you can just check the status of the radiobutton or checkbutton later on in the program.

The boolean status of the checkbutton is stored in a variable that you give via the `-variable` option when it is created. Each checkbutton should have its own status stored in its own unique variable. When the checkbutton is clicked, the status is updated. In addition, any callback associated with the `-command` option is invoked (regardless of the new status of the checkbutton). The options that change a checkbutton's behavior are listed below and explained in greater detail afterwards.

Checkbutton Options

The following checkbutton options work exactly the same as a standard button, so I won't go over them in detail again. Refer to Chapter 3, for complete descriptions of these options: `-activebackground`, `-activeforeground`, `-anchor`, `-background`, `-borderwidth`, `-cursor`, `-disabledforeground`, `-font`, `-foreground`, `-height`, `-highlightbackground`, `-highlightcolor`, `-highlightthickness`, `-justify`, `-padx`, `-pady`, `-state`, `-takefocus`, `-text`, `-textvariable`, `-underline`, `-width`, and `-wraplength`.

The rest of the options behave a little differently or are exclusive to the checkbutton widget. They are covered in the following list. Some options deal with only the indicator (such as `-selectimage`). Remember that the `-state` option refers to the entire checkbutton widget, and the status of the indicator is governed by the options `-onvalue`, `-offvalue`, `-indicatoron`, and `-variable`.

`-activebackground` => *color*
> Sets the color the widget's background should be when the mouse is over it.

`-activeforeground` => *color*
> Sets the color the widget's text should be when the mouse is over it.

`-anchor` => `'n'` | `'ne'` | `'e'` | `'se'` | `'s'` | `'sw'` | `'w'` | `'nw'` | `'center'`
> Sets the position of the text within the widget. Most noticeable when the widget is resized larger.

-background => *color*

   Sets the color of the widget background (behind the text).

-bitmap => *bitmap*

   Displays this bitmap instead of text.

-borderwidth => *amount*

   Sets the edge thickness of the widget. Also changes the thickness of the indicator. Default is 2.

-command => *callback*

   Associates a subroutine to the button. Called when button is clicked.

-cursor => *cursorname*

   Sets the cursor to change to *cursorname* when it is over the widget.

-disabledforeground => *color*

   Sets the color of the text when -state is 'disabled'.

-font => *fontname*

   Sets the font to use when displaying text in the widget.

-foreground => *color*

   Sets the color of the text.

-height => *amount*

   Sets the height of the button; *amount* is a valid screen distance.

-highlightbackground => *color*

   Sets the color the highlight rectangle around the widget should be when the widget does not have focus.

-highlightcolor => *color*

   Sets the color the highlight rectangle around the window should be when the widget does have focus.

-highlightthickness => *amount*

   Sets the thickness of the highlight rectangle.

-image => *imgptr*

   Displays image instead of text.

-indicatoron => 0 | **1**

   Determines whether to display the indicator.

-justify => 'left' | 'right' | **'center'**

   Sets the justification of the text within the widget.

-offvalue => *newvalue*

   Sets the value used when the button is off. Must be a scalar. Default is 0.

-onvalue => *newvalue*

   Sets the value used when the button is on. Must be a scalar. Default is 1.

-padx => *amount*

> Sets the amount of space left between text/indicator and left/right edges of widget.

-pady => *amount*

> Sets the amount of space left between text/indicator and top/bottom edges of widget.

-relief => '**flat**'|'groove'|'raised'|'ridge'|'sunken'|'solid'

> Changes the look of the widget edges.

-selectcolor => *color*

> Sets the color of the indicator when on.

-selectimage => *imgptr*

> Indicates the image to display instead of text when button is on. Ignored if -image is not used.

-state => '**normal**' | 'disabled' | 'active'

> Sets the state of the widget. If disabled, it will not respond to any input.

-takefocus => 0 | 1 | **undef**

> Determines if the widget is available for focus or not.

-text => "text"

> Sets the text displayed in the widget.

-textvariable => \\$variable

> Indicates that text in $variable is displayed as text in widget.

-underline => *n*

> Underlines the *n*th character in the text string.

-variable => \\$value

> Associates the on/off value of indicator with $variable.

-width => *amount*

> Sets the widget to this width. Can be any valid screen distance.

-wraplength => *amount*

> Indicates that the text will wrap when it exceeds this amount.

Storing the Indicator's Status

The option -variable will associate a variable with the status of the indicator by sending a reference as the value. To use the scalar $value, you would add this to the option list of the Checkbutton call:

```
-variable => \$value
```

Just as the -textvariable option sets the variable that is associated with the text of the checkbutton, this option sets the variable associated with the indicator.

When the checkbutton is clicked, $value will now contain the status of the indicator (the value placed in $value is defined by -onvalue and -offvalue and by default are 1 and 0 respectively).

In addition to using the mouse to change the status, you can also change the contents of $value directly. If your code contains $value = 1 at some point, the indicator will be turned on. You can specify $value = 1 before creating the checkbutton, which will draw the checkbutton for the first time with the indicator on. If you change the value in $value at any time after you create the checkbutton in your program, the checkbutton will change to reflect the new value. The subroutine associated with -command (if there is one) is *not* invoked when the value of $value is changed.

Utilizing -variable is usually the easiest way to check the status of the indicator on the button. Here is an example that has two buttons that change the value in $cb_value:

```
$cb_value = 0;
$cb = $mw->Checkbutton(-text => "Checkbutton",
                       -variable => \$cb_value,
                       -command => sub { print "Clicked! $cb_value\n" }
                       )->pack(-side => 'top');

$mw->Button(-text => "CB on",
            -command => sub { $cb_value = 1 })->pack(-side => 'left');
$mw->Button(-text => "CB off",
            -command => sub { $cb_value = 0 })->pack(-side => 'left');
```

See Figure 4-2 for the resulting window.

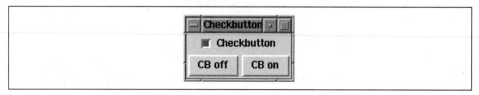

Figure 4-2. Buttons changing the value of a checkbutton

The value stored in $cb_value can be changed in three ways: clicking on the checkbutton, clicking on the "CB off" button, or clicking on the "CB on" button. Only when you click on the checkbutton will you see the word "Clicked!" written in the shell window from which it was run.

There are other ways to change the value associated with the checkbutton. See invoke, select, deselect, and toggle in "Checkbutton Methods" later in this chapter.

Assigning a Callback

The -command option works just like it does for a standard button, but usually the function associated with a checkbutton's callback does something less obvious. Many times, there is no callback at all associated with the checkbutton because the important information is the status of the checkbutton rather than whether the checkbutton was just clicked.

One of the things a checkbutton might do is alter the appearance of the window. The checkbutton might look something like the one in Figure 4-3.

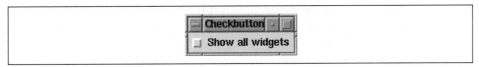

Figure 4-3. Checkbutton that will display other widgets on the screen when clicked

When the user clicks on the checkbutton to turn it on, our window magically changes to look like Figure 4-4.

Figure 4-4. Window after clicking the checkbutton

Here's the code that makes the magic happen:

```perl
#!/usr/bin/perl -w
use Tk;
$mw = MainWindow->new;
$mw->title("Checkbutton");

## Create other widgets, but don't pack them yet!
for ($i = 1; $i <= 5; $i++) {
  push (@buttons, $mw->Button(-text => "Button$i"));
}

$mw->Checkbutton(-text => "Show all widgets",
                 -variable => \$cb_value,
                 -command => sub {
                   if ($cb_value) {
                     foreach (@buttons) {
                       $_->pack(-side => 'left');
                     }
                   } else {
                     foreach (@buttons) {
```

```
                   $_->pack('forget');
              }
         }
    })->pack(-side => 'top');
MainLoop;
```

So we can display some widgets later on in the program, we create them ahead of time and store references to them in the @buttons array. The buttons in this example aren't very useful because they don't even have a -command associated with them. Normally, they would each have a specific task they would perform when pressed; however, for our example, we just want them to exist.

Then we create our magic checkbutton. When the button is clicked (regardless of the status of its indicator), it will call the subroutine pointed to by -command. Our subroutine looks at the current value of $cb_value, shows the buttons if it is on, and hides them if it is off. The value in $cb_value is changed before this subroutine is called. When our checkbutton is clicked again, the extra buttons will be removed from the window and the window will shrink back to the size it was previously.

This type of setup is great when you want to keep a basic window uncluttered but want the ability to show more widgets if the user can handle the advanced functions of the extra widgets. For example, you can create a Find window that has a place to enter some text, a button to start the find, and an Advanced Search checkbutton. Clicking on Advanced Search would add some more widgets to the bottom of the window allowing you to match case, use regular expressions, and use other fancy search mechanisms.

On and Off Values

If you don't like the default on value of 1, you can use the -onvalue option to change it:

```
-onvalue => newvalue  ## Default is 1
```

The same is true of the off value:

```
-offvalue => newvalue  ## Default is 0
```

These options will change the values stored in $variable. Depending on how you would like the checkbutton to interact with the rest of your application, sometimes it makes sense to use different values. The *newvalue* could be anything, as long as it is a scalar value. This means that you can use references to arrays and hashes if you really want to.

It is good practice to keep the meaning of -onvalue the opposite of -offvalue. If -onvalue is now the string "ON", logically -offvalue should be "OFF". Of course, if the purpose of this checkbutton is to use a more accurate value of π, then –onvalue could be "3.14159265359", and –offvalue could be "3.14".

Be careful when you use unusual values for –onvalue and –offvalue. If you set the variable to something that doesn't equal either one of them, the checkbutton will be considered off, even though the value of the $variable will not equal the –offvalue value. For instance, if you set –onvalue => 1, –offvalue => 0, and you set $variable to 3, then the checkbutton will be considered off.

Indicator Color

You can use the –selectcolor option to alter the color that fills in the indicator when the checkbutton is selected:

```
-selectcolor => color
```

The default value is "#b03060" (a dark pink color). Changing the value for –selectcolor will also change the background of the button when the button is selected and –indicatoron => 0 .

Hiding the Indicator

One of the ways a checkbutton is different from a standard button is the indicator. Use the –indicatoron option to tell Perl/Tk not to draw that funny little square button at all:

```
-indicatoron => 0 | 1
```

As we have seen from the previous examples, the default for –indicatoron is 1 (i.e., show the indicator). If we change this –indicatoron to 0, the checkbutton will look almost like a normal button (without quite as much space around the text, though). Even though it looks a lot like a regular button, its behavior when it is clicked (to turn the indicator, which is hidden, to on) is completely different (see Figure 4-5). Note that the –relief option is ignored completely when –indicatoron is set to 0.

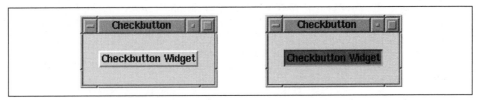

Figure 4-5. Checkbutton with -indicatoron => 0. Window on left is unchecked. Window on right is checked.

In this example, the color for the background on the checked button is the -selectcolor, not the -backgroundcolor. You might want to use the nonindicator configuration if you change the text of the button to reflect the new state of the checkbutton. For instance, change Logging Enabled to Logging Disabled.

Displaying a Picture Instead of Text

As you can with a normal button, you can use the -image option to display an image in place of the text on a checkbutton. Another option, -selectimage, is available to display a different image when the checkbutton has been clicked:

```
-image => $imgptr [ , -selectimage => $imgptr ]
```

The usage statement shows -selectimage as optional because it will be ignored if -image is not used.

The imgptrs can be created by using the same methods as those used in Chapter 3 with a button's -image option: $arrow = $mw->Photo(-file => "nextart.gif");

The image will be put in place of the text on the checkbutton. These options have precedence over the -text option, so if both -text and -image are listed, the -text option will be ignored.

Which image is displayed depends on whether the button is on or off. If only the -image option is specified, this image will be displayed no matter what. If -selectimage is also specified, the image associated with it will be displayed when the button is checked. Figure 4-6 shows an example that uses both options.

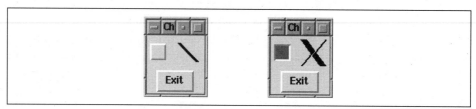

Figure 4-6. The same window with the checkbutton unchecked (on the left) and checked (on the right)

The checkbuttons in Figure 4-6 were created with this code snippet:

```
$img1 = $mw->Bitmap(-file =>
                    "/usr/X11R6/include/X11/bitmaps/lineOp.xbm");
$img2 = $mw->Bitmap(-file => "/usr/X11R6/include/X11/bitmaps/xlogo32");

$mw->Checkbutton(-text => "Checkbutton",
                 -image => $img1,
                 -selectimage => $img2,
                 -variable => \$cb_value)->pack(-side => 'top');
```

Using two different images to indicate whether the checkbutton is off or on might make more sense if you also use -indicatoron and set it to 0. For instance, if you want to indicate that a document is locked (read-only) or unlocked you could use a picture of a lock for -image and a picture of a lock with a line through it for -selectimage.

For this example, I chose to use bitmap files as our images. Instead of using the -image option to display a bitmap, you could use the -bitmap option directly. The -bitmap option is exactly the same as the standard button -bitmap option; it replaces the text of the button with the specified bitmap (see Figure 4-7).

Figure 4-7. Checkbutton with -bitmap => 'warning'

Unlike -image and -selectimage, using -bitmap will not change the image when the button is clicked on or off.

You might think that using images instead of text would make your application easier for non-English speakers to understand. However, if you use too many checkbuttons with images, you might confuse people even more. A few easily understood icons are better than a large collection of vague icons.

Checkbutton Style

Although the button and checkbutton both share the -relief and -borderwidth options, and they mean the exact same thing, when they are used with a checkbutton, the effects are visually different because of the indicator. As a reminder, the possible values are:

```
-relief => 'flat'|'groove'|'raised'|'ridge'|'sunken'|'solid'
-borderwidth => amount
```

Figure 4-8 shows the different relief types when a default -borderwidth value is used. The default for a checkbutton is 'flat' because the relief of the outside edge of the checkbutton doesn't change when the checkbutton is clicked; only the indicator changes. Figure 4-8 also shows that the edges of the checkbutton are much closer to the text; the -padx and -pady default values are smaller than the default for a button. The -relief option does not affect the indicator.

The -borderwidth option affects both the outside edge of the checkbutton and the indicator inside the checkbutton. The indicator itself stays the same size no

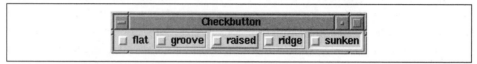

Figure 4-8. Example of all possible -relief types

matter what the borderwidth of the widget is, but the indicator's edges change in width. When you use a large `-borderwidth`, you get some interesting results, as shown in Figure 4-9.

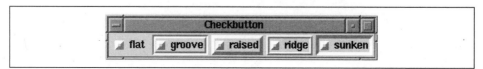

Figure 4-9. Example using -borderwidth => 4

We used a `-borderwidth` of 4, and you can see that the outside edges got a bit thicker, and so did the edges of the indicator. With a larger `-borderwidth`, there is much less room to show the indicator's color when it is on (see the tiny square in the middle of those indicators?).

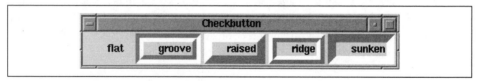

Figure 4-10. Example using -borderwidth => 10

In Figure 4-10, we used a `-borderwidth` of 10. Notice the remarkable difference! We can no longer see the indicator at all, even though there is still space left for it. When these checkbuttons are checked or unchecked, there is no way to tell what the current state it is because the indicator is essentially invisible.

I highly recommend that you do not use the `-borderwidth` option associated with a checkbutton because of this interesting side effect.

Configuring a Checkbutton

Like the button widget, the checkbutton has methods that can manipulate it after it is created. These methods can be invoked at any time after the checkbutton is created, even before it is displayed on the screen.

You can use both `configure` and `cget` methods with a checkbutton as well. These methods are explained in Appendix A, *Configuring Widgets with configure and cget*.

Turning a Checkbutton On and Off

You can force the checkbutton to go from on to off or vice versa using the **deselect** and **select** methods.

The **deselect** method will always set the indicator to the off state and the variable assigned by **-variable** to the value in **-offvalue**:

```
$cb->deselect();
```

The opposite of **deselect**, **select** will cause the indicator to be set to the on state and the variable assigned by **-variable** to the **-onvalue**:

```
$cb->select();
```

Both methods are ignored if **-state** is '**disabled**'.

You can also toggle the indicator from on to off or vice versa using the **toggle** method:

```
$cb->toggle();
```

Calling **toggle** does not cause the subroutine associated with the **-command** value to be called.

Flashing the Checkbutton

You can make the indicator flash with the **-background** and **-foreground** colors by calling **flash**:

```
$cb->flash();
```

Invoking the Checkbutton

To perform the same action as clicking the checkbutton with the left mouse button, call **invoke**:

```
$cb->invoke();
```

It will cause any callback associated with **-command** to be called; it will also switch the state of the indicator from on to off or vice versa.

The Radiobutton Widget

A radiobutton looks similar to a checkbutton because it also has an indicator on the left side. The radiobutton indicator is a diamond, rather than a square. Both look 3D and are slightly raised when unselected.

The main difference between a radiobutton and a checkbutton is the function they serve in an application. A radiobutton is used to select one of several different choices:

- In a multiple choice test, the answers A, B, C, D, or E

- Which version of a tool you would like to use

- Your income range: 0–20,000; 20,001–30,000; 30,001–40,000; 40,000 and up

- Which type of entree you prefer: beef, chicken, or vegetarian

In each example, only one answer is appropriate. For instance, it wouldn't make sense to have a salary of both $18,000 and $33,000. And when you are taking a multiple-choice test, you can't select all the answers and hope that the teacher gives you credit. You have to pick only one.

Because radiobuttons are used to decide between several choices, you should always create at least two.* It doesn't make sense to ask a question at all if there is only one choice. Radiobuttons should always be created in groups of two or more.

Creating Radiobuttons

So far, you have learned to create one widget at a time. Because radiobuttons are always in a group, we generally need to create more than one at a time. So you can be efficient and create all the widgets as quickly and painlessly as possible, I'll show you some quick ways to make up a group of radiobuttons.

(To show you how to take advantage of the widgets in the best way, the examples will start to get a bit more complicated. By now, you should know the basics of widget creation and how to specify options during the creation. I'll often say that an option works exactly like it did with widget X and refer you to that chapter for a more complete discussion.)

Radiobuttons are similar to checkbuttons; they also have a $variable associated with the state of the indicator (using the option -variable). When you create a group of radiobuttons, use the same $variable for every radiobutton in the group. The value put into the $variable will change according to which radiobutton is selected. To create a new group of radiobuttons, simply associate the new group with a different $variable.

Because each radiobutton in a group points to the same $variable, there isn't a concept of onvalue and offvalue. The offvalue would be whatever the other radiobutton wanted it to be. To accomplish this, radiobuttons use the option -value instead of -onvalue and -offvalue.

---

* If you did create only one radiobutton, it would start out unselected (unless the variable you associated with it contained the on value). Once that radiobutton was selected, you would never be able to deselect it.

For our first example, we'll create a group of radiobuttons that indicate the background color of our window. We need to use colors that are valid to the $mw-> configure(-background => *color*) command. Simple color names usually work, so we will use red, yellow, green, blue, and gray.

As always, the basic usage for creating a radiobutton is as follows:

```
$rb = $parentwidget->Radiobutton( [ option => value, . . . ] )->pack;
```

Here is the code that will create the radiobutton group that controls the background color:

```
# setup the default value we would like
$rb_value = "red";
$mw->configure(-background => $rb_value);

# create the radiobuttons that will let us change it
foreach (qw(red yellow green blue grey)) {
  $mw->Radiobutton(-text => $_,
                   -value => $_,
                   -variable => \$rb_value,
                   -command => \&set_bg)->pack(-side => 'left');
}

# function to change the background color using $rb_value
sub set_bg {
  print "Background value is now: $rb_value\n";
  $mw->configure(-background => $rb_value);
}
```

We are storing the status of our radiobutton group in $rb_value. We set it to an initial value of "red", which happens to match the first radiobutton we are creating. When any of the radiobuttons are clicked, including the one currently selected, the subroutine set_bg will be called. This subroutine will print the new value of $rb_value and then change the background of our main window to that color.

One thing to note: Although we set the default value of our radiobutton group to "red", that doesn't mean that the background of the window has been set to red as well. We do this by calling the configure command and sending it the value in $rb_value. We could also do it by an explicit call to the set_bg routine, or we could have done it when we created the MainWindow.

The window we have created looks like Figure 4-11.

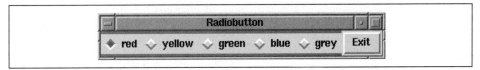

Figure 4-11. Radiobuttons that will change the background color of the window

The best way to understand how this window works is to type in the code and run it. This will be true for a lot of the examples shown in this book. When you click on each radiobutton, you'll see a strip of the window at the top and bottom change color. You'll only see this small strip because we only changed the background of $mw, not of each radiobutton or the exit button.

Now that we've seen a basic application of radiobuttons, we can go over each of the options.

Radiobutton Options

As with the checkbutton, the following options are the same for any of the three types of buttons: -activebackground, -activeforeground, -anchor, -background, -borderwidth, -cursor, -disabledforeground, -font, -foreground, -height, -highlightbackground, -highlightcolor, -highlightthickness, -padx, -pady, -state, -takefocus, -text, -textvariable, -underline, and -width.

In addition, the following options are the same between checkbutton and radiobutton: -command, -indicatoron, -image, -selectimage, -bitmap, -wraplength, -justify, and -selectcolor.

The rest I will discuss because they behave a bit differently because of the context in which we are using them.

-activebackground => *color*
> Sets the color the widget's background should be when mouse is over it.

-activeforeground => *color*
> Sets the color the widget's text should be when the mouse is over it.

-anchor => 'n' | 'ne' | 'e' | 'se' | 's' | 'sw' | 'w' | 'nw' | **'center'**
> Sets the position of the text within the widget. Most noticeable when the widget is resized larger.

-background => *color*
> Sets the color of the widget background (behind the text).

-bitmap => *bitmapname*
> Displays this bitmap instead of text.

-borderwidth => *amount*
> Sets the edge thickness of the widget. Also changes the thickness of the indicator. Default is 2.

-command => *callback*
> Associates a subroutine to the button. Called when the button is clicked.

`-cursor => ` *cursorname*
> Indicates that the cursor will change to *cursorname* when it is over the widget.

`-disabledforeground => ` *color*
> Sets the color of the text when `-state` is `'disabled'`.

`-font => ` *fontname*
> Sets the font to use when displaying text in the widget.

`-foreground => ` *color*
> Sets the color of the text.

`-height => ` *amount*
> Sets the height of the button; *amount* is a valid screen distance.

`-highlightbackground => ` *color*
> Sets the color the highlight rectangle around the widget should be when the widget does *not* have focus.

`-highlightcolor => ` *color*
> Sets the color the highlight rectangle around the window should be when the widget *does* have focus.

`-highlightthickness => ` *amount*
> Sets the thickness of the highlight rectangle.

`-image => ` *imgptr*
> Indicates that an image is displayed instead of text.

`-indicatoron => 0 | `**`1`**
> Indicates the status of the indicator; 0 means indicator is not displayed.

`-justify => `**`'center'`**` | 'left' | 'right'`
> Sets the justification of the text within the widget.

`-padx => ` *amount*
> Sets the amount of space left between text/indicator and left/right edges of the widget.

`-pady => ` *amount*
> Sets the amount of space left between text/indicator and top/bottom edges of widget.

`-relief => `**`'flat'`**`|'groove'|'raised'|'ridge'|'sunken'|'solid'`
> Changes the look of the widget edges.

`-selectcolor => ` *color*
> Sets the color the indicator should be when on.

-selectimage => *imgptr*

> Indicates that an image should be displayed instead of text when the button is on. Ignored if -image is not used.

-state => 'normal' | 'active' | 'disabled'

> Sets the state of the widget. If disabled, it will not respond to any input.

-takefocus => 0 | 1 | undef

> Determines whether the widget is available for focus or not.

-text => *textstring*

> Sets the text displayed in the widget.

-textvariable => \$variable

> Indicates that the text in $variable is displayed as text in the widget.

-underline => *n*

> Underlines the *n*th character in the text string.

-value => *newvalue*

> Sets the value assigned to $variable (set with -variable option) when this radiobutton is selected (default is 1).

-variable => \$variable

> Sets the variable to use when this radiobutton is clicked.

-width => *amount*

> Sets the width of the widget. Can be any valid screen distance.

-wraplength => *amount*

> Indicates that the text will wrap when it exceeds this amount.

Using the -variable Option

The -variable option will look the same in each radiobutton creation command, except logically, we are using it differently. We should have several radiobuttons sharing the same $variable instead of each one having their own distinct $variable. The example for Figure 4-11 shows how this works.

Setting the Value

With checkbuttons, we had two options, -onvalue and -offvalue, because we had to worry about the state of each individual checkbutton. With radiobuttons, we only care about the state of the whole group. Each radiobutton should have a different -value to it, so a glance at $variable will tell us which radiobutton is selected.

The default -value is 1. (Remember: When you use a group that consists of only one radiobutton, that one is always checked.)

To make sure you understand the difference between the **-variable** option and the **-value** option, let's walk through a short example.

```
$mw->Radiobutton(-text => "Beef", -value => "Beef",
                 -variable => \$entree);
$mw->Radiobutton(-text => "Chicken", -value => "Chicken",
                 -variable => \$entree);
$mw->Radiobutton(-text => "Vegetarian", -value => "Vegetarian",
                 -variable => \$entree);
```

Here we have created three radiobuttons that all use the variable $entree to store their values in. If the user selects Beef, then $entree will contain the value of **"Beef"**. If the user selects Chicken, then $entree will contain the value of **"Chicken"**. Later in the program when we build the physical menu for the printer, we can just check to see what is in $entree to find out what that user wants for dinner.

Radiobutton Style

Okay, so the **-relief** option does the same thing it does in a checkbutton. But it is worthwhile to show a screen shot of what happens when different relief types are used (see Figure 4-12).

Figure 4-12. Different relief types for a radiobutton

As with the checkbutton, changing **-borderwidth** can cause the radiobutton to look drastically different (see Figure 4-13).

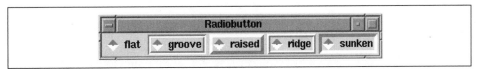

Figure 4-13. Radiobuttons with -borderwidth of 4

Remember how the indicator completely disappeared in a checkbutton when we used a **-borderwidth** of 10? Well, in a radiobutton, it makes it look kind of like a kite (see Figure 4-14). You still won't be able to tell which radiobutton is checked or not, so I don't recommend using the **-borderwidth** option.

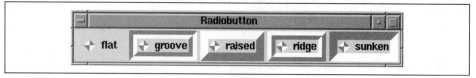

Figure 4-14. Radiobuttons with -borderwidth of 10

Configuring a Radiobutton

Just as you can with our other widgets, you can use `configure` and `cget` to get or set option values for each radiobutton widget. See Appendix A for more details on how to use these methods.

Selecting and Unselecting a Radiobutton

A radiobutton also has both `select` and `deselect` methods:

```
$rb->deselect();
$rb->select();
```

Using `select` causes the radiobutton to be selected. (Using `deselect` will cause the radiobutton to be unselected. It sets the `$variable` to an empty string. If you use this method, make sure you account for it in any code that evaluates the value of `$variable`). Any command associated via the `-command` option will also be invoked with both `select` and `deselect`.

Flashing the Radiobutton

The `flash` method will flash the radiobutton's background/foreground colors off and on, but otherwise, it does nothing interesting:

```
$rb->flash();
```

Invoking a Radiobutton

To programmatically select a radiobutton, use the `invoke` method:

```
$rb->invoke();
```

It causes the radiobutton to be selected and will also invoke any callback associated with the radiobutton via the `-command` option. Essentially, it does the same thing it would do if you clicked on the radiobutton with the mouse.

Fun Things to Try

- Create a bunch of checkbuttons and a Go button that will report the status of all the checkbuttons.

- Make up a survey that uses checkbuttons for questions that have one or more options and radiobuttons with only one appropriate choice.

- Create three different groups of checkbuttons: Favorite Color, Favorite Song, and Shoe Size. Then create a radiobutton to represent each group. The currently selected radiobutton dictates which checkbuttons the user can see and use.

5

Label and Entry Widgets

There are times you'll want users to type in specific information such as their name, address, or even a serial number. The simplest way to do this is to use entry widgets. You can use a label widget with an entry to clearly communicate to the user what should be typed in the entry. Most often, you'll see the label and entry combination used multiple times in a database entry–type window where there are many different pieces of information the user must enter.

The Label Widget

Label Widget So far, all we have talked about are buttons, buttons, and more buttons. What if we just want to put some informative text on the screen? The label widget does just that. A label is like a button that doesn't do anything. It is a noninteractive widget and by default cannot have the keyboard focus (meaning you can't tab to it) and it does nothing when you click on it.

The label widget is probably *the* simplest widget. It is similar to a button in that it can show text (or a bitmap), have relief (default is flat), display multiple lines of text, have a different font, and so on. Figure 5-1 shows a simple window, with both a button and label, created with this code:

```
use Tk;
$mw = MainWindow->new();
$mw->Label(-text => "Label Widget")->pack();
$mw->Button(-text => "Exit", -command => sub { exit })->pack();
MainLoop;
```

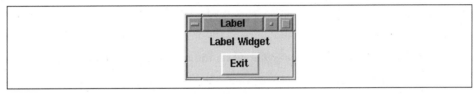

Figure 5-1. A simple window with label and button

Here are some typical uses for a label:

- Put a label to the left of an entry widget so the user knows what type of data is expected.

- Put a label above a group of radiobuttons, making their purpose more clear (e.g., "Background Color:"). You can do the same thing with checkbuttons if they happen to be related or along the same theme.

- Use a label to tell users what they did wrong: "The number entered must be between 10 and 100." (Typically, you would use a Dialog composite widget to give messages to the user like this, but not always.)

- Put an informational line across the bottom of your window. All the other widgets would have a mapping that displays a string containing information about that widget.

Creating a Label

The command to create a label is, of course, `Label`. Here's the basic usage:

```
$label = $parent->Label( [ option => value . . . ] )->pack();
```

Hopefully, you are starting to see a trend in the creation command. As you might expect, when you create a label, you can specify options that will change its appearance and how it behaves.

Label Options

The following list is a comprehensive list of options for labels:

`-anchor => 'n' | 'ne' | 'e' | 'se' | 's' | 'sw' | 'w' | 'nw' |`
  `'center'`
  Causes the text to stick to that position in the label widget. This won't be obvious unless the label is forced to be larger than standard size.

`-background => color`
  Sets the background color of the label to *color*.

`-bitmap => bitmap`
  Displays the bitmap contained in *bitmap* instead of text.

-borderwidth => *amount*

    Changes the width of the edges of the label.

-cursor => *cursorname*

    Changes the cursor to *cursorname* when the mouse is over this widget.

-font => *fontname*

    Indicates that the text in the widget will be displayed with *fontname*.

-foreground => *color*

    Changes the text of the button (or the bitmap) to be color *color*.

-height => *amount*

    Sets the height of the label to *amount*; *amount* is a valid screen distance.

-highlightbackground => *color*

    Sets the color of the focus rectangle when the widget is not in focus to *color*.

-highlightcolor => *color*

    Sets the color of the focus rectangle when the widget has focus to *color*.

-highlightthickness => *amount*

    Sets the width of the focus rectangle. Default is 0 for the label.

-image => *imgptr*

    Displays the image to which *imgptr* points instead of text.

-justify => 'left' | 'right' | **'center'**

    Sets the side of the label against which the text will justify.

-padx => *amount*

    Adds extra space inside the edge to the left and right of the label.

-pady => *amount*

    Adds extra space inside the edge to the top and bottom of the label.

-relief => **'flat'** | 'groove' | 'raised' | 'ridge' | 'sunken'

    Changes the type of edges drawn around the button.

-takefocus => **0** | 1 | undef

    Changes the ability of the label to have the focus or not.

-text => *text*

    Displays in the label a text string.

-textvariable => \\$variable

    Points to the variable containing text to be displayed in the label. Label will change automatically as $variable changes.

-underline => *n*

    Causes the *n*th character to be underlined. Allows that key to invoke the widget when it has the focus. Default value is −1 (no character underlined).

-width => *amount*
> Causes the label to be width *amount.*

-wraplength => *amount*
> Indicates that the text in the label will wrap when it gets longer than *amount.*

This list briefly describes each option and what it does. Some of the options have different defaults for the label widget than we are used to seeing with the button-type widgets, causing the label to behave a bit differently.

How a Label Differs from Other Widgets

When we created button-type widgets, we could either click them with the mouse or tab to them and then use the keyboard to cause the button to be pressed. A label widget, on the other hand, does not interact with the user. It is there for informational purposes only, so there is no -command option. We also can't tab to a label widget because nothing would happen.

The default value for the -takefocus option is 0, making the label noninteractive. When tabbing between widgets on the screen, the highlight rectangle shows us which widget currently has the keyboard focus. Since we don't allow the label to have the focus (remember, -takefocus is set to 0), it doesn't make sense to have a visible highlight rectangle. The default value for the -highlightthickness option in a label widget is 0. You can make a rectangle appear around a label by setting -highlightthickness to something greater than 0, and setting -highlightbackground to a color such as blue or red.

The label widget also doesn't have a -state option. Since we shouldn't be able to click a label, we should never have to disable it.

Relief

In Figure 5-2, you can see what happens when you change the label's -relief option. Notice that the edges of the widget are very close to the text. Unlike a button, you usually don't want much extra space around the label (space is controlled by the -padx and -pady options). Normally, you want the label widget to sit right next to the widget (or widgets) it is describing.

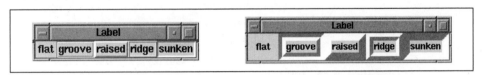

Figure 5-2. Labels with different relief values. Window on right has a -borderwidth of 10.

You'll notice that I like seeing what widgets look like with the different relief values. This sometimes helps determine where the widget ends, especially with widgets that have a default value of "flat". Also, I often change the relief of different widgets to make sure I know which widgets are where on the screen. After creating 10 entries and labels with less than creative variable names, it's easy to lose track. Also, changing the borderwidth is bound to make that one widget stand out. Of course, I always change the relief and borderwidth back to something non-obnoxious before I give the program to anyone else to run! Color is also a good way to do a diagnostic message.

Status Message Example

I often use the groove or ridge relief when I'm making a help or status label along the bottom of my window. I make a label that is packed with `-side => 'bottom'` and `-fill => 'x'`. There are two different ways you can use a status label:

- Set the variable associated with it so it changes as your program progresses, announcing to the user that it is busy, or something is happening.

- Have the help label give information on each of the different widgets in your application when it gets the focus, using the `bind` command.

Both types are demonstrated in the following sample code.

This code shows the "What I'm doing now" type of help label:

```
$mw->Label(-textvariable => \$message, -borderwidth => 2,
           -relief => 'groove')->pack(-fill => 'x',
                                      -side => 'bottom');
$mw->Text()->pack(-side => 'top',
                  -expand => 1,
                  -fill => 'both');

$message = "Loading file index.html...";
...
$message = "Done";
```

The label is created across the bottom of the screen. We pack it first because we want it to stay on the screen if we resize the window (remember, the last widgets packed will get lower priority if the window runs out of room). As the program executes (represented by the `...`), it changes the label accordingly.

This code shows an example of using a widget-helper help label:

```
$mw->title("Help Label Example");

$mw->Label(-textvariable => \$message)
   ->pack(-side => 'bottom', -fill => 'x');

$b = $mw->Button(-text => "Exit", -command => \&exit)
        ->pack(-side => 'left');
&bind_message($b, "Press to quit the application");
```

```
$b2 = $mw->Button(-text => "Do Nothing")->pack(-side => 'left');
&bind_message($b2, "This button does absolutely nothing!");

$b3 = $mw->Button(-text => "Something",
  -command => sub { print "something\n"; })->pack(-side => 'left');
&bind_message($b3, "Prints the text 'something'");

sub bind_message {
  my ($widget, $msg) = @_;
  $widget->bind('<Enter>', [ sub { $message = $_[1]; }, $msg ]);
  $widget->bind('<Leave>', sub { $message = ""; });
}
```

This example is a bit longer because we are using the bind method (the bind method is explained in more detail in Chapter 14, *Binding Events*). For each widget we create, we want to associate a help message with it. We do this by adding bindings to each widget that change the variable $message to a specified string when the mouse enters the widget, and to an empty string if the mouse leaves the widget. We used a subroutine to avoid writing the same two bind lines over and over again. Figure 5-3 shows what our window looks like with the mouse over the center button.

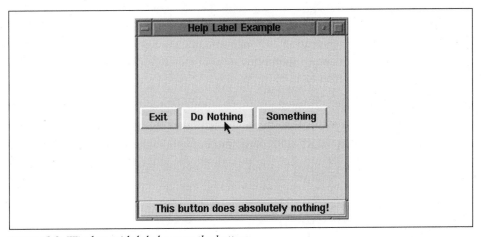

Figure 5-3. Window with label across the bottom

Container Frames

In Figure 5-3, you can see that the example text is centered within the label widget. For some reason, when you fill the widget across the screen, the text remains centered, even if you add the -justify => 'left' option. You can get around this by creating a container frame, giving it the desired relief, filling the frame across the screen (instead of the label), and placing the label widget within the frame:

```
$f = $mw->Frame(-relief => 'groove',
              -bd => 2)->pack(-side => 'bottom',
```

```
                              -fill => 'x');
   $f->Label(-textvariable => \$message,)->pack(-side => 'left');
```

This allows the label to grow and shrink within the frame as necessary, while the text sticks to the left side. If you've typed this short little example in and played with the strings bound to each widget, you might have noticed that the window will resize itself if the text assigned to $message is too long to display in the label. This can get annoying if your window is fairly small to begin with. There are two ways to deal with this: First, you can always use really short text strings, and second, you can tell the window to not resize when the label changes size.

The drawbacks with each approach aren't too bad, and which one you pick just depends on the application you are working on. If you can make really short sentences that make sense, great. Telling the window to not resize is almost as easy, though—it is accomplished by adding one line to your program:

```
   $mw->packPropagate(0);
```

Using **packPropagate** will cause your window to not resize when a widget is placed inside the window (we first talked about packPropagate in Chapter 2, *Geometry Management*). This means that your window might not be showing all your widgets right away. You can deal with this by keeping it on until you get all your widgets in it, figuring out a good starting size for your window and using $mw->geometry(*size*) to request that size initially. (See Chapter 13, *Toplevel Widgets*, for info on the **geometry** method.)

Label Configuration

Label is a pretty boring widget, so there are only two methods available to change or get information on it: **cget** and **configure**. Both methods work for Label the same way they work for the Button widget. Please refer to Appendix A for the details on arguments and return values.

The Entry Widget

Until now, the only input we know how to get from the user is a mouseclick on a button widget (Button, Checkbutton, or Radiobutton), which is handled via the **-command** option. Getting input from a mouseclick is useful, but it's also limiting. The entry widget will let the user type in text that can then be used in any way by the application. Here are a few examples of where you might use an entry widget:

- In a database form that requires one entry per field (e.g., Name, Last name, Address)

- In a software registration window that requires a serial number

- In a login window that requires a username and password

- In a configuration window to get the name of a printer

- In an Open File window that requires the path and name of a file

Normally, we don't care what users type in an entry widget until they are done typing, and any processing will happen "after the fact" when a user clicks some sort of Go button. You could get fancy and process each character as it's typed by setting up a complicated bind—but it is probably more trouble than it is worth.

The user can type anything into an entry widget. It is up to the programmer to decide if the text entered is valid or not. When preparing to use the information from an entry, we should do some error checking. If we want an integer and get some alphabetic characters, we should issue a warning or error message to the user.

An entry widget is a much more complex widget than it first appears to be. The entry widget is really a simplified one-line text editor. Text can be typed in, selected with the mouse, deleted, and added. I would classify an entry widget as a middle-of-the-line widget. It's more complicated than a button, but much less complicated than the text or canvas widgets.

Creating the Entry Widget

No surprises here:

```
$entry = $parent->Entry( [ option => value . . . ] )->pack;
```

When the entry widget is created, it is initially empty of any text, and the insert cursor (if the entry had the keyboard focus) is at the far-left side.

Entry Options

The following list contains a short description of each option available for configuring an entry widget. Several of them are discussed in more detail later in this chapter.

-background => *color*
> Sets the background color of the entry widget. This is the area behind the text.

-borderwidth => *amount*
> Changes the width of the outside edge of the widget. Default value is 2.

-cursor => *cursorname*
> Changes the cursor to *cursorname* when it is over the widget.

-exportselection => 0 | **1**
> If the Boolean value specified is true, any text selected will be exported to the windowing system's clipboard.

`-font => ` *fontname*
>   Changes the font displayed in the entry to *fontname*.

`-foreground => ` *color*
>   Changes the color of the text.

`-highlightbackground => ` *color*
>   Sets the color the highlight rectangle should be when the widget does not have the keyboard focus.

`-highlightcolor => ` *color*
>   Sets the color the highlight rectangle should be when the widget does have the keyboard focus.

`-highlightthickness => ` *amount*
>   Sets the thickness of the highlight rectangle around the widget. Default is 2.

`-insertbackground => ` *color*
>   Sets the color of the insert cursor.

`-insertborderwidth => ` *amount*
>   Sets the width of the insert cursor's border. Normally used in conjunction with `-ipadx` and `-ipady` options for the geometry manager.

`-insertofftime => ` *milliseconds*
>   Sets the amount of time the insert cursor is off in the entry widget.

`-insertontime => ` *milliseconds*
>   Sets the amount of time the insert cursor is on in the entry widget.

`-insertwidth => ` *amount*
>   Sets the width of the insert cursor. Default is 2.

`-justify => ` **`'left'`** `| 'right' | 'center'`
>   Sets the justification of the text in the entry widget. The default is left.

`-relief => 'flat'|'groove'|'raised'|'ridge'|`**`'sunken'`**`|'solid'`
>   Sets the relief of the outside edges of the entry widget.

`-selectbackground => ` *color*
>   Sets the background color of any selected text in the entry widget.

`-selectborderwidth => ` *amount*
>   Sets the width of the selection highlight's border.

`-selectforeground => ` *color*
>   Sets the text color of any selected text in the entry widget.

`-show => ` *char*
>   Sets the character that should be displayed instead of the actual text typed.

`-state => ` **`'normal'`** `| 'disabled' | 'active'`
>   Indicates the state of the entry. Default is `'normal'`.

```
-takefocus => 0 | 1 | undef
```
    Allows or disallows this widget to have the keyboard focus.

```
-textvariable => \$variable
```
    Sets the variable associated with the information typed in the entry widget.

```
-width => amount
```
    Sets the width of the entry in characters.

```
-xscrollcommand => callback
```
    Assigns a callback to use when scrolling back and forth.

The following options behave as we expect them to, and aren't worth further discussion: `-background`, `-cursor`, `-font`, `-highlightbackground`, `-highlight-color`, `-highlightthickness`, `-foreground`, `-justify`, `-takefocus`, and `-state`. For more detailed information on these how these options affect a widget, see Chapter 3.

Assigning the Entry's Contents to a Variable

The `-textvariable` option lets you know what the user typed in the entry widget:

```
-textvariable => \$variable
```

By now, you should be familiar with this option from several of our button examples. Any text input into the entry widget will get assigned into $variable. The reverse also applies. Any string that gets assigned to $variable will show up in the entry widget.

It is important to remember that no matter what the user enters, it will be assigned to this variable. This means that even though you are expecting numeric input (e.g., "314"), you might get something like "3s14" if the user accidentally (or on purpose!) presses the wrong key(s). Before using any information from an entry widget, it's a good idea to do some error checking to make sure it's the information you expect or, at the very least, in the correct format. Trying to use "3s14" in an equation would most likely produce undesired results.

The other way you can find out what is in the entry widget is by using the `get` method:

```
$stuff = $entry->get();
```

You can use `get` whether or not you have used the `-textvariable` option.

Relief

As with all the widgets, you can change the way the edges are drawn by using the
-relief and/or -borderwidth options:

```
-relief => 'flat' | 'groove' | 'raised' | 'ridge' | 'sunken'
-borderwidth => amount
```

The default for an entry is 'sunken', which is also a change from what we've
seen so far. Figure 5-4 shows the different relief types at different -borderwidth
values incrementing from the default, 2, to 4, to 10.

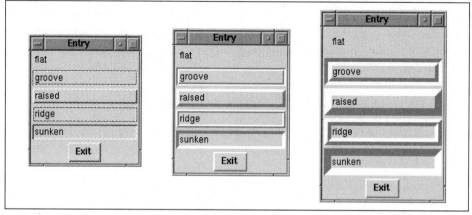

Figure 5-4. Different relief types for an entry widget: -borderwidth of 2 (the default), 4, and 10

This is the code snippet that created the five entry widgets and used the relief
name as the entry widget's text:

```
foreach (qw/flat groove raised ridge sunken/) {
  $e = $mw->Entry(-relief => $_)->pack(-expand => 1);
  $e->insert('end', $_);  # put some text in the entry
}
```

Entry Indexes

In order to manipulate the text in the entry widget, you need some way to iden-
tify specific portions or positions within the text. The last example actually used an
index in it. The line $e->insert('end', $_) uses the index 'end'. Just like the
insert method (covered later in the chapter), all of the methods that require
information about a position will ask for an index (or two, if the method requires
a range of characters). This index can be as simple as 0, meaning the very beginning of the text, or something more complicated like 'insert'.

Here are the different forms of index specification and what they mean:

n (any integer)

A numerical character position. 0 is the first character in the string. If the entry contains the string `"My mother hit your mother right on the nose"` and we used an index of 12, the character pointed to would be the "t" in the word "hit."

`'insert'`

Indicates the character directly following the insertion cursor. The insertion cursor is that funny-looking little bar thing that shows up inside the entry widget when text is typed. You can move it around with the arrow keys or by clicking on a different location in the entry widget.

`'sel.first'`

The first character in the selection string. This will produce an error if there is no selection. The selection string is the string created by using the mouse or shift-arrow.. The selected text is slightly raised from the background of the entry.

If our selected text were the word "nose" in this string (shown here in bold)

My mother hit your mother right on the **nose**

`'sel.first'` would indicate the "n".

`'sel.last'`

The character just after the last character in the selection string. This will also produce an error if there is no selection in the entry widget. In the preceding example, this would mean the space after the "e" in nose.

`'anchor'`

The `'anchor'` index changes depending on what has happened with the selection in the entry widget. By default, it starts at the far left of the entry: 0. It will change if you click anywhere in the entry widget with the mouse. The new value will be at the index you clicked on. The `'anchor'` index will also change when a new selection is made—either with the mouse (which means the `'anchor'` will be wherever you clicked with the mouse) or by Shift-clicking—and `'anchor'` will be set to where the selection starts. Mostly, this index is used internally, and you'll rarely find a case where it would be useful in an application.

`'end'`

This indicates the character just after the last one in the text string. This value is the same as if you specified the length of the entire string as an integer index.

'@x'

> This form uses an x coordinate in the entry widget. The character that contains this x coordinate will be used. **"@0"** indicates the leftmost (or first) character in the entry widget. This form of index specification is also one you'll rarely use.

Text Selection Options

You can select the text in an entry widget, and several things happen. The indices **'sel.first'** and **'sel.last'** point to the beginning and end of the selected text respectively. You can also make the selected text available on the clipboard on a Unix system by using the **-exportselection** option:

```
-exportselection => 0 | 1
```

The **-exportselection** option indicates whether or not any selected text in the entry will be also be put in the selection buffer in addition to being stored internal to the entry as a selection. By leaving this option in its default value, you can paste selected text into other applications.

The selected text also has some color options associated with it: **-selectbackground**, **-selectforeground**, and **-selectborderwidth**:

```
-selectbackground => color
-selectforeground => color
-selectborderwidth => amount
```

The **-selectbackground** and **-selectforeground** options change the color of the text and the area behind the text when that text is highlighted. In Figure 5-5, the word "text" is selected.

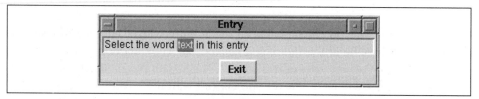

Figure 5-5. Entry with -selectbackground => 'red' and -selectforeground => 'yellow'

You can change the width of the edge of that selection box by using **-selectborderwidth**. If you left the size of the entry widget unchanged, you wouldn't see the effects of it. The entry widget cuts off the selection box. To actually see the results of increasing the **-selectborderwidth** value use the **-selectborderwidth** option in the entry command and the **-ipadx** and **-ipady** in the geometry management command.

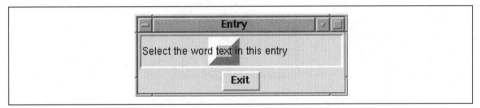

Figure 5-6. Entry widget with -selectborderwidth => 5

You might want to change the `-selectborderwidth` option if you like a little extra space around your text or if you really want to emphasize the selected text. Here's the code that generated the entry widget in Figure 5-6:

```
$e = $mw->Entry(-selectborderwidth => 10)->pack(-expand => 1,
                                                -fill => 'x',
                                                -ipadx => 10,
                                                -ipady => 10);
$e->insert('end', "Select the word text in this entry");
```

Notice the `-ipadx` and `-ipady` options in the `pack` command.

The Insert Cursor

The insert cursor is that funny-looking little bar that blinks on and off inside the entry widget when it has the keyboard focus. It will only show up when the entry widget actually has the keyboard focus. If another widget (or none) has the keyboard focus, the insertion cursor is still there, but it is invisible. In Figure 5-7, the insertion cursor is immediately after the second "n" in the word "Insertion."

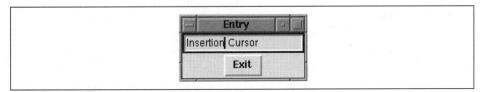

Figure 5-7. Default insertion cursor

You can change the thickness, border width, and width of the insertion cursor by using these options:

```
-insertbackground => color
-insertborderwidth => amount
-insertwidth => amount
```

The `-insertwidth` option simply changes the width of the cursor so it looks fatter. The `-insertbackground` option changes the overall color of the insertion cursor. Figure 5-8 shows an example.

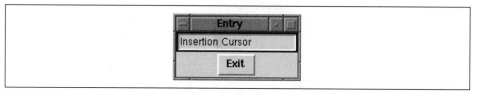

Figure 5-8. Insertion cursor with -insertbackground => 'green' and -insertwidth => 10

No matter how wide the cursor, it is always centered over the position between two characters. The insertion cursor in Figure 5-8 is in the same location it was in Figure 5-7. This can look distracting to users and might just confuse them unnecessarily, so you most likely won't change the **-insertwidth** option.

You can give the insertion cursor a 3D look by using **-insertborderwidth** (as in Figure 5-9). Like the **-insertwidth** option, the **-insertborderwidth** option doesn't have much practical use.

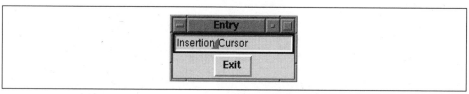

Figure 5-9. Insertion cursor with -insertborderwidth => 5, -insertbackground => 'green' and -insertwidth => 10

You can also change the amount of time the cursor blinks on and off by using these options:

```
-insertofftime => time
-insertontime => time
```

The default value for **-insertofftime** is 300 milliseconds. The default for **-insertontime** is 600 milliseconds. The default values make the cursor's blink stay on twice as long as it is off. Any value specified for these options must be nonnegative.

For a really frantic-looking cursor, change both values to something much smaller. For a relaxed and mellow cursor, double the default times. If you don't like a blinking cursor, change **-insertofftime** to 0.

Password Entries

There are times when you'll request information from the user that shouldn't be displayed on the screen. To display something other than the actual text typed in, use the **-show** option:

```
-show => char
```

The *char* is a single character that will be displayed instead of the typed-in characters. For a password entry, you might use asterisks (see Figure 5-10). If you specify a string, just the first character of that string will be used. By default, this value is undefined, and whatever the user actually typed will show.

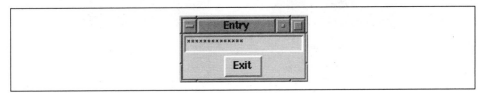

Figure 5-10. Entry displaying a password

When using the **-show** option, the information stored in the associated **$variable** will contain the real information, not the asterisks.

If you use this feature, the user can't cut and paste the password (regardless of the value of **-exportselection**). If it is cut and pasted to another screen, what the user saw on the screen (the asterisks, for example) is actually pasted, not the information behind it. You might think that if you did a configure on the entry widget such as **$entry->configure(-show => "");**, the words the user entered would suddenly appear. Luckily, this isn't true. A bunch of **\x0s** (essentially gibberish) show up instead. Any variable that uses the **-textvariable** option and is associated with the entry will still contain the correct information. If you perform an **$entry->get()**, the correct (nongibberish) information will be returned as well. The **get** method is described later in this chapter.

Using a Scrollbar

If the information requested from the user could get lengthy, the user can use the arrow keys to manually scroll through the text. To make it easier, we can create and assign a horizontal scrollbar to the entry widget by using the **-xscrollcommand** option:

```
-xscrollcommand => [ 'set' => $scrollbar ]
```

For now, I'm going to show you the most basic way to assign a scrollbar to the entry widget. For more details on the scrollbar see Chapter 6, *Scrollbars*.

To create a scrollbar and associate it with the entry widgets, do this:

```
$scroll = $mw->Scrollbar(-orient => "horizontal"); # create scrollbar
$e = $mw->Entry(-xscrollcommand => [ 'set' => $scroll ])->
  pack(-expand => 1, -fill => 'x'); # create entry
$scroll->pack(-expand => 1, -fill => 'x');
$scroll->configure(-command => [ $e => 'xview' ]); # link them
$e->insert('end', "Really really really long text string");
```

Figure 5-11 shows the resulting window in two states: on the left, the window as it looked when it was created, and on the right, how it looks after scrolling all the way to the right.

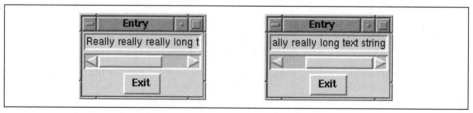

Figure 5-11. Scrollbar and an entry widget

You'll very rarely want to use a scrollbar with an entry widget. The scrollbar doubles the amount of space taken, and you can get the same functionality without it by simply using the arrow keys when the entry widget has the focus. If the user needs to enter multiple lines of text, you should use a text widget instead. See Chapter 8, *The Text Widget,* for more information on what it can do.

Configuring an Entry Widget

Both `cget` and `configure` are the same for the entry widget as they are for any of the other widgets. The default options for the entry widget are listed in Appendix A, *Configuring Widgets with configure and cget.*

Deleting Text

You can use the `delete` method when you want to remove some or all of the text from the entry widget. You can specify a range of indices to remove two or more characters or a single index to remove one character:

```
$entry->delete(firstindex, [ lastindex ])
```

To remove all of the text, you can use `$entry->delete(0, 'end')`. If you use the `-textvariable` option, you can also delete the contents by reassigning the variable to an empty string: `$variable = ""`.

Here are some other examples of how to use the `delete` method:

```
$entry->delete(0);          # Remove only the first character
$entry->delete(1);          # Remove the second character

$entry->delete('sel.first', 'sel.last')  # Remove selected text
   if $entry->selectionPresent();        # if present
```

Getting the Contents of an Entry Widget

There are two ways to determine the contents of the entry widget: the `get` method or the variable associated with the `-textvariable` option. Using the `get` method, `$entry_text = $entry->get()` will assign the entire contents of the entry widget into `$entry_text`.

Which way you find out the content depends on what you are going to do with the information. If you only need to reference it once in order to write it to a file or insert it into a database, it doesn't make sense to waste memory by storing it in a variable. Simply use the `get` method in the `print` statement (or wherever it would be appropriate). If the information in the entry widget is going to be a frequently used value such as a number for a mathematical calculation, then it makes sense to initially store it in a variable for easy access later.

Moving the Insertion Cursor

The `icursor` method will place the cursor at the specified *index*:

```
$entry->icursor(index);
```

By default, the insertion cursor starts out wherever the last `insert` took place. To force the insertion cursor to show up elsewhere, you could do something like this:

```
$e_txt = "Entry Text";
$e = $mw->Entry(-textvariable => \$e_txt)->pack();
$e->focus;
$e->icursor(1); # put cursor at this index
```

We use the `focus` method (which is not specific to the entry widget; it's generic to all widgets) to have the application start with the focus on our entry widget. Then we place the insertion cursor between the first and second characters (indices 0 and 1) in the entry. See Chapter 16, *Methods for Any Widget*, for more information on `focus`.

You might want to move the starting position of your cursor if you are starting the text with a specific string. For instance, set `$e_txt = "http://"` and then do `$e->icursor('end')`.

Getting a Numeric Index Value

The `index` method will convert a named index into a numeric one:

```
$numindex = $entry->index(index) ;
```

One of the uses of `index` is to find out how many characters are in the entry widget: `$length = $entry->index('end')`. Of course, if we used the `-textvari-`

able option, we could get the same result by using $length = length($variable).

As an example of using **index** to find out where the current selection starts, use this code:

```
$startindex = $entry->selectionPresent() ?
            $entry->index('sel.first') : -1;
```

We discuss **selectionPresent** later in the chapter.

Inserting Text

The **insert** function will let you insert any text string at the specified index:

```
$entry->insert(index, string);
```

Here's a simple application that uses **insert**:

```
#!/usr/bin/perl
use Tk;
$mw = MainWindow->new;
$mw->title("Entry");

$e_txt = "Entry Text";     # Create entry with initial text
$e = $mw->Entry(-textvariable => \$e_txt)->pack(-expand => 1,
                                                -fill => 'x');
$mw->Button(-text => "Exit",
            -command => sub { exit })->pack(-side => 'bottom');

# Create a Button that will insert a counter at the cursor
$i = 1;
$mw->Button(-text => "Insert #", -command =>
            sub {
                if ($e->selectionPresent()) {
                  $e->insert('sel.last', "$i"); $i++;
                }
            })->pack;
MainLoop;
```

We fill the entry widget with **"Entry Text"** as a default. Then we create two buttons. The first one is the obvious Exit button that will allow us to quit the application. The second one is a bit more complicated. When pressed, it will check to see if any text is selected in the entry $e. If text is selected, it will insert a number that keeps track of the number of times we have pressed the Insert # button.

In Figure 5-12, we first selected the word "Entry" and then pressed the Insert # button four times. Each time it was pressed, it inserted a number at the index **"sel.last"**. This index didn't change in between button presses, so it looks as if we are counting backward!

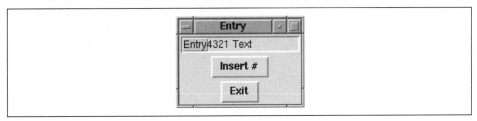

Figure 5-12. Using the insert method

Scanning Text

Both **scanMark** and **scanDragto** are used within the entry widget. They allow fast scrolling within the entry widget. A call to **scanMark** simply records the x coordinate passed in for use later with **scanDragto**. It returns an empty string.

```
$entry->scanMark(x);
$entry->scanDragto(x);
```

The companion function to **scanMark** is **scanDragto**, which also takes an x coordinate. The new coordinate is compared to the **scanMark** x coordinate. The view within the entry widget is adjusted by 10 times the difference between the coordinates.

Working with the Selection

The **selection** method has several possible argument lists. If you look at the web-page documentation, you'll see that you can use:

```
$entry->selectionAdjust(index).
```

You might also see the form `$entry->selection('adjust', index)`, where `'adjust'` is the first argument. Be aware that they mean the same thing as you read code written by other people.

You can adjust the selection to a specified index by using **selectionAdjust**:

```
$entry->selectionAdjust(index);
```

The selected text is extended toward the *index* (from whichever end is closest).

To clear out the selection:

```
$entry->selectionClear();
```

Any selection indicator will be removed from the entry widget, and the indices `'sel.first'` and `'sel.last'` are now undefined. The selected text remains.

To reset the `'anchor'` index to the specified index, use **selectionFrom**:

```
$entry->selectionFrom(index);
```

This does not affect any currently selected text or the indexes `'sel.first'` and `'sel.last'`.

The only way to check to see if there is a selection in the entry widget is to use `selectionPresent`:

```
if ($entry->selectionPresent()) {
}
```

It returns a 1 if there is a selection, which means that you can safely use the `'sel.first'` and `'sel.last'` indices (if there isn't a selection, an error will be printed when you refer to either index). `selectionPresent` will return a 0 if there is no current selection.

You can change the selection range by calling `selectionRange`:

```
$entry->selectionRange(startindex, endindex);
```

The two indices indicate where you would like the selection to cover. If *startindex* is the same or greater than *endindex*, then the selection is cleared, causing `'sel.first'` and `'sel.last'` to be undefined. Otherwise `'sel.first'` and `'sel.last'` are defined to be the same as *startindex* and *endindex* respectively.

The `selectionTo` method will cause the new selection to be set from the current `'anchor'` point to the specified index:

```
$entry->selectionTo(index);
```

Changing the View in the Entry Widget

`xview` is a method that will change its purpose based on what arguments are passed in.

With no arguments, it will return a two-element list containing numbers from 0 to 1. These two numbers define what currently is visible in the entry widget. The first number indicates how much of the text is off to the left and not visible. If it were .3, then 30% of the text is to the left of the entry widget. The second number returned is how much of the text is not visible on the left side of the entry widget plus the amount that is visible in the widget. In this case, 50% of the text is actually visible in the entry widget (see Figure 5-13).

```
($left, $right) = $entry->xview();
```

When passing an index value to `xview`, the text in the entry widget will shift position so that the text at the specified index is visible at the far-left edge:

```
$entry->xview(index);
```

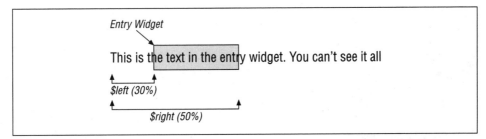

Figure 5-13. What $left and $right mean

The rest of the forms of **xview** have to do directly with scrolling (and are explained in detail in Chapter 6):

```
$entry->xviewMoveto (fraction);
$entry->xviewScroll (number,  what);
```

Fun Things to Try

There aren't too many exciting things you can do with label widgets, but it's a good idea to practice using the entry widget.

- Create an entry and label combination and display the same information in both. When you put something new in the entry, the label should display it simultaneously.

- Create a database entry form, labeling each entry with Name, Address, City, State, Zip, Phone. Add an Update button that will perform some error checking on the information in the entry widgets based on the information expected.

- Create a window with an entry widget and several buttons, each of which does something different to the entry widget. Some suggestions: Clear, Delete Selection, or Default (replace with original string).

- Create an entry widget and type something in it. Put a button in the window that will reverse the string in the entry widget when pressed.

6

Scrollbars

Scrollbars are used with widgets when there is more to see than can be shown at once. One or two scrollbars allow a user to scroll a widget's contents horizontally and/or vertically. You've seen a scrollbar on many different types of applications. Every major word processor has scrollbars. A drawing program has scrollbars. Even your web browser has scrollbars. This chapter will show you how you can use scrollbars with certain Perl/Tk widgets.

Defining Scrollbar Parts

Figure 6-1 shows all the different parts of a scrollbar and their names.

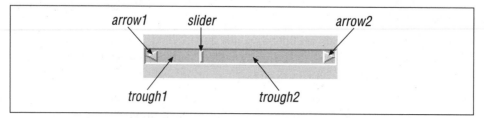

Figure 6-1. Different parts of a scrollbar

The trough is the sunken part between the two arrows. It is divided into two parts, trough1 and trough2, by the slider. The slider is the rectangle that indicates how much of the window is available for scrolling. If you were in the middle of the list, you would see the slider rectangle in the center of the trough with space on either side of it. The arrows on either end are called arrow1 and arrow2. If the scrollbar were vertical (rotated 90 degrees clockwise), arrow1 would be the top arrow.

Clicking on either arrow will move the information in the associated widget one unit at a time. What the unit is depends on what type of widget the scrollbar is associated with. With an entry widget, the units are characters. With a listbox widget and a vertical scrollbar, the units are lines. Clicking in the trough on either side of the slider will page the information in the widget in that direction. You can also click directly on the slider and, holding the mouse button down, move it directly.

Scrollbars can be horizontal or vertical. Typically, they reside on the bottom and/or to the right of the widget they are scrolling, but not always.

Some of the Perl/Tk widgets that can be configured for use with scrollbars are text, listbox, canvas, entry, ghostview, hlist, and tiler. Only the first four widgets (text, listbox, canvas, entry) are covered in this book. See Figures 6-2 through 6-5 for examples of scrollbars with each of the covered widgets.

Figure 6-2. Entry widget with a scrollbar

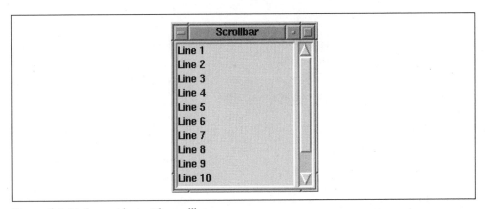

Figure 6-3. Listbox widget with scrollbar

There are two ways to create and configure scrollbars for use with widgets. You can use the `Scrollbar` widget creation command, or you can use the `Scrolled` method to create the widget and associated scrollbars. Both have their advantages and disadvantages. Using `Scrolled` is much less work and requires less coding, but it won't let you do anything fancy like associate the same scrollbar with two different widgets. Creating the scrollbar widgets yourself takes more code, but you can do much fancier things with them since you'll have direct control over where

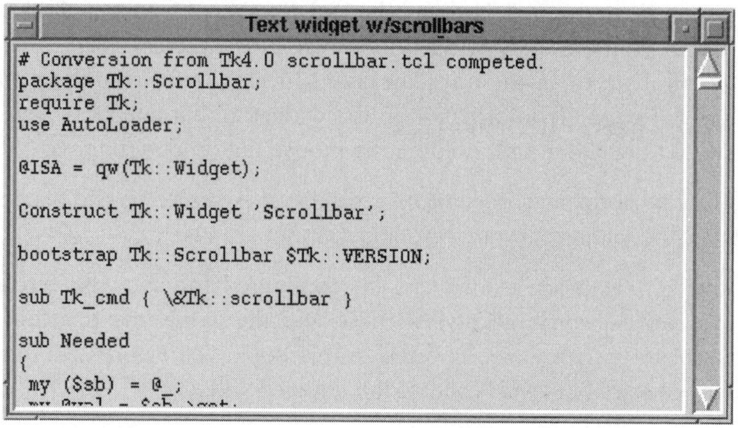

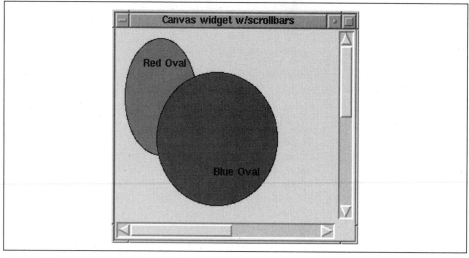

Figure 6-4. Text widget with scrollbar. Text widget is displaying Scrollbar.pm file

Figure 6-5. Canvas widget with scrollbars

they go and which widget(s) they are associated with. This chapter will cover both
methods of creating scrollbars.

The Scrolled Method

To create a widget and scrollbars at the same time, use the `Scrolled` method.
`Scrolled` returns a pointer to the widget created. It is the easiest way to add
scrollbars to a scrollable widget. The method creates a frame, which contains the
widget and scrollbar(s). You create them all in one command.

The usage for the `Scrolled` method is:

```
$widget = $parent->Scrolled('Widget',
                          -scrollbars => 'string' [, options ]);
```

The first argument is the widget to create, such as `"Listbox"` or `"Canvas"`. The other argument you'll need to use is the `-scrollbars` option, which takes a string that tells it which scrollbars to create and where to put them.

The possible values for `-scrollbars` are `"n"`, `"s"`, `"e"`, `"w"`, or `"on"`, `"os"`, `"oe"`, `"ow"`, or some combination of those that combines *n* or *s* with an *e* or *w*. The `"n"` means to put a horizontal scrollbar above the widget. An `"s"` means to put a horizontal scrollbar below the widget. The `"e"` means to put a vertical scrollbar to the right of the widget. The `"w"` means to put a vertical scrollbar to the left of the widget.

You can have a maximum of two scrollbars for each widget. For instance, we can create one scrollbar on the `"n"` side of the widget. It is possible to use `"nw"` to create two scrollbars, one on the top and one on the left of the widget. It is not legal to use `"ns"` because `"n"` and `"s"` scroll in the same direction.

The `"o"` in front of the direction makes that scrollbar optional. Optional scrollbars will only display when the size of the widget makes it necessary to scroll the information in the widget. Always list the north or south value first (if you use either) to avoid complaints from the subroutine. Here are some examples to make this clearer:

```
# Create optional scrollbar east (to the right) of widget
$lb = $mw->Scrolled("Listbox", -scrollbars => 'oe')->pack;

# Create scrollbars to south (below) and east (to the right) of widget
$lb = $mw->Scrolled("Listbox", -scrollbars => 'se')->pack;

# Create optional scrollbars south (below) and east (right) of widget
$lb = $mw->Scrolled("Listbox", -scrollbars => 'osoe')->pack;

# Create scrollbars to the north (above) and west (to the left) of widget
$lb = $mw->Scrolled("Listbox", -scrollbars => 'nw')->pack;
```

Configuring the Scrollbar(s) Created with Scrolled

Any other options sent with the `Scrolled` method will configure only the widget created. If you need to configure the scrollbars, use the `Subwidget` method from the widget reference. The `Subwidget` method can be used because a `Scrolled` widget is really a composite widget. Composite widgets are covered in Chapter 15, *Composite Widgets*.

To turn the background of your horizontal scrollbar green, use this code:

```
$lb->Subwidget("xscrollbar")->configure(-background => "green");
```

To configure a vertical scrollbar, use **"yscrollbar"** in place of **"xscrollbar"**. If you try to configure a scrollbar that you didn't create (for instance, you used **-scrollbars => "e"** and tried to configure the **"xscrollbar"**), nothing will happen.

To configure just the widget, you can use **$widget->configure** after calling **Scrolled()**, or you can use:

```
$widget->Subwidget("widget")->configure(...);
```

Using **Subwidget** this way is silly because you can just use **$widget**. The **"widget"** string is the same as the first argument sent to **Scrolled**, except it's all lowercase. For instance, in the preceding example we called **Scrolled** with **"Listbox"**, but we would use **"listbox"** with the **Subwidget** method.

The Scrollbar Widget

Instead of automatically creating one or more scrollbars with the **Scrolled** method, you can use the **Scrollbar** widget method and perform the configuration yourself. It is better to create and configure your own scrollbars when you need to do something nonstandard, such as having one scrollbar scroll two listboxes.

Creating a Scrollbar Widget

To create the scrollbar, invoke the **Scrollbar** method from the parent widget. It returns a reference to the newly created scrollbar that you can use for configuration:

```
$scrollbar = $mw->Scrollbar([ options ...])
```

There are at least two other things you need to do to get a scrollbar working with another widget. First, create the to-be-scrolled widget and use the scrollbar with its **-xscrollcommand** or **-yscrollcommand** option. Then configure the scrollbar so that it knows to talk to that widget. Here's an example that creates a listbox widget (don't worry if you don't quite follow all of this now; I just want to show a complete example before we go on to talk about all the options):

```
# Create the vertical scrollbar
$scrollbar = $mw->Scrollbar();
$lb = $mw->Listbox(-yscrollcommand => ['set' => $scrollbar]);
#Configure the scrollbar to talk to the listbox widget
$scrollbar->configure(-command => ['yview' => $lb]);

#Pack the scrollbar first so that it doesn't disappear when we resize
$scrollbar->pack(-side => 'right', -fill => 'y');
$lb->pack(-side => 'left', -fill => 'both');
```

Creating the scrollbar is pretty simple; we want all the default options for it. As we create the listbox, we have to set up a callback so the listbox can communicate with the scrollbar when the contents of the listbox move around. Our scrollbar is vertical, so the `-yscrollcommand` option has the `set` command and our scrollbar assigned to it (if it is horizontal, use `-xscrollcommand`). When the contents of the listbox are scrolled by the user without using the scrollbar, the listbox will alert the scrollbar by invoking `$scrollbar->set(...)`.

The line `$scrollbar->configure(-command => ['yview' => $lb])` does almost the opposite; it configures the scrollbar to communicate with the listbox. When the user clicks on the scrollbar, the scrollbar will invoke `$lb->yview(...)` to tell the listbox how to change the view of the contents. We use the "y" version of the view command because this is a vertical scrollbar.

There is more information on the details of `yview` in "How the Scrollbar Communicates with Other Widgets," later in this chapter. The last two lines in this example pack the scrollbar and the listbox in the window so that the scrollbar is the same height as the listbox and lies to the right of the listbox.

Always pack your scrollbars first within the window or frame. This allows the scrollbars to remain visible when the user resizes the window smaller. It will then resize the listbox (or other widget) but leave the scrollbars visible on the edges of the screen.

Now that we've seen a complete example of how to create a scrollbar and how to set up the widget it will scroll, we can go over the options with an idea of how they are used.

Scrollbar Options

This list contains the options available with a scrollbar, and their quick definitions. The important options are discussed in more detail later in this chapter.

`-activebackground => ` *color*
Sets the color the scrollbar should be when the mouse pointer is over it.

`-activerelief => 'flat' | 'groove' | `**`'raised'`**` | 'ridge' | 'sunken'`
The `-activerelief` option determines how active elements are drawn. The elements in question are `arrow1`, `arrow2`, and the `slider`.

`-background => ` *color*
Sets the background color of the scrollbar (not the trough color).

`-borderwidth => ` *amount*
Sets the width of the edges of the scrollbar and the `arrow1`, `arrow2`, and `slider` elements.

-command => *callback*
  Sets the callback that is invoked when the scrollbar is clicked.

-cursor => *cursorname*
  Sets the cursor that is displayed when the mouse pointer is over the scrollbar.

-elementborderwidth => *amount*
  Sets the width of the borders of the **arrow1**, **arrow2**, and **slider** elements.

-highlightbackground => *color*
  Sets the color the highlight rectangle around the scrollbar widget should be when it does not have the keyboard focus.

-highlightcolor => *color*
  Sets the color the highlight rectangle around the scrollbar should be when it does have the keyboard focus.

-highlightthickness => *amount*
  Sets the thickness of the highlight rectangle. Default is 2.

-jump => **0** | 1
  Indicates whether or not the scrollbar will jump scroll.

-orient => "horizontal" | **"vertical"**
  Sets the orientation of the scrollbar.

-relief => 'flat'|'groove'|'raised'|'ridge'|**'sunken'**|'solid'
  Changes the edges of the widget.

-repeatdelay => *time*
  Sets the number of milliseconds required to hold down an arrow before it will auto-repeat. Default is 300 ms.

-repeatinterval => *time*
  Sets the number of milliseconds in between auto-repeats. Default is 100 ms.

-takefocus => 0 | 1| **undef**
  Controls whether the scrollbar can obtain the keyboard focus.

-troughcolor => *color*
  Changes the color of the trough (both **trough1** and **trough2**).

-width => *amount*
  Sets the width of the scrollbar.

Scrollbar Colors

Within the scrollbar, we have a new part of the widget called a trough. This trough gets its own coloring through the -troughcolor option. The trough is considered the part behind the arrows and slider. Figure 6-6 shows an example.

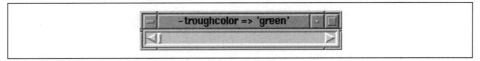

Figure 6-6. Scrollbar with -troughcolor set to 'green'

The background of the scrollbar consists of the arrows, the slider, and a small portion around the outside of the trough. You change the color of the background by using the -background option. The -activebackground option controls the color that is displayed when the mouse cursor is over one of the arrows or the slider. Figure 6-7 shows two examples of -background; the second window uses both -background and -troughcolor.

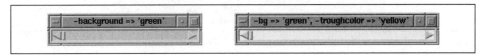

Figure 6-7. Examples of -background option

Scrollbar Style

The -relief and -borderwidth options affect both the outside edges of the scrollbar and the arrow1, arrow2, and slider elements. This is similar to how the checkbutton and radiobutton widgets are affected by the -relief and -borderwidth options. See Figure 6-8 for a screen shot of different values for these two options.

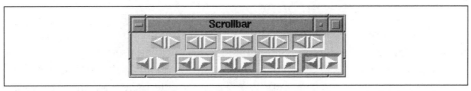

Figure 6-8. First row shows different relief values; second row different relief values with -borderwidth => 4

The -activerelief option affects the decoration of three elements—arrow1, arrow2, and the slider—when the mouse cursor is over them. The -element-borderwidth also affects the same three elements: arrow1, arrow2, and the slider. The width of the edges of these elements can be changed with this option. The -borderwidth option also changes the width of these elements but also changes the width of the edges of the widget. Notice in Figure 6-9 how the edges of the scrollbar remain at a width of 2.

Figure 6-9. Example of -elementborderwidth set to 4

The **-width** of the scrollbar is the distance across the skinny part of the scrollbar, not including the borders. Figure 6-10 demonstrates how the scrollbar changes when you alter the **-width**.

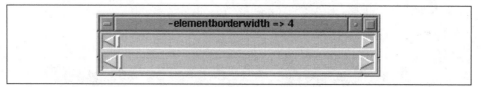

Figure 6-10. Top scrollbar has default width of 15, bottom scrollbar has width of 20

Scrollbar Orientation

As mentioned earlier, a scrollbar can be vertical or horizontal. The default for a scrollbar is **'vertical'**. To change this, use the **-orient** option:

```
$scrollbar = $mw->Scrollbar(-orient => 'horizontal');
```

You could also use **-orient => 'vertical'**, but since this is the default, it is not necessary.

Using the Arrows and Slider

When you click on one of the arrows in a scrollbar, you cause the slider to move in that direction by one unit. If you continue to hold the mouse button down, after a bit of a delay, the slider will auto-repeat that movement. The amount of time you must wait before the auto-repeat kicks in is determined by the **-repeatdelay** option. The default is 300 milliseconds.

Once you have held the mouse button down long enough to start auto-repeating, there is a short delay between each time it repeats the action. This delay is controlled by the **-repeatinterval** option. The default for **-repeatinterval** is 100 milliseconds.

Normally, when you click on the slider and move it around, the data within the widget will move accordingly. This is because the scrollbar is updating the widget continuously as you move the slider. To change the scrollbar so that it will only update the widget when you let go of the slider, use the **-jump** option and set it to 1. The default for **-jump** is 0. You would most likely want to use **-jump => 1** when your scrolled widget contains a large amount of data, and waiting for the screen to update while you slide through it would make the application seem slow.

Assigning a Callback

When you create a scrollbar, you tell it which widget to talk to and which method in that widget to call by using the **-command** option with an anonymous list. The list contains the name of the method to call and the widget from which that method should be invoked. In this code snippet, we can see that we want to use the **yview** command to scroll the widget **$lb** (a listbox):

```
$scrollbar->configure(-command => ['yview' => $lb])
```

Now when the scrollbar gets clicked on by the user, it will invoke **$lb->yview**. We know that the scrollbar associated with **$lb** is vertical because it uses the **yview** command. For a horizontal scrollbar, use **xview**. Both **yview** and **xview** tell the widget to move the widget contents an amount that is determined by where the user clicked in the scrollbar. The **yview** and **xview** methods are covered in the next section.

How the Scrollbar Communicates with Other Widgets

As described earlier, you use the **-command** option with the scrollbar so it knows which widget and method to use when the scrollbar is clicked. The command should be **xview** for horizontal scrollbars and **yview** for vertical scrollbars. You can call these methods yourself, but most of the time you won't want to.

Both **xview** and **yview** take the same type of arguments. Where the user clicked in the scrollbar determines the value used, but the value will always be sent as one of the following forms:

```
$widget->xviewMoveto(fraction); # or
$widget->yviewMoveto(fraction);
```
This form is used when the user clicks on the slider, moves it around, and drops it again. The argument is a fraction, a real number from 0 to 1 that represents the first part of the data to be shown within the widget. If the user moved the slider all the way to the top or left of the scrollbar, the very first part of the data in the widget should be seen on the screen. This means the argument should be 0:

```
$widget->xviewMoveto(0);
```
If the slider were moved to the center of the scrollbar, the argument is 0.5:

```
$widget->xviewMoveto(0.5);
```

```
$widget->xviewScroll(number, "units"); # or
$widget->yviewScroll(number, "units");
```

This form is used when the user clicks on one of the arrow elements in the scrollbar. The widget should move its data up/down or left/right unit by unit.

The first argument is the *number* of units to scroll by. The value for *number* can be any number, but it's typically either 1 or –1. A value of 1 means that the next unit of data on the bottom or right of the widget becomes visible (scrolling one unit of data off the left or top). A value of –1 means that a previous unit of data will become visible in the top or right of the widget (one unit will scroll off the bottom or right of the widget). For example, every time the user clicks on the down arrow in a vertical scrollbar associated with a listbox, a new line shows up at the bottom of the listbox.

The second argument is the string **"units"**. What a unit is depends on the widget. In a listbox, a unit would mean one line of text. In an entry widget, it would be one character.

Here are some example calls:

```
# User clicked down arrow
$listbox->yviewScroll(1, "units");

# User clicked up arrow
$listbox->yviewScroll(-1, "units");

# User clicked right arrow
$entry->xviewScroll(1, "units");
```

```
$widget->xviewScroll(number, "page"); # or
$widget->yviewScroll(number, "page");
```

This form is exactly like our previous one except the last argument is **"page"** instead of **"units"**. When users click in the trough area of the scrollbar (between the slider and arrows), they expect to see the data move by an entire page.

The type of page is defined by the widget being scrolled. For example, a listbox would page up/down by the number of lines. It would page right/left by the width of the listbox.

Scrollbar Configuration

You can get and set any of the options available with a scrollbar by using cget and configure. See Appendix A, *Configuring Widgets with configure and cget*, for complete details on these methods.

Defining What We Can See

The **set** method, which we tell the scrolled widget about when we create it, defines what is visible. In our first example, we created a listbox and told it to use our scrollbar and the **set** method:

```
$scrollbar = $mw->Scrollbar();   # Vertical scrollbar
$lb = $mw->Listbox(-yscrollcommand => ['set' => $scrollbar ]);
```

When the widget invokes the **set** command, it sends two fractions (*first* and *last*) as the arguments:

```
$scrollbar->set(first, last);
```

This will change the position in the data that we are seeing. The arguments *first* and *last* are real numbers between 0 and 1. They represent the position of the first data item we can see and the position of the last data item we can see, respectively. If we can see all of the data in our widget, they would be 0 and 1. The *first* value gets larger as more data is scrolled off the top, and the *last* value gets smaller as more data is scrolled off the bottom. You will probably never find a case in which to call *set* yourself, so just try to get an idea of what it does behind the scenes.

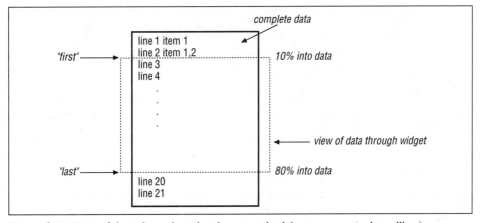

Figure 6-11. View of data through widget by set method (assumes vertical scrollbar)

Figure 6-11 shows a hypothetical document that we are viewing with a vertically scrolled widget. The dashed rectangle represents the view of what we can currently see within the widget. When the widget calls **set**, it determines how far into the document the first viewable item is and sends this as the first argument. In Figure 6-11, this would be 10%, or 0.10. The second argument to **set()** is how far into the document the last viewable item is. From our example, this would be 80%, or 0.80.

Getting the Current View

The `get` method returns in a list whatever the latest arguments to `set` were:

```
($first, $last) = $scrollbar->get();
```

This data can change if the widget requests a change in position of the data or if the scrollbar requests a change.

Activating Elements in a Scrollbar

To determine which part of the scrollbar is active, you can use the `activate` method:

```
$elem = $scrollbar->activate();
```

The value returned is an empty string (which means no element is currently active) or the name of the currently active element. The possible elements are `"arrow1"`, `"arrow2"`, or `"slider"`.

If you send an element name as the argument to `activate`, that element will change to the color and relief specified by the `-activebackground` and `-activerelief` options. The element will continue to display that color and relief until an event (such as the mouse cursor passing over the element) causes it to change. Contrary to what you might believe, using `activate` does not invoke that element. Here are some examples:

```
$scrollbar->activate("arrow1");
$scrollbar->activate("arrow2");
$scrollbar->activate("slider");
```

There is no `activate` for `"trough"` because the trough doesn't change color when the mouse is over it.

Calculating Change from Pixels

The number returned by `delta` indicates how much the scrollbar must change to move the slider *deltax* pixels for horizontal scrollbars and *deltay* pixels for vertical scrollbars. (The inapplicable argument is ignored for each type of scrollbar).

```
$amount = $scrollbar->delta(deltax, deltay)
```

The amount returned can be positive or negative.

Locating a Point in the Trough

Given a point at (x,y), `fraction` will return a real number between 0 and 1 indicating where that coordinate point would fall in the trough of the scrollbar:

```
$loc = $scrollbar->fraction(x, y);
```

The point (x,y) must be relative to the scrollbar. Figure 6-12 shows the location of three possible results from fraction: 0.0, 0.5 and 1.0.

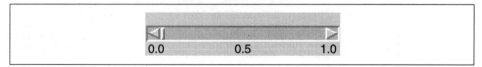

Figure 6-12. Example of values returned by the fraction method

Identifying Elements

The `identify` method returns a string containing the name of the element located at the x,y coordinate:

```
$elem = $scrollbar->identify(x,y);
```

If x,y is not in any element, the string will be empty. Both *x* and *y* must be pixel coordinates relative to the scrollbar. The possible element names are `"arrow1"`, `"arrow2"`, `"trough"`, and `"slider"`.

Examples

These examples are included to hopefully clear up any confusion about how to use scrollbars in the real world. Each example uses the `Scrolled` method if possible; then we do the same thing manually. We haven't covered all the widget types we are using here, but we aren't doing anything fancy with them either. If you see an option or method you don't recognize, just see the appropriate chapter for that widget to learn more.

Entry Widget

The entry widget can only be scrolled horizontally. The entry can only contain one line of text at most, so a vertical scrollbar would do nothing. Using `Scrolled` to create a scrolled entry widget is easy:

```
$mw->Scrolled("Entry", -scrollbars => "s", -width => 30)->pack();
```

If you want to make the scrollbar only show when the data in the entry widget requires it, use `-scrollbars => "os"`. Using the `Scrollbar` method is a bit more work:

```
$scrollbar = $mw->Scrollbar(-orient => 'horizontal');
$entry = $mw->Entry(-width => 30,
                    -xscrollcommand => ['set' , $scrollbar]);
$scrollbar->configure(-command => ['xview', $entry]);
$scrollbar->pack(-side => 'bottom', -fill => 'x');
$entry->pack(-side => 'bottom', -fill => 'x');
```

Both will create an entry that looks similar to the one in Figure 6-13.

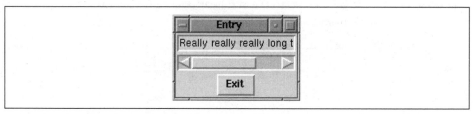

Figure 6-13. Entry widget with a scrollbar

Listbox, Text, and Canvas Widgets

A listbox widget can be scrolled both horizontally and vertically, although you might not always want to use both options. If you know how wide your data is going to be and the window can accommodate it, a horizontal scrollbar is unnecessary. Our first example uses the `Scrolled` method and creates two scrollbars:

```
$mw->Scrolled("Listbox", -scrollbars => "se",
            -width => 50, -height => 12)->pack();
```

To do the same thing manually, we need to use `Scrollbar` to create two scrollbars and configure them to work with the widget:

```
$f = $mw->Frame()->pack(-side => 'top', expand => 1, -fill => 'both');
$xscroll = $f->Scrollbar(-orient => 'horizontal');
$yscroll = $f->Scrollbar();
$lb = $f->Listbox(-width => 50, -height => 12,
                    -yscrollcommand => ['set', $yscroll],
                    -xscrollcommand => ['set', $xscroll]);
$xscroll->configure(-command => ['xview', $lb]);
$yscroll->configure(-command => ['yview', $lb]);
$xscroll->pack(-side => 'bottom', -fill => 'x');
$yscroll->pack(-side => 'right', -fill => 'y');
$lb->pack(-side => 'bottom', -fill => 'both', -expand => 1);
```

As you can see, using `Scrolled` saves a lot of extra work. In Figure 6-14, we see a listbox with two scrollbars, one on the south and one on the east. This window was created using `Scrolled`. There is a subtle difference: the small square of open space where the two scrollbars meet in the southeast corner. When we create the scrollbars ourselves, we don't get that small space (whichever scrollbar gets packed first takes it).

Scrolled text and canvas widgets are created the same exact way a scrolled listbox widget is created, so we won't bother repeating the same code again.

One Scrollbar, Multiple Widgets

There are times when you want to use one scrollbar with more than one widget. When the user clicks on the scrollbar, it should scroll all the widgets in the same direction at the same time. For this example, we will create three listboxes, each

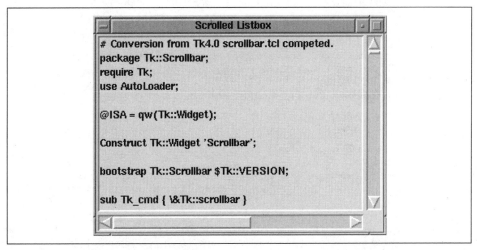

Figure 6-14. A listbox with two scrollbars

with eleven items. There will be one scrollbar that will scroll all three lists when the user clicks on it. When the user tabs to the listboxes and scrolls up and down by using the arrow keys or the pageup/pagedown keys, the other listboxes are also scrolled. Figure 6-15 shows what the window looks like.

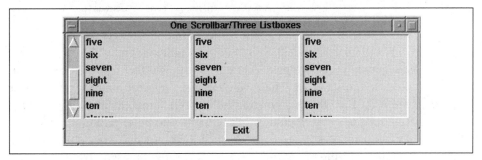

Figure 6-15. A window with three listboxes all controlled by the same scrollbar

The code for Figure 6-15 is as follows:

```
use Tk;

$mw = MainWindow->new();
$mw->title("One Scrollbar/Three Listboxes");
$mw->Button(-text => "Exit",
            -command => sub { exit })->pack(-side => 'bottom');

$scroll = $mw->Scrollbar();
# Anonymous array of the three listboxes
$listboxes = [ $mw->Listbox(), $mw->Listbox(), $mw->Listbox() ];
```

```perl
# This method is called when one listbox is scrolled with the keyboard
# It makes the scrollbar reflect the change, and scrolls the other lists
sub scroll_listboxes {
  my ($sb, $scrolled, $lbs, @args) = @_;
  $sb->set(@args); # tell the scrollbar what to display
  my ($top, $bottom) = $scrolled->yview();
  foreach $list (@$lbs) {
    $list->yviewMoveto($top); # adjust each lb
  }
}

# Configure each listbox to call &scroll_listboxes
foreach $list (@$listboxes) {
  $list->configure(-yscrollcommand => [ \&scroll_listboxes, $scroll,
                                        $list, $listboxes ]);
}

# Configure the scrollbar to scroll each listbox
$scroll->configure(-command => sub { foreach $list (@$listboxes) {
                                      $list->yview(@_);
                                    }});

# Pack the scrollbar and listboxes
$scroll->pack(-side => 'left', -fill => 'y');
foreach $list (@$listboxes) {
  $list->pack(-side => 'left');
  $list->insert('end', "one", "two", "three", "four", "five", "six",
                       "seven", "eight", "nine", "ten", "eleven");
}

MainLoop;
```

In order to connect multiple widgets to one scrollbar, we first use the `Scrollbar` command to create the scrollbar. Then we configure the scrollbar so it calls `yview` for each of the listboxes we are scrolling (the listboxes are kept in an anonymous array so that all methods can reference them easily). The other part that makes the listboxes truly connected is to configure each listbox to call a special subroutine that scrolls all three listboxes in addition to adjusting the scrollbar. Normally, `-yscrollcommand` would only have `['set', $lb]` assigned to it. Instead, we use a callback to `\&scroll_listboxes` and call `set` from within that subroutine.

Fun Things to Try

- Create two of each scrollable widget type, make one `Scrolled`, and create your own scrollbars for the second of each type. This will show you which method you prefer to use.

- Create two scrollbars and attach them to the same widget (the opposite of our one scrollbar/multiple widgets example). For instance, create a listbox with a scrollbar on the left and one on the right, both of which will scroll the listbox vertically.

7

The Listbox Widget

 A listbox widget is designed to list strings of text, one text string per line. You can then select a line or multiple lines from the listbox to perform other operations on. Some examples of things to place inside a listbox:

- An alphabetized list of cities.

- A list of servers to log in to. Select a server name and then enter a name and password into some entry widgets. Click the OK button to log in.

- A list of operating systems.

- A list of payment options: MasterCard, American Express, Visa, Check, Cash.

A listbox is ideal for replacing radiobuttons or checkboxes that have become too numerous to display on the screen. Usually 3 or 4 checkbuttons or radiobuttons aren't a big deal, but if you had to try to display 10 at a time, the window could get a little crowded. A group of radiobuttons can be replaced by a listbox that limits the number of selections to one and has a default selection. A bunch of checkbuttons can be replaced by a listbox that allows multiple selections.

Creating and Filling a Listbox

To create a listbox widget, use the `Listbox` method on the parent of the listbox:

```
$lb = $parent->Listbox( [ options ...] )->pack;
```

The `Listbox` method returns a reference to the listbox that has been created. You can now use this reference to configure the listbox, insert items into the listbox,

and so on. The most common thing to do after creating a listbox is to use the
insert method to insert items into it:

```
$lb->insert('end', @listbox_items);
# or...
$lb->insert('end', $item1, $item2, $item3);
```

The **insert** method takes an index value as the first argument; the rest of the
arguments will be considered items to be put into the listbox. Listbox indexes are
similar to the entry widget indexes except they refer to lines instead of individual
characters.

We could use a listbox instead of radiobuttons to select our window background
color (see Chapter 4, *Checkbuttons and Radiobuttons*, for the radiobutton example). The listbox code looks like this:

```
$lb = $mw->Listbox(-selectmode => "single")->pack();
$lb->insert('end', qw/red yellow green blue grey/);
$lb->bind('<Button-1>',
          sub { $lb->configure(-background =>
                             $lb->get($lb->curselection()) );
              });
```

The **-selectmode** option limits the number of selections to one. We **insert**
some colors to choose from. There is no **-command** option for a listbox, so we use
bind (see Chapter 14, *Binding Events*) to have something happen when the user
clicks on an item with the left mouse button. Using the listbox methods **get** and
curselection, we determine which item the user clicked on and then set the
background of the listbox to that color. There are only five colors in our example
here; you can use more colors and add a scrollbar to make it more useful. You
can add a scrollbar by changing the line with **Listbox** in it:

```
$lb = $mw->Scrolled("Listbox", -scrollbars => "e",
                    -selectmode => "single")->pack();
```

All the other lines in the program remain unchanged. For more information about
adding and utilizing scrollbars, see Chapter 6, *Scrollbars*. Now that we've looked at
an example, let's go over the options and methods that let us use the listbox the way
we want to.

Listbox Options

As with any of the widgets, you can configure the listbox using options. The standard widget options are **-cursor**, **-font**, **-height**, **-highlightbackground**,
-highlightcolor, **-highlightthickness**, **-takefocus**, **-width**, **-xscroll-
command**, and **-yscrollcommand**. The options that behave the same for each
widget will only be listed in the following list. Those options specific to listbox
widgets will be discussed later in this chapter.

-background => *color*
    Sets the color of the area behind the text.

-borderwidth => *amount*
    Sets the width of the edges of the widget. Default is 2.

-cursor => *cursorname*
    Sets the cursor to display when the mouse is over the listbox.

-exportselection => 0 | **1**
    Determines if the current listbox selection is made available for the X selection as well. If set to 1, prevents two listboxes from both having selections at the same time.

-font => *fontname*
    Sets the font of any text displayed within the listbox.

-foreground => *color*
    Sets the color of nonselected text displayed in the listbox.

-height => *amount*
    Sets the height of the listbox.

-highlightbackground => *color*
    Sets the color the highlight rectangle should be when the listbox does not have the keyboard focus.

-highlightcolor => *color*
    Sets the color the highlight rectangle should be when the listbox does have the keyboard focus.

-highlightthickness => *amount*
    Sets the thickness of the highlight rectangle. Default is 2.

-relief => 'flat'|'groove'|'raised'|'ridge'|'**sunken**'|'solid'
    Sets the relief of the edges of the listbox.

-selectbackground => *color*
    Sets the color behind any selected text.

-selectborderwidth => *amount*
    Sets the width of the border around any selected text.

-selectforeground => *color*
    Sets the color of the text in any selected items.

-selectmode => "single" | "**browse**" | "multiple" | "extended"
    Affects how many items can be selected at once; also affects some key/mouse bindings for the listbox (such as Shift-select). Default is "**browse**".

-setgrid => **0** | 1
    Turns gridding off or on for the listbox. Default is 0.

-takefocus => 0 | 1 | undef
> Determines the ability of the widget to get the keyboard focus or not. 0 means never, 1 means always, undef means dynamic decision.

-width => *amount*
> Sets the width of the listbox in characters. If amount is 0 or less, the listbox is made as wide as the longest item.

-xscrollcommand => *callback*
> Assigns horizontal scrollbar to widget. See Chapter 6.

-yscrollcommand => *callback*
> Assigns vertical scrollbar to widget. See Chapter 6.

Selection Modes

As part of the listbox widget, you are given several choices in the way you can select items in the listbox. You can have it so only one item at a time can be selected (emulating radiobuttons), or you can have many different contiguous or noncontiguous items selected (emulating checkbuttons). You control this behavior with the -selectmode option.

The possible select modes are "browse", "single", "multiple", or "extended". The default mode is "browse".

browse & single
> The "browse" and "single" modes are similar in that only one item can be selected at a time; clicking on any item will deselect any other selection in the listbox. The browse mode has a slight difference: when the mouse is held down and moving around, the selection moves with the mouse. For bind purposes, a "<Button-1>" bind will be invoked when you first click down. If you want to catch the event when the mouse is released, define a Button-Release binding (binding events to widgets is discussed in Chapter 14).

extended
> The "extended" mode lets you select more than one item at a time. You can click on a single item with the left mouse button, but it will deselect any other selection. To select more than one item, you must Shift-click or Control-click more items. Shift-clicking (holding down the Shift key while pressing a mouse button) will extend the selection from the already selected item to the newly selected item. Control-clicking (holding down the Control key while pressing a mouse button) will add the item being clicked on to the selection, but it won't alter any of the other selections. You can also click an item with the mouse button, hold down the button, and then move the pointer over other items to select them. This is what I call a click-drag motion. Using "extended" allows for very fast selection of many different items in the listbox.

`multiple`

> The `"multiple"` mode also allows you to select more than one item. Instead of Shift-clicking or Control-clicking, you have to select items one at a time. Selecting an unselected item will select it, and selecting an already selected item will unselect it.

Operating System Differences

When testing the `-selectmode` feature, I discovered that Windows 95 does not allow the `"multiple"` selection mode to behave properly. It behaves the same as `"single"` mode on Windows 95 only. On Unix and Windows NT, `"multiple"` mode works correctly.

When you select an item in a listbox, by default it is made available as an X selection (meaning you can cut and paste it like any X selection in any window). Even though this doesn't do anything with the clipboard on Win32 systems, it still affects the selection in multiple listboxes. Items can be selected in only one listbox at a time, even if you have more than one listbox. The option `-export-selection` controls this. Use `-exportselection => 0` to allow items to be selected in more than one listbox at the same time.

Colors

In most widgets there is a `-background` and a `-foreground` color. In addition to those, we also have the `-selectbackground` and the `-selectforeground` color options in a listbox. When a listbox entry is selected, it appears in a different color.

Although you can change the color of the selected text, you can only use *one* color. You cannot make different lines in the listbox different colors.

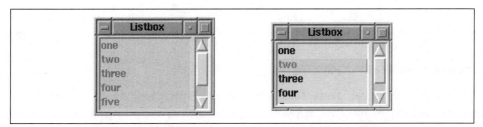

Figure 7-1. Examples of -foreground, -background, -selectforeground, and -selectbackground

In Figure 7-1, the listbox on the left has `-foreground => 'red'`, `-background => 'green'`. The listbox on the right has `-selectforeground => 'red'`, `-selectbackground => 'green'`. Make sure that the foreground and background values contrast with each other if you change these options.

Listbox Style

The default -relief of a listbox is 'sunken'. The default -borderwidth is 2. Figure 7-2 shows the five different relief types (flat, raised, ridge, groove, and sunken). In the first window, the default -borderwidth is used; in the second window, a -borderwidth of 4 is used. To save space in the windows, I didn't draw any scrollbars.

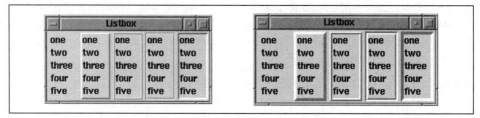

Figure 7-2. Examples of -relief and -borderwidth in listboxes

Style of Selected Items

There is also a borderwidth associated with any selected text. This is controlled by the -selectborderwidth option. Figure 7-3 shows what changing the selection borderwidth to 4 does to the listbox.

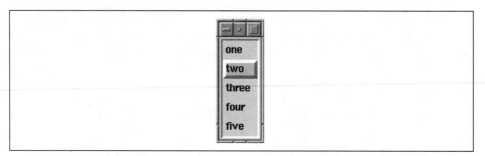

Figure 7-3. Example of -selectborderwidth => 4

Special Listbox Resizing

The -setgrid option changes how the window is drawn when it's resized. Using -setgrid => 1 causes the window to stay resized to the grid created by the listbox widget. Essentially, this means that the listbox will display only complete lines (no half lines) and complete characters. A side benefit is that the listbox will always display at least one line and can't get resized off the visible window. This option has nothing to do with which geometry manager you use to put the listbox in the window.

Listbox Indexes

The items in an entry widget are ordered. The first listbox item is at index 0, and the numbers increment by 1. These values are valid for any of the methods that require an index value.

n

> An integer index. The first item in a listbox is at index 0.

`"active"`

> The index within the listbox that has the location cursor. If the listbox has the keyboard focus, it will be displayed with an underline.

`"anchor"`

> This index is set with the `selectionAnchor(...)` method.

`"end"`

> The end of the listbox. Depending on which method is using this index, it could mean just after the last element (such as when `insert` is used), or it could mean the last element in the listbox (such as when `delete` is used).

`"@x,y"`

> The listbox item that covers the point at the coordinate x,y (pixel coordinates). The closest item will be used if x,y is not at a specific item.

Configuring a Listbox

You can use the `cget` method to find out the current value of any of the listbox options. You can use `configure` to query or set any of the listbox options. See Appendix A, *Configuring Widgets with configure and cget*, for more information on using the `configure` and `cget` methods.

Inserting Items

Use the `insert` method to add items to the listbox:

```
$lb->insert(index, element, element ... );
```

Each *element* is another line in the listbox. The *index* is a valid index (see "Listbox Indexes" later in this chapter) that the new elements will be inserted before. For instance, to insert items at the end of the listbox:

```
$lb->insert('end', @new_elements);
# Or
$lb->insert('end', "Item1", "Item2", "Item3");
```

To insert items at the beginning of the listbox:

```
$lb->insert(0, @new_elements);
```

Deleting Items

You can use the `delete` method to delete items from the listbox:

```
$lb->delete(firstindex [, lastindex ]);
```

The first argument is the index from which to start deleting. To delete more than just that one item, you can add a second index. The *firstindex* must be less than or equal to the *lastindex* specified. To delete all the elements in the listbox:

```
$lb->delete(0, 'end');
```

To delete the last item in the listbox:

```
$lb->delete('end');
```

Retrieving Elements

The `get` method returns a list of listbox elements specified by the indexes *first* to *last:*

```
$lb->get(firstindex [,  lastindex ]);
```

If only the *firstindex* is specified, only one element is returned. The *firstindex* must be less than or equal to the *lastindex*. To get a list of all elements in the listbox:

```
@elements = $lb->get(0, 'end');
```

To get the last item in the listbox:

```
$lastitem = $lb=>get('end');
```

To find out which items in the listbox are selected, use the `curselection` method:

```
@list = $lb->curselection();
```

It returns a list containing the indexes of all currently selected items in the listbox. If no items are selected, `curselection` returns an empty string. Here is an example of how the `curselection` method is used:

```
@selected = $lb->curselection;
foreach (@selected) {
  # do something with the index in $_
}
```

Make sure to remember that `curselection` returns a list on indexes, not elements.

Selection Methods

The `curselection` method, discussed in the preceding section, only tells you what the user has selected. You can also change the selection by using a form of the `selection` method.

Selecting Items

To select a range of items in a listbox, you can use the "set" form of the `selection` method (`selectionSet`). `selectionSet` takes either a single index or a range. Any items not in the range are not affected. If you use a range, the *first* index must be less than or equal to the *last* index. Here are some examples:

```
# select everything
$lb->selectionSet(0, 'end' );
#select the first item
$lb->selectionSet(0);
```

Even if you have used `-selectmode` to limit the selection to only one item, you can force more than one item to be selected by using `selectionSet(...)`.

Unselecting Items

To clear any selections in the listbox, use the "clear" form of the `selection` method (`selectionClear`). Pass in an index or a range or indexes from which to clear the selection. For instance, to remove all the selections in the listbox, you would do the following:

```
$lb->selectionClear(0, "end");
```

Any indexes outside the specified range will not be unselected—this allows you to unselect one item at a time. You can also clear the selection from just one item:

```
$lb->selectionClear("end");
```

Testing for Selection

To test to see if a specific index is already selected, use the "includes" form of `selection` (`selectionIncludes`). Calling `selectionIncludes` returns 1 if the item at the specified index is selected and 0 if it is not. For instance, to see if the last item in the list is selected:

```
if ($lb->selectionIncludes('end')) {
  ...
}
```

Anchoring the Selection

Using the "anchor" form of selection (`selectionAnchor`) to set the index `"anchor"` to the specified index. The `"anchor"` is used when you are using the mouse cursor to select several items within the listbox. The first item you click (without letting up on the mouse button) becomes the `"anchor"` index. For example, you would use this to set the anchor as the first item in the list:

```
$lb->selectionAnchor(0);
```

Moving to a Specific Index

To cause the listbox to show a specific item, you can use the **see** method.

```
$lb->see(index);
```

Given an index, **see** will cause the listbox to page up or down to show the item at that index. For an example of using **see**, look at the Listbox Example later in this chapter.

Translating Indexes

The **index** method translates an index specification (such as `"active"`) into the numerical equivalent. For instance, if the listbox contained 12 items, `$index = $lb->index("end")` would set the variable `$index` to 11. (Remember the first item in a listbox is at index 0.)

Counting Items

The **size** method returns the total number of items in the listbox:

```
$count = $lb->size();
```

Active Versus Selected

The **activate** method will set the listbox item at index *index* to the active element. This allows you to access this item later using the `"active"` index. Figure 7-4 shows two windows with active elements underlined. Each listbox also has the black highlight rectangle around it, which indicates it has the keyboard focus (the active element isn't seen as marked unless the listbox has focus).

```
# The first window activates the item "four"
$lb->activate(3);
$lb->focus();
# The second window activates the item "three"
$lb2->activate(2);
$lb2->focus();
```

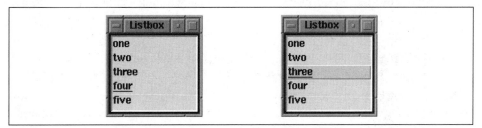

Figure 7-4. Windows showing a listbox with an "active" element

Bounding Box

The method **bbox** returns a list of four elements that describes the bounding box around the text at *index*:

```
($x, $y, $w, $h) = $lb->bbox(index);
```

The four elements are (in order): x, y, w, and h. The x,y coordinates are the upper left corner of the bounding box. The w is the width of the text in pixels. The h is the height of the text in pixels. These measurements are shown in Figure 7-5.

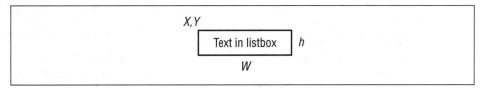

Figure 7-5. Bounding box values around text

Finding an Index by Y Coordinate

If you know a y coordinate in the listbox, you can determine the index of the nearest listbox item to it by using the **nearest** method:

```
$index = $lb->nearest(y)
```

The **nearest** method returns a number that corresponds to the index of the closest visible listbox item.

Scrolling Methods

The listbox can be scrolled both horizontally and vertically so it has both **xview** and **yview** methods and all their associated forms. These forms and how to use them are described in detail in Chapter 6.

The **scan** method allows you to use a really fast scrolling method. It is automatically bound to the second mouse button by the listbox. Here is how you can do the same thing within your window:

```
$mw->bind("Listbox", "<2>",['scan','mark',Ev('x'),Ev('y')]);
$mw->bind("Listbox", "<B2-Motion>",['scan','dragto',Ev('x'),Ev('y')]);
```

When you click in the window with the second mouse button and then move your mouse around, you'll see the contents of the listbox zip by at super-fast speed. You could change the second argument of each **bind** statement if you wanted to bind this to another combination of keys/mouse actions. The **bind** method is explained in Chapter 14.

Listbox Example

Sometimes when you put a lot of items in a listbox, it takes a long time to scroll through the listbox. If you insert the items in the listbox sorted, you can implement a search routine. Here's a quick script that shows you how to use an entry widget to input the search text and then search the listbox every time you get a new character in the entry:

```
use Tk;

$mw = MainWindow->new;
$mw->title("Listbox");
# For example purposes, we'll use one word for each letter
@choices = qw/alpha beta charlie delta echo foxtrot golf hotel india
              juliet kilo lima motel nancy oscar papa quebec radio sierra
              tango uniform victor whiskey xray yankee zulu/;

# Create the entry widget, and bind the do_search sub to any keypress
$entry = $mw->Entry(-textvariable => \$search)->pack(-side => "top",
                                                     -fill => "x");
$entry->bind("<KeyPress>", [ \&do_search, Ev("K") ]);

# Create listbox and insert the list of choices into it
my $lb = $mw->Scrolled("Listbox", -scrollbars => "osoe",
                       )->pack(-side => "left");
$lb->insert("end", sort @choices);

$mw->Button(-text => "Exit",
            -command => sub { exit; })->pack(-side => "bottom");

MainLoop;

# This routine is called each time we push a keyboard key.
sub do_search {
  my ($entry, $key) = @_;
```

```
# Ignore the backspace key and anything that doesn't change the word
# i.e. The Control or Alt keys
return if ($key =~ /backspace/i);
return if ($oldsearch eq $search);

# Use what's currently displayed in listbox to search through
# This is a non-complicated in order search
my @list = $lb->get(0, "end");
foreach (0 .. $#list) {
  if ($list[$_] =~ /^$search/) {
    $lb->see($_);
    $lb->selectionClear(0, "end");
    $lb->selectionSet($_);
    last;
  }
}
$oldsearch = $search;
}
```

Fun Things to Try

Use a listbox to create a mini file viewer. Use an entry field to read a filename and a button that, when you click on it, loads the file into your listbox (each line in the file becomes one entry in the listbox).

8

The Text Widget

When you think about what a text widget might do, you automatically think, "it displays text." This is true, yet it can do quite a bit more. The text widget is one of the most powerful standard widgets available in Perl/Tk. It is flexible, configurable, and easy to use for simple tasks. Here are some examples of how you can use text widgets:

- Display and edit a plain text file.

- Display formatted text from an HTML document.

- Create a scrollable color key, with buttons that allow you change the colors

- Gather multiline, formatted text (including colors) from a user (mini word processor).

- Display text with different colors based on the input.

- Make certain portions of text "clickable" and perform an action when clicked on. This could be HTML, or it could be similar to the widget demo.*

You can put simple text, formatted text, and other widgets inside a text widget. A text widget can be used in conjunction with scrollbars to allow many pages of information to be viewed in much less space.

Creating and Using a Text Widget

To create a text widget, use the **Text** method from the desired parent widget:

```
$text = $parent->Text( options ... )->pack;
```

---

* When you installed the Tk module with Perl, you also installed the *widget* demo. Type *widget* on the command line to see the capabilities of widgets in Perl/Tk.

After the text widget is created, there are several different ways to place text in it. The user can type directly into it, or you can use the **insert** method:

```
$text->insert('end', "To be or not to be...\nThat is the question");
```

The basic form of the **insert** method takes two arguments. The first is an index value that indicates where to start placing the text. The second argument is the string to insert. Unlike the listbox **insert** method, you can't use an array as the second argument. If you do, only the first item in the array is inserted into the text box.

A typical use of the text widget is to read a file and place it in the text widget as it's read:

```
$text = $mw->Scrolled("Text")->pack();
open (FH, "chapter1") || die "Could not open chapter1";
while (<FH>) {
  $text->insert('end', $_);
}
close(FH);
```

You can use the text widget to display the file backward (line by line) by changing the insert line to **$text->insert(0, $_)**. This will put the next line read at the top of the text widget instead of at the end.

The text widget can do a lot more than just display a file or two lines from a Shakespearean play. In addition to options, we also have tags, indexes, and marks to control how the contents of a text widget are displayed.

Text Widget Options

Options used with the **Text** method change the way the text is displayed within the text widgets. The following options are standard for all the widgets: -background, -borderwidth, -cursor, -exportselection, -foreground, -highlightbackground, -highlightcolor, -highlightthickness, -insert-background, -insertborderwidth, -insertofftime, -insertontime, -insertwidth, -padx, -pady, -selectbackground, -selectborderwidth, -selectforeground, -setgrid, -state, -takefocus, -wrap, -xscrollcom-mand, and -yscrollcommand.

To find out more about what these options do, check back to Chapter 3, *The Basic Button*, where they were first covered.

-background => *color*
    Changes the color of the screen displayed behind the text.

-borderwidth => *amount*
    Sets the width of the edges of the widget.

-cursor => *cursorname*
    Sets the cursor displayed when the mouse cursor is in front of the text widget.

`-exportselection => 0 | 1`

> Determines if the text selected within the widget can also be used by the windowing system (such as X windows).

`-font => ` *fontname*

> Sets the font in which the text is displayed.

`-foreground => ` *color*

> Sets the color of the text.

`-height => ` *amount*

> Sets the height of the widget. Default is 24.

`-highlightbackground => ` *color*

> Sets the color the highlight rectangle around the widget should be when it does not have the keyboard focus.

`-highlightcolor => ` *color*

> Sets the color the highlight rectangle around the widget should be when it does have the keyboard focus.

`-highlightthickness => ` *amount*

> Sets the thickness of the highlight rectangle around the widget. Default is 2.

`-insertbackground => ` *color*

> Changes the color of the insert cursor.

`-insertborderwidth => ` *amount*

> Changes the width of the insert cursor.

`-insertofftime => ` *time*

> Sets the time the insert cursor blinks in the off position. Default is 300.

`-insertontime => ` *time*

> Sets the time the insert cursor blinks in the on position. Default is 600.

`-insertwidth => ` *amount*

> Sets the width of the insert cursor.

`-padx => ` *amount*

> Adds extra space to the left and right of the text inside the text widget's edge.

`-pady => ` *amount*

> Adds extra space to the top and bottom of the text inside the text widget's edge.

`-relief => 'flat'|'groove'|'raised'|'ridge'|'sunken'|'solid'`

> Sets the relief of the edges of the widget. Default is `'sunken'`.

`-selectbackground => ` *color*

> Sets the color of the area behind the selected text.

`-selectborderwidth => ` *amount*

> Sets the width of the border of the selected area.

-selectforeground => *color*

    Sets the color of the selected text.

-setgrid => **0** | 1

    Enables gridding for the text widget. Default is 0.

-spacing1 => *amount*

    Sets the amount of additional space left on top of a line of text that begins on its own line. Default is 0.

-spacing2 => *amount*

    Sets the amount of additional space left on top of a line of text after it has been wrapped around automatically by the text widget. Default is 0.

-spacing3 => *amount*

    Sets the amount of additional space left after a line of text has been ended by a "\n". Default is 0.

-state => **'normal'** | 'disabled'

    Indicates the state of the text widget. Default is 'normal'. If set to 'disabled', no text can be inserted by either the user or the application (via the insert method).

-tabs => *list*

    Specifies a list of tab stops to use in the text widget. Default is undefined (or no tab stops).

-takefocus => 0 | 1 | **undef**

    Determines if widget can obtain keyboard focus.

-width => *amount*

    Sets the width of the text widget in characters. Default is 80.

-wrap => "none" | **"char"** | "word"

    Sets the mode used to determine automatic line wrapping. Default is **"char"**.

-xscrollcommand => *callback*

    Determines the callback used when the text widget is scrolled horizontally.

-yscrollcommand => *callback*

    Determines the callback used when the text widget is scrolling vertically.

Fonts

You can use the -font option to change the font, including how large or small the text is (see Figure 8-1). This defines the default font for the entire text widget. Text that is inserted without a text tag (a tag allows you specify special formatting that applies only to certain portions of the text) will use this font.

The use of fonts was covered in Chapter 3, the first time we saw the -font option.

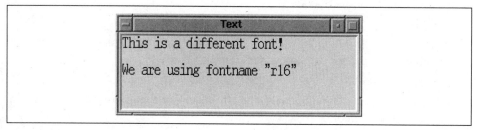

Figure 8-1. Text widget using -font => "r16"

Widget Size

When you first create a text widget, it will usually have a height of 24 lines and a width of 80 characters. Depending on how you put the text widget in the window (whether you use **pack** with the **-expand** and **-fill** options or **grid** with **—sticky => "nsew"**), it can change size when the window changes size. To force a certain size, you can use the **-width** and **-height** options:

```
# Text widget 20 characters wide and 10 lines tall
$mw->Text(-width => 20, -height => 10)->pack;
```

The values associated with **-width** are in characters, and the values associated with **-height** are lines of text. It is possible that the text widget will not be that exact width and height if you force the window to be larger via the **minsize** routine (i.e., **$mw->minsize(400,400)**), especially if you used **-expand => 1** and **-fill => 'both'** with the **pack** command. So if you don't see what you expect on the screen the first time out, keep this in mind.

Widget Style

As with other widgets, you can change how the edges of the text widget are drawn using **-relief** and **-borderwidth** options. The examples shown in Figure 8-2 might not look much like text widgets, but trust me—they are!

Line Spacing

When text is displayed in a text widget, it can wrap around automatically if the line becomes longer than the text widget can display. The amount of room left between lines is defined by using the **-spacing***N* options. Figure 8-3 shows the different areas that **-spacing1**, **-spacing2**, and **-spacing3** affect.

The **-spacing1** option affects how much room is above a new line of text (the first line in a paragraph). The **-spacing2** option affects the space between lines when text that is wrapped automatically is too long to fit on one line. The **-spacing3** option determines how much room is left after a paragraph is finished (right after an explicit newline).

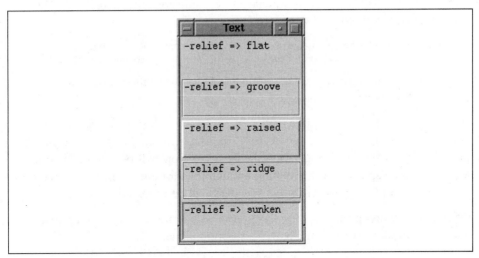

Figure 8-2. Text widgets showing different -relief values (also shows use of -width and -height options to force smaller size)

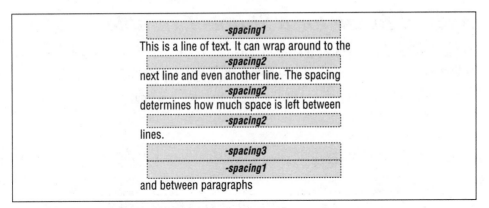

Figure 8-3. Example of -spacingN options

Tab Stops

The default setup for text widget tab stops is every eight characters. Each tab equals eight spaces (but it doesn't actually use spaces). You can replace this default setting by using the **-tabs** option as follows:

```
-tabs => [qw/2 center/]    # Place tabs every 2 pixels
-tabs => [2, "center"]     # The same thing, different syntax
```

The argument that goes with **-tabs** is an anonymous list that specifies positions in which to place each of the tab stops. You can also specify an optional justification value for each tab stop (as in the preceding example) after each tab stop's numerical value. This all sounds much more confusing than it really is. Here are some examples to help clarify things:

```
-tabs => [qw/1i center/]    # every inch, text centered on tab-stop
-tabs => [qw/1i 1.5i/]      # ts at 1 inch, 1.5 inch and every_inch after
```

The default justification is `"left"`. The possible justification values are `"left"`, `"right"`, `"center"`, or `"numeric"`.

When you specify the values (whether in centimeters, inches, or pixels), they are not cumulative. The list `["1i", "1.5i"]` translates to one tab stop at 1 inch from the left edge of the text widget, and the next tab stop will be 1.5 inches from the left edge. If the specified list isn't long enough to span the entire window, the distance between the last two tab stops specified will be repeated across the screen.

Of course, setting up new tab stops is pretty useless unless you're doing major text editing, so in most cases, you'll leave this option alone.

You can reset the tab stops back to the default by setting `-tabs` to `undef`:

```
$text->configure(-tabs => undef);
```

A Short Break for a Simple Example

Before we get into some of the more complex (and more fun) things you can do with a text widget, let's look at complete use of the text widget.

This is a short program that will display a file, let you make changes to it, and then save it:

```
use Tk;
$mw = MainWindow->new;
# Create necessary widgets
$f = $mw->Frame->pack(-side => 'top', -fill => 'x');
$f->Label(-text => "Filename:")->pack(-side => 'left', -anchor => 'w');
$f->Entry(-textvariable => \$filename)->pack(-side => 'left',
    -anchor => 'w', -fill => 'x', -expand => 1);
$f->Button(-text => "Exit", -command => sub { exit; } )->
   pack(-side => 'right');
$f->Button(-text => "Save", -command => \&save_file)->
   pack(-side => 'right', -anchor => 'e');
$f->Button(-text => "Load", -command => \&load_file)->
   pack(-side => 'right', -anchor => 'e');
$mw->Label(-textvariable => \$info, -relief => 'ridge')->
   pack(-side => 'bottom', -fill => 'x');
$t = $mw->Scrolled("Text")->pack(-side => 'bottom',
   -fill => 'both', -expand => 1);

MainLoop;

# load_file checks to see what the filename is and loads it if possible
sub load_file {
```

```
    $info = "Loading file '$filename'...";
    $t->delete("1.0", "end");
    if (!open(FH, "$filename")) {
      $t->insert("end", "ERROR: Could not open $filename\n");
            return;
    }
    while (<FH>) { $t->insert("end", $_); }
    close (FH);
    $info = "File '$filename' loaded";
}

# save_file saves the file using the filename in the entry box.
sub save_file {
    $info = "Saving '$filename'";
    open (FH, ">$filename");
    print FH $t->get("1.0", "end");
    $info = "Saved.";
}
```

Figure 8-4* shows the window when a document has been loaded and saved.

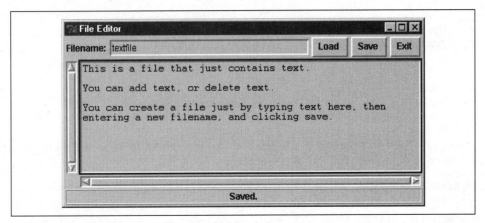

Figure 8-4. Simple file editor with a "textfile" loaded

Text Indexes

When we talked about listbox index values, each index referred to a line in the listbox. The first line in the listbox was at index 0, and so on. With a text widget, the index can point to a specific line, but it can also point to a character within that line. An index for a text widget is built by using a base index and then optionally modifying that index with a modifier. The entire index, base, and modifier should be put in double quotes.

---

* For those of you paying attention, you'll notice this screenshot looks slightly different. That's because this was taken off of Windows 95 instead of X Windows. Note the "Tk" in the upper left-hand corner, and the Windows controls in the upper-right.

Base Index Values

"*n.m*"

> This format allows you to explicitly specify a line number and a character number within that line. Lines start at 1 (which is different than the listbox widget), and characters start at 0.

"@*x,y*"

> The character in the widget that is closest to the x,y coordinate.

"end"

> The very end of the text widget, after any "\n" characters as well.

"*mark*"

> Specifies the character after the location named *mark*. The two mark names provided by Tk are **"current"** and **"insert"**. What they refer to is discussed later in this chapter.

"*tag*.first"

> A tag name is simply a placeholder for some special formatting instructions (discussed in the very next section). After creating tags, you can use this index form. *tag*.first is the first character in the text widget that is of type *tag*. That is, you could create a **"heading"** tag and use **"heading.first"** index.

"*tag*.last"

> Specifies the character directly after the text marked with *tag*.

$widget

> If you have an embedded widget, you can refer to its location within the text widget by the variable referring to it.

$image

> You can have embedded images as of Tk8.0. You can refer to its location by using the variable referring to it.

Index Modifiers

The index modifiers can be used following a base index value.

[+ | -] *count* [chars | lines]

> You can use the + and − to add/subtract lines and characters to a base index. The index **"end − 1 chars"** refers to text on the line before the **"end"**. Be careful when you use this, though, because any **"\n"** lines also count as a complete line.

linestart

> Modifies the index to refer to the first character on that line; i.e., **$t->insert("end linestart", $string)** will insert the string at the front of the last line in the text widget. **insert** will place the new text before the index given.

`lineend`

> Refers to the last character in the line (usually the newline). It is useful when you don't know the exact number of characters in a line but want to insert text at the end of it.

`wordstart`

> Adjusts the index to refer to the first character at the start of the word that contains the base index.

`wordend`

> Adjusts the index to refer to the character after the end of the word that contains the base index.

Text Index Examples

`"end"`

> The position right after the last line of text in the widget, no matter how much text is in the widget.

`"1.0"`

> The first character on the first line in the text widget. The 1 represents the line, and 0 represents the character.

`"2.0 − 1 chars"`

> The last character on the end of the first line. We reference it by using the first character on the second line (`2.0`) and subtracting one character value from that. If we used the `insert` method with this item, we would insert the text right before the `"\n"` at the end of the first line.

`"1.end"`

> Also the last character on the end of the first line. This is a simpler way of getting to it.

`"2.0 lineend"`

> The end of the second line. It is necessary to specify `2.0`, not just `2`, because 2 is an invalid base index.

The basic indexes are easy. When you start doing index arithmetic, it becomes a little more complicated. You just have to remember that you are referring to a position in the text widget that may change if other text has been inserted or deleted (either by the user or the application).

Although some of the combinations may seem silly (for example, `"1.0 linestart"`), keep in mind that you will most likely be calling methods that return indeterminate information about an event. For example, a user clicks in the text widget and presses a button that will increase the font size of that entire line. The index arithmetic allows you to reference that entire line without even knowing for sure which line it is on.

Text Tags

Text tags give you another way to address portions of text in the text widget. A tag has three purposes, and the same tag can serve all three or only one:

- Assigning formatting information to a portion(s) of text

- Associating a binding with text in the widget

- Managing selected text

Tags are also used to change how the text appears on the screen: font, size, coloring, and spacing are among a few of the text properties affected by tags. You change text properties by creating your own tags (with their own names), and using option/value pairs to assign formatting information. In addition to changing the formatting, you can use a tag to apply a specific binding (such as perform a task when the user clicks on that text). A special tag `"sel"` manages the selected text. Anytime the user selects some text, the location of that text is marked with the tag `"sel"`.

Any of the text within the text widget can have one or more tags associated with it. If you apply two tags to the same piece of text and they both alter the font, the last tag applied wins.

Options Used With Tags

The options you can use to configure tagged text are mostly a subset of the configuration options of the text widget itself. There are some options that can only be used through tagged text.

`-background =>` *color*
> Sets the color of the area behind the text.

`-bgstipple =>` *pattern*
> Sets the pattern used to draw the area behind the text. Can create a shaded look.

`-borderwidth =>` *amount*
> Sets the width of the relief drawn around the edges of the text, line by line.

`-fgstipple =>` *pattern*
> Sets the pattern used to draw the text.

`-font =>` *fontname*
> Sets the font used for the text.

`-foreground =>` *color*
> Sets the color of the text.

`-justify =>` **`'left'`** `| 'right' | 'center'`
  Sets the position of the text within the text widget.

`-lmargin1=>` *amount*
  Sets the amount of indentation from the left edge for the first line of a paragraph.

`-lmargin2=>` *amount*
  Sets the amount of indentation from the left edge for the second and greater lines of a paragraph. Sometimes called a hanging indent.

`-offset =>` *amount*
  Sets the amount the text is raised or lowered from the baseline. Can be used to create superscripts and subscripts.

`-overstrike =>` **`0`** `| 1`
  If a true value, causes the text to have a line drawn through it.

`-relief =>` **`'flat'`** `| 'groove' | 'raised' | 'ridge' | 'sunken'`
  Determines the way the edges of the text are drawn, line by line.

`-rmargin =>` *amount*
  Sets the amount of space left between the text and the right edge of the widget.

`-spacing1 =>` *amount*
  Sets the amount of additional space left on top of a line of text that begins on its own line. Default is 0.

`-spacing2 =>` *amount*
  Sets the amount of additional space left on top of a line of text after it has been wrapped around automatically by the text widget. Default is 0.

`-spacing3 =>` *amount*
  Sets the amount of additional space left after a line of text has been ended by a `"\n"`. Default is 0.

`-tabs =>` *list*
  Indicates the set of tab stops for this text. See "Tab Stops" earlier in this chapter for more detailed information.

`-underline =>` *boolean*
  Indicates that the text should be drawn with an underline.

`-wrap =>`**`'none'`** `|` **`'char'`** `| 'word'`
  Determines the mode in which the text is wrapped. `'none'` means lines that are longer than the text widget is wide are not wrapped. `'char'` will wrap at each character. `'word'` will wrap between words.

A Simple Tag Example

Let's look at an example of how a simple tag is created and use it to insert some
text into a text widget (the resulting screen is shown in Figure 8-5):

```
$t = $mw->Text()->pack();
$t->tagConfigure('bold', -font =>
                 "-*-Courier-Medium-B-Normal--*-120-*-*-*-*-*-*");
# Use -font => "{Courier New} 24 {bold}" for Win32 systems
$t->insert('end', "This is some normal text\n");
$t->insert('end', "This is some bold text\n", 'bold');
```

Line 1 creates the Text widget and places it on the screen.

Line 2 creates the `'bold'` tag. Don't be fooled by the use of the word "configure" instead of "create." When you configure a tag, you are creating it. We created a tag named `'bold'` and associated a different font with it (it happens to be
the same as our Unix text widget default font, just the bold version).

At this point, we haven't changed anything in the text widget. We are just setting
up to use the tag later in the code. You can use any name to indicate a tag as long
as it is a valid text string. We could have named the tag "bold_font" or "big_bold_
font" or "tag1." If you have good programming style (and want to be able to maintain your code), use a name that indicates what the tag does.

Line 3 inserts some text into the text widget.

Line 4 inserts some more text into the text widget, but uses the `'bold'` tag. The
`insert` method allows us to specify a tag as the third argument. This causes that
string of text to be inserted into the text widget and assigned the tag `'bold'`. The
`'bold'` tag was configured to change the font, so any text with the `'bold'` tag
will be shown with the different font.

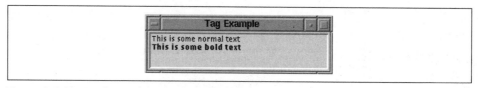

Figure 8-5. Text widget with normal and bold text

This is a pretty simplified example. What if we want to alter text that has been typed
in by the user? We can't use the `insert` method then. We use the `tagAdd` method:

```
$t->tagAdd('bold', '1.0', 'end');
```

This applies the `'bold'` tag to all of the text within the text widget.

Using the "sel" Tag to Manipulate the Selection

The **"sel"** tag is a special tag that is maintained by the text widget. Any text that is selected by the user will be assigned the **"sel"** tag. You can also force the selection by using some of the tag methods (which we haven't covered yet) to put the **"sel"** tag on some text. For instance, to select the third line:

```
$t->tagAdd("sel", "3.0", "3.0 lineend");
```

Here's an example that shows how to add another tag to the currently selected text:

```
$t->tagAdd('bold', 'sel.first', 'sel.last') if ($t->tagRanges('sel'));
```

When you use the **"sel"** tag as part of an index, you need to make sure the tag exists (using **tagRanges**) within the text widget first or you'll get a really nasty huge error.

Configuring and Creating Tags

The first thing you'll do with a tag is create it by using **tagConfigure** (unless you're using the automatically defined **"sel"** tag). The first argument to **tagConfigure** is the name of the tag. The rest of the arguments (which are optional) are option/value pairs as described in the earlier section, "Options Used with Tags." Here are some examples:

```
# creating a tag with no options
$text->tagConfigure("special");
# Creating a tag that will change the color
$text->tagConfigure("blue", -foreground => "blue");
# Creating a tag that will make underlined text
$text->tagConfigure("underline", -underline => 1);
# Creating a tag that changes the color and spacing
$text->tagConfigure("bigblue", -foreground => "blue",
                    -spacing2 => 6);
```

You can change the settings for an already created tag by using **tagConfigure** a second time. Any changes you make to the tag immediately affect any text on the screen that has that tag:

```
# Add background color to "blue" tag
$text->tagConfigure("blue", -background => "red");
# Change the spacing for "bigblue"
$text->tagConfigure("bigblue", -spacing2 => 12);
```

As with widget **configure** methods, you can use **tagConfigure** to find out the current settings for a specific tag. To get all the tag options and their values in a list of lists:

```
@listoflists = $text->tagConfigure("blue");
foreach $l (@list) { print "@$l\n"; }  # print it out
```

Each list within the list contains two elements: the option name and the value. You can also limit the information you retrieve to a single option:

```
($option, $value) = $text->tagConfigure("blue", -font);
```

If you only want information on the value for a particular option, use `tagCget`:

```
$value = $text->tagCget("bigblue", -spacing2)
```

Adding a Tag to Existing Text

We've already seen an example of using the `tagAdd` method. It allows you to add a tag to portions of text in the text widget. The usage of `tagAdd` is as follows:

```
$text->tagAdd('tagname', index1 [ , index2, index1, index2, ... ] )
```

You can add a tag to a single index or a range of indexes. This means you can add a tag to the text widget to multiple places at the same time. Let's say you wanted to add the tag 'heading' to the 1st, 12th, and 30th lines because they are the location of some heading information that you want to look different than the rest of the text. The `tagAdd` line would look like this:

```
$text->tagAdd('heading', '1.0', '1.0 lineend',
                         '12.0', '12.0 lineend',
                         '30.0', '30.0 lineend');
```

Now, assuming the formatting of 'heading' makes the font bigger, those lines now show up differently than the defaults from the rest of the text in the widget.

You can add more than one tag to a section of text. For example, you can have both a 'heading' tag and a 'color' tag. If both tags try to alter the same option (such as -font), the last setting for that option wins.

Once you place a tag on a range of text, any text inserted between the beginning and ending indices of that text will automatically get the tag of the characters surrounding it. This happens whether you are using `insert` without any specific tags or the user just types text into the text widget. If you specify a tag with `insert`, it overrides the surrounding tag.

Using Bind with Tags

One of the main reasons for tags is the ability to assign a binding to certain portions of the text. After creating a tag with `tagConfigure`, you can use `bind` so a callback will execute when a sequence of events happens (such as a mouse click) on that tagged text. On our button widgets, we have a default binding of `<Button-1>` that invoked the callback associated with the `-command` option. We can do the same thing with tagged text.

The best example is using text like a web hyperlink. When you click on the link, something happens: a new document is loaded or another window is created and presented to the user. The basic form of a **tagBind** call is as follows:

```
$text->tagBind(tagname [, sequence, callback ] )
```

The callback is similar to that specified for the **-command** callback on a button. The sequence is a description of the event that triggers the script. The only sequences you can specify are those that are keyboard or mouse related. (See Chapter 14, *Binding Events*, for more details on available events.)

The following code shows a psuedo-link example. All the link does when we click on it is show the end of the text widget:

```
$t = $mw->Scrolled("Text", -width => 40)->pack(-expand => 1,
                                               -fill => 'both');
$t->tagConfigure('goto_end', -underline => 1, -foreground => 'red');
$t->tagBind('goto_end', "<Button-1>", sub { shift->see('end'); } );

# Setup Bindings to change cursor when over that line
$t->tagBind('goto_end', "<Any-Enter>",
            sub { shift->configure(-cursor => 'hand2') });
$t->tagBind('goto_end', "<Any-Leave>",
            sub { shift->configure(-cursor => 'xterm') });
$t->insert('end', "END\n", "goto_end");

# Insert a bunch of lines
for ($i = 1; $i <= 100; $i++) {
  $t->insert('end', "$i\n");
}
```

Inside the subs in the **tagBind** calls, we use the **shift** command to invoke a method. We can do this because the first argument sent to the **bind** callback is the text widget. This is done implicitly for you. Whichever widget **tagBind** is invoked on is the widget that will be sent as the first argument to the callback. To use the text widget more than once in the callback, assign it to a local variable; for example, **my $widget = shift**.

If we created our text widget in the global scope of the program and placed a reference to the widget in the variable $t, we could also access the text widget in the callback via the $t variable. This is only possible because $t is in the global scope and available during the callback. If you have two different text widgets that you want to use the same callback with, use **shift** to get the correct text widget:

```
$t1->tagBind('goto_end', "<Button-1>", \&goto_end );
$t2->tagBind('goto_end', "<Button-1>", \&goto_end );
sub goto_end {
  my $text = shift;
  $text->see('end');
}
```

Using the same callback for both text widgets helps save space in your program.

To determine what the bindings are for a tagname, just use `tagBind` with only the tag name argument:

```
@bindings = $text->tagBind("tagname");
```

The list will be empty if there are no bindings currently for that tag.

Deleting All Instances of a Tag

Once a tag is created, you can use the `tagDelete` method to delete the tag:

```
$text->tagDelete(tagname [ , tagname ... ])
```

The tags are deleted completely when you use `tagDelete`. This means the text reverts back to the default configuration values, and any bindings or other information associated with those tags is also deleted.

The `tagDelete` method can be used if you are creating temporary tags dynamically within the program and you need to delete the tags later when the information is no longer valid.

Removing a Tag from the Text

To remove the tag from a specific block of text, you can use the `tagRemove` method:

```
$text->tagRemove(tagname, index1 [, index2, index1, index2 ...])
```

Specify the name of the tag and an index or range of indexes from which to remove the tag. This leaves the tag intact; it merely removes it from the specific text indicated with the indices.

Raising and Lowering Tags

When there are several tags applied to the same text, the last tag added to the text overrides the previous ones, and its configuration options are given priority. You can change the priority of the tags by using `tagLower` and `tagRaise`:

```
$text->tagLower(tagname [, belowtag ])
$text->tagRaise(tagname [ , abovetag ])
```

These methods take a tag name as the first argument. If there is no second tag argument, the first tag is given the highest or lowest priority. This affects the entire text in the text widget no matter where the tags are applied. If a second tag is specified, the first tag is specifically placed before or after the second tag.

Think of it as reordering a stack of tags (all applied to the same text). The tag on the top has the most say, and if it has a `-foreground` option of `'red'`, then all the text with that tag will be red, regardless of what the other text tags set **-fore-ground** to. If we use **tagRaise** to move a tag with **-foreground** of **'blue'** to the top, the tagged text will change to blue.

Getting Tag Names

You can find out all the different tags that apply to a specific index or to the whole text widget by using the **tagNames** method:

```
$text->tagNames([ index ])
```

If you specify an index, the list returned contains tags that only apply to that index. If a specific index isn't given, then the list returned contain all the tags that apply to the entire text widget whether or not that tag has been applied to text within the widget.

Determining Where a Tag Applies

If you know the name of the tag, you can find out where it applies in the text widget by using the range methods. The first method, **tagRanges**, returns a list that contains pairs of index values for the whole text widget:

```
@list = $text->tagRanges("tagname")
# returns ( begin1, end1, begin2, end2 ... )
```

If no text in the text widget has that tag, the returned list will be empty.

You can get the pairs of index values one at a time by using the **tagNextrange** method:

```
($start, $end) = $text->tagNextrange("tagname", index1 [ , index2 ])
```

The search for **"tagname"** will begin at *index1* and go no farther than *index2*. If *index2* is not specified, then the search will continue until the end of the text widget or until it finds the tagname, whichever comes first.

Inserting Text

Now that we've gone over text indexes and marks, we can talk in more detail about the methods for manipulating the widget's contents.

As we've seen from the many examples in this chapter, we use **insert** to put text into the text widget. The first argument is an index and indicates where the text will be inserted. The second argument is the string to insert. The next argument (which is optional) is a single tag name or a list of tag names to assign to the inserted text. The usage is:

```
$text->insert(index, string, [ taglist, string, taglist ...] )
```

So far we've only seen single tags used with `insert`. If you want to specify more than one tag, put the tag names into square brackets, creating a list:

```
$t->insert('end', "This is a very tagged line",
          [ 'tag1', 'tag2', 'tag3' ]);
```

To use different sets of tags, you can supply additional text lines and additional tag lists:

```
$t->insert('end', "This is the heading", ['heading', 'underline'],
                  "Second line", ['bold', 'blue']);
```

When you use the `insert` command to insert more than one set of text with different tags, make sure they always come in pairs: text, tags, text, tags, etc. If the tag used isn't defined (with `tagConfigure`), there will be no effect on the text but the tag will still be assigned to that text. You can create the tag later if you wish.

Deleting Text

To remove text from the text widget, you can use the `delete` method:

```
$text->delete(index1 [ , index2 ]);
```

The first index argument is required; the second is optional. If both are specified, then the first index must be less than or equal to the second. All the characters from *index1* to (but not including) *index2* are removed from the text widget. If you want to delete everything from the text widget, you can use `$text->delete("1.0", 'end')`.

Retrieving Text

The `get` function is one you'll use a lot. It returns the text located from *index1* to *index2*. If *index2* isn't specified, just the character located at *index1* is returned. The usage of `get` is as follows:

```
$t = $text->get(index1 [ , index2 ]);
```

As with any index ranges, *index1* must be less than or equal to *index2* or an empty string will be returned.

Translating Index Values

When you work with indexes, it is useful to be able to convert a complicated index form into a simpler one. The `index` method returns an index with the form *line.char*.

```
$newvalue = $text->index(index1);
```

The *index1* value can be any valid index expression.

Comparing Index Values

You can compare two index values by using the **compare** method.

```
$text->compare(index1, op, index2);
```

You pass the first index, the test operation to perform, and the second index. The values for *op* are: `"<"`, `"<="`, `"=="`, `">="`, and `"!="`. The function returns 1 if the test was true and 0 if it wasn't. The call

```
$status = $text->compare("1.0", "<=", "end");
```

returns a 1 because the index `"1.0"` is less than `"end"`.

Showing an Index

By using the **see** method, you can cause the text widget to show the portion of it that contains *index*:

```
$text->see(index);
```

The text within the widget will be scrolled up or down as a result of this call. If the *index* is already visible, nothing happens.

Getting the Size of a Character

The **bbox** method returns a list containing four items that describe the box around the character at *index*:

```
($x, $y, $w, $h) = $text->bbox(index);
```

The first two items returned are the x and y coordinates of the upper-left corner. The last two are the width and height of the box. The bounding box only describes the visible portion of the character, so if it is half hidden or not visible at all, the values returned will reflect this.

Getting Line Information

The **dlineinfo** method returns a list of five items. These items describe the area of the line that contains *index*:

- X coordinate of the upper-left corner
- Y coordinate of the upper-left corner
- Width of the area
- Height of the area
- Baseline position of the line, measured from x

Here is an example call:

```
($x, $y, $w, $h, $base) = $text->lineinfo("index");
```

Unlike the **bbox** method, even areas not shown (due to nonwrapped characters) are used in the calculations as long as some of the line is showing. However, if the line is not visible at all on the screen, the list will be empty. If the line happens to wrap to multiple lines, the entire area is used.

Searching the Contents of a Text Widget

You can use the **search** method to search the text widget for a pattern or regular expression. The **search** method takes some optional switches, the pattern to search for, and an index at which to start searching:

```
$index = $text->search([switches], pattern, index, [ stopindex ])
```

If a match is made, the index returned will point to the first character in the match. If no match is made, an empty string is returned.

The possible switches are:

-forwards

> Tells **search** to search forward through the text widget starting at *index*. This is the default.

-backwards

> Tells **search** to search backward through the text widget starting at the character before *index*.

-exact

> The *pattern* must match the text exactly. This is the default.

-regexp

> The *pattern* will be considered as a regular expression.

-nocase

> Ignores case between *pattern* and the text within the text widget.

-count => *varname*

> *varname* is a pointer to a variable (i.e., \\$**variable**). The number of characters matched will be stored within that variable.

--

> This option does nothing except force the next argument to be taken as the *pattern* even if the next string starts with a "**-**".

Here is a simple example of using **search**:

```
$result = $text->search(-backwards, "find me", 'end');

$location = $text->search(-nocase, "SWITCHES", "1.0");
```

Scrolling

The text widget can be scrolled both horizontally and vertically, so it implements both `xview` and `yview` methods. These two methods are described in Chapter 6, *Scrollbars*.

Marks

There are several ways to refer to different positions throughout the text widget. Index values refer to a character. Tags are named references to a specific character or characters. The term *mark* is used to refer to the spaces in between characters. Similar to tags, a mark has a name. For example, the `"insert"` mark refers to the position of the insert cursor. However, tags refer to the actual characters, and if those characters are deleted, the tag is no longer associated with those characters. The mark stays in place whether the characters surrounding it are deleted or other characters are added. Marks can only refer to one location within the text widget at a time.

Once it is created, you can use a mark as an index. The *gravity* of the mark will affect on which side the text will be inserted. If the gravity is `'right'` (the default), the text will be inserted to the left of the mark because the mark is glued to the character to the right of the mark. If the gravity is `'left'`, the text will be inserted to the left of the mark and the mark will refer to the left of the last character inserted.

There are two special marks that are set automatically by the text widget: `"insert"` and `"current"`. The `"insert"` mark is wherever the insert cursor is. The `"current"` mark is the position closest to the mouse and adjusts as the mouse moves (as long as a mouse button is pressed). Both marks are maintained internally and cannot be deleted.

You will also see a mark called `"anchor"` that shows up in the `getNames` method after you click in the text widget. It always has the same index value as the `"insert"` mark, but `"anchor"` might not always exist.

Setting and Getting the Gravity

To set the gravity of the mark, you can use `markGravity`:

```
$text->markGravity(markname [ , direction ])
```

The possible values for *direction* are `"right"` and `"left"`. The default gravity for new marks is `"right"`. If you don't specify a gravity, the current gravity for that mark is returned.

Determining Mark Names

To get a list of all the marks in the text widget, you can use `markNames`:

```
@names = $text->markNames()
```

There are no arguments to the `markNames` function, and it returns a list. Here is an example of how to report the marks within the text widget:

```
$f->Button(-text => "Report",
           -command => sub { my @m = $t->markNames();
                             foreach (@m) {
                                 print "MARK: $_ at ", $t->index($_), "\n";
                             }})->pack(-side => 'left');
```

The results after clicking in the window to set the insertion cursor are as follows:

```
MARK: insert at 2.15
MARK: anchor at 2.15
MARK: current at 3.0
```

Creating and Deleting Marks

You can create a mark and set it at a specific index by using the `markSet` method.

```
$text->markSet(markname, index)
```

In addition to the *markname* you want to create, specify the *index* where the mark should be placed. For instance, if you always want to be able to insert at the end of line 3:

```
$text->markSet("end of line3", "3.0 lineend");
...
$text->insert("end of line3", "text to insert");
```

The `markUnset` method removes the mark from the text widget and deletes the mark completely. It will no longer show up in the `markNames` list after it has been unset, and it can't be used as an index value either. You can specify more than one markname in `markUnset`:

```
$text->markUnset(markname [, markname, markname ... ])
```

Embedding Widgets

One of the best things you can do with a text widget is put other widgets (such as button or entry widgets) inside it. One advantage of embedding widgets is you can create a scrolled set of widgets on a line-by-line basis.

Before we go over all the different functions that are available to work with embedded widgets, let's look at a quick example. We often want to do a lot of data entry in a program, which means we need a lot of label and entry widgets.

Sometimes there are so many of them that it's hard to fit them all on the screen
without making a mess of the window. By using a scrolled text widget and put-
ting the label and entry widgets inside it, we can create a lot more widgets within
a smaller space. Here's the code:

```
use Tk;

$mw = MainWindow->new;
$mw->title("Data Entry");
$f = $mw->Frame->pack(-side => 'bottom');
$f->Button(-text => "Exit",
           -command => sub { exit; })->pack(-side => 'left');
$f->Button(-text => "Save",
           -command => sub {  # do something with %info;
                   })->pack(-side => 'bottom');
$t = $mw->Scrolled("Text", -width => 40,
                   -wrap => 'none')->pack(-expand => 1, -fill => 'both');

foreach (qw/Name Address City State Zip Phone Occupation
            Company Business_Address Business_Phone/) {
        $w = $t->Label(-text => "$_:", -relief => 'groove', -width => 20);
        $t->windowCreate('end', -window => $w);
        $w = $t->Entry(-width => 20, -textvariable => \$info{$_});
        $t->windowCreate('end', -window => $w);
        $t->insert('end', "\n");
}
$t->configure(-state => 'disabled'); # disallows user typing

MainLoop;
```

Figure 8-6 shows the Win32 version of this window.

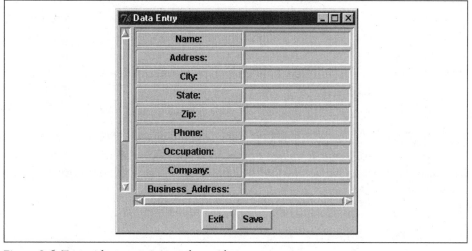

Figure 8-6. Text widget containing other widgets

We disable the text widget before running `Mainloop` because we don't want the user to be able to type text directly into the text widget. This only disables the ability to enter or delete text—the internal widgets still function normally. We also turned off the `-wrap` option so the label and entry widgets don't accidentally drop down to the next line when the window is resized.

You could put a text widget inside another text widget, but you probably wouldn't want to.

The window Method

As you can see from the preceding example, we use the `windowCreate` method to insert an embedded widget. The widget should have already been created, and it should be a child of the text widget. The general syntax is:

```
$widget = $text->Widget(   );
$text->windowCreate(index, -window => $widget,[option => value ] );
```

In our example above, we used the `'end'` index. You can use any valid text widget index to insert the embedded widgets. The only option we used was a `-window` option with the reference to the new `$widget`.

Here are the available options for the `window` method:

—align => *where*
Possible values of `'baseline'`, `'bottom'`, `'center'`, or `'top'`. It determines where the widget is placed within the line if it is not as tall as the line itself. The default is `'center'`.

—padx => *amount* and -pady => *amount*
Add space around the widget in the x and y directions respectively (`-padx =>` 10).

—stretch => 0 | 1
Takes a boolean value (1 or 0). A true value will stretch the widgets to fill the line from top to bottom.

—window => $widget
Takes a reference to another widget.

There are several different forms of the `window` method. The first one, the "Create" form, creates the widget within the text widget. The "Names" form lets you know what types of widgets are embedded in the text widget:

```
@types = $text->windowNames();
```

The results look like this:

```
.text.radiobutton .text.label .text.button .text.entry .text.checkbutton
```

Use the `windowCget` function to get information about the options that were used when the window was created in the text widget:

```
$value = $text->windowCget(index, option);
```

In order to use `windowCget` you need to know the index the widget is currently occupying (each widget occupies one character in the text widget, even if it looks like it takes more space).

The "Configure" form of `window` will allow you change the options associated with the widget at *index* or retrieve the value of the configuration option:

```
$text->windowConfigure(index [, option => value ] );
```

Remember that the only options you can use with this method are `-align`, `-padx`, `-pady`, `-stretch`, and `-window`. Other than this, `windowConfigure(...)` behaves just like a regular widget's `configure` method. To make changes on the $widget directly, use `$widget->configure(...)`.

Internal Debug Flag

The `debug` function takes an optional boolean argument:

```
$text->debug( [ boolean ] );
```

If the value passed in is true, then internal consistency checks will be turned on in the B-tree code associated with text widgets. If false, the checks will be left off. Without any argument, the `debug` method will return the value `"on"` if it has been turned on, and `"off"` if not. All text widgets in the application share the same debug flag.

Scanning

The `scanMark` and `scanDragto` methods are used internally within the text widget. A call to `scanMark` simply records the x, y passed in for use later with `scanDragto`. It returns an empty string:

```
$text->scanMark(x, y);
```

`scanDragto` also takes x, y coordinates, which are compared to the `scanMark` x,y coordinates. The view within the text widget is adjusted by 10 times the difference between the coordinates.

```
$text->scanDragto(x, y);
```

Fun Things to Try

- Create a scrollable text widget. Insert a button widget that has text describing the foreground color of the text widget and when you click the button, have it cycle between several different colors, updating the button's `-foreground` color and text. For a practical application, have several buttons, each associated with a different color in your application. When the user clicks the button, you can change the color to a different value (possibly using the ColorEdit composite widget).

- Create a text widget that will display a read-only file. Create two buttons on the window, one to decrease the font within the text widget, the other to increase it.,

9

The Canvas Widget

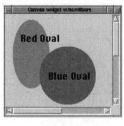

The canvas widget is mainly used for drawing items such as arcs, lines, rectangles, circles, and so on. You can also place text and other widgets inside a canvas widget. Think of it as a painter's canvas: It is blank until you decide to draw something on it. But unlike a painter's canvas, which is limited in size, this canvas is scrollable in any direction. Here are some examples of how you can use a canvas widget:

- Create a drawing program.
- Display a graph based on input from the user.
- Create a customized slider.

Each item you create in a canvas widget can have bindings attached to it to allow for easy interaction with the user.

Creating a Canvas

I recommend that you always use the `Scrolled` method to create a canvas unless you know for sure that your canvas is going to be a fixed size that will fit in the window:

```
$canvas = $mw->Canvas( [ option => values, ... ] )->pack();
# or...
$canvas = $mw->Scrolled('Canvas', [ option => values, ... ])->pack();
```

The first line creates just a canvas and the second creates a canvas with scrollbars. (See Chapter 6, *Scrollbars*, for more information on what else you can do with the `Scrolled` method.) To create a canvas widget, use the desired parent widget to invoke the `Canvas` method and pass any initial options in with their values. The `Canvas` method returns a reference to the newly created canvas widget.

Before we get into the options and methods available with a canvas widget, here are a few miscellaneous things you should know about using a canvas widget.

Coordinate System

A canvas widget uses a coordinate system to locate items inside of it, but the coordinate system isn't a normal one. It's more like an upside-down coordinate system.

Figure 9-1 shows a diagram that demonstrates the coordinate system a canvas widget uses.

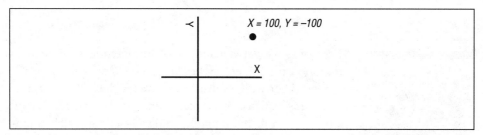

Figure 9-1. Canvas coordinate system

The x coordinates behave normally; the larger coordinates are to the right and the smaller ones are to the left. The y coordinates look like they have been drinking vodka; the larger y coordinates are on the bottom rather than on the top because the 0,0 point is in the upper-left corner. Although it is rare, you can use negative coordinates in a canvas.

The coordinate system isn't too hard to deal with once you realize what is happening, but if you try to draw a building with a standard coordinate system in mind (that is, with the larger y coordinates higher up), your building will come out upside down.

There are several ways to deal with this. First, adjust your way of thinking so you always think y coordinates are larger at the bottom (never mind all those years we all struggled through geometry classes). Or, you are just as stubborn as I am, you can think in normal coordinates, and have your program do a quick little calculation before sending y coordinates to the canvas functions. (Multiply all y coordinates by –1. Tricky, huh?)

Whichever way you decide to deal with it, be consistent and make sure you comment your code.

The x and y coordinates can be specified in any valid screen unit. They are pixels by default. If you follow the coordinate number with a letter m, then you are measuring distance in millimeters. The other letters you can use are p for printer points, i for inches, and c for centimeters. The default is pixels, which is what we'll use for all of the examples in this chapter.

The Scrollable Region

The scrollable area is the portion of the canvas widget that you want the user to be able to see. If you don't create a scrollable area (by using the -scrollregion option), the user can scroll infinitely in any direction and the scrollbars don't reflect where items on the canvas are.

Figure 9-2 shows an example of the scrollable area compared with the area that is visible in the canvas. If these two areas are the same size, you don't need scrollbars on the canvas (if you use scrollbars, their sliders will completely fill the trough area).

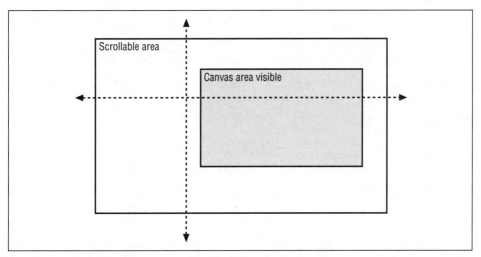

Figure 9-2. Scrollable area compared with visible area

The arrows on the axis markers in Figure 9-2 indicate that the canvas can still be larger than the indicated scrolling area. For instance, if you decide to insert a circle beyond the scrolling area, you have to adjust the scrollable area so the user will be able to see the new circle.

The best way to do this is to use the **bbox** method, which returns a bounding box for all items that match the tags you send it. Here's what the code looks like:

```
$canvas->configure(-scrollregion => [ $canvas->bbox("all") ]);
```

Calling this after you add or remove items to the canvas resets the scroll region to where it needs to be. Of course, if you are adding many different items all at once, you should wait until after you have added them all and then update the scroll region.

Using Bind with a Canvas

When you try to use the **bind** method with a canvas widget, you'll run into some unexpected problems. You'll either get an error and your script won't run, or your script will run but your **bind** won't seem to have any effect. In order to get around this, you'll need to use the explicit **Tk::bind** instead of just **bind** (because the canvas has its own **bind** method that you have to avoid using):

```
$canvas = $mw->Canvas();
$canvas->Tk::bind("<Button-1>", sub { print "bind!\n"; });
```

You can also use **SUPER::bind** instead of **Tk::bind**. Either way will work.[*]

If you used the **Scrolled** method to create your canvas, you'll have an added difficulty; you'll have to use the **Subwidget** method to get to the canvas widget:

```
$canvas = $mw->Scrolled("Canvas");
$real_canvas = $canvas->Subwidget("canvas");
$real_canvas->Tk::bind("<Button-1>", sub { print "bind!\n" });
```

Other than this one small annoyance, **bind** works just as you would expect it would. Here's a quick (and fairly useful) example that will print out the coordinate you clicked on:

```
$c = $mw->Scrolled("Canvas")->pack();
$canvas = $c->Subwidget("canvas");
$canvas->Tk::bind("<Button-1>", [ \&print_xy, Ev('x'), Ev('y') ]);
sub print_xy {
  my ($canv, $x, $y) = @_;
  print "(x,y) = ", $canv->canvasx($x), ", ", $canv->canvasy($y), "\n";
}
```

This example prints out the coordinates (in canvas coordinates) when you click the left mouse button.

Canvas Options

The options listed in this section affect the entire canvas widget and the items within it. Items are circles, lines, rectangles, text, or other widgets. These options act as you would expect them to (as explained in Chapter 3, *The Basic Button*, for

---

[*] For those using Tk8.0: You can use **canvasBind** instead of **Tk::bind**. I'll refer to Tk::bind throughout the rest of the chapter, but note that you should use **canvasBind** instead.

most options and in Chapter 6 for the scrollbar options): `-background`, `-border-width`, `-cursor`, `-height`, `-highlightbackground`, `-highlightcolor`, `-high-lightthickness`, `-relief`, `-takefocus`, `-width`, `-xscrollcommand`, and `-yscrollcommand`.

New Options

When selecting items in the canvas with the mouse cursor, the canvas widget does calculations to determine if the mouse cursor is inside or outside the item. The `-closeenough` option controls how close the mouse must be to the item before it is considered inside the item. The default value for `-closeenough` is `"1.0"`, which is 1.0 pixels away. Any floating point number is a valid value (and will always be in pixels) for `-closeenough`.

I discussed the `-scrollregion` option briefly in "The Scrollable Region" earlier in this chapter. It takes a list reference, and that list must contain four coordinates. The coordinates indicate a bounding region for the scrollable area in the canvas. The coordinates are in this order: [*minx*, *miny*, *maxx*, *maxy*]. You can also think of the coordinates as if they were defining the [left, top, right, bottom] edges of the scrollable region.

Normally, the canvas widget limits the user to seeing only the area defined by the `-scrollregion` option. You can allow the user to scroll beyond this area by using `-confine => 0`. The default for `-confine` is 1.

Additional Scrolling Options

The `-xscrollcommand` and `-yscrollcommand` options both work as described in Chapter 6, but there are two additional options that affect how the canvas scrolls its contents: `-xscrollincrement` and `-yscrollincrement`. Each option takes a valid screen distance for a value. This distance is the unit the canvas will use to scroll in the associated direction. For instance, if you specify `-xscrollincrement => 10`, each time you click an arrow on the horizontal scrollbar, the contents of the canvas will shift so that the left edge of the contents is an even multiple of 10. Essentially, the canvas will shift the contents 10 pixels in the arrow's direction.

If the value associated with `-xscrollincrement` or `-yscrollincrement` is 0 or less, scrolling is done in normal increments.

Options for Text Items

The following options are applied to the entire canvas widget, but they really only affect the text items inside the canvas widget: -insertbackground, -insertbor-derwidth, -insertofftime, -insertontime, -insertwidth, -selectback-ground, -selectborderwidth, and -selectforeground. These options work the same as they would for an entry widget or a text widget. See Chapter 5, *Label and Entry Widgets*, and Chapter 8, *The Text Widget*, for more details.

Canvas Widget Option List

These options all are used with the **Canvas** method:

-background => *color*
  Sets the background of the canvas to *color*.

-borderwidth => *amount*
  Changes the width of the edges of the canvas to *amount*.

-closeenough => *float_amount*
  Sets the amount of distance from the item when the cursor is considered inside the item.

-confine => **1** | 0
  Indicates that the canvas will limit itself to the area defined by -scroll-region if set to 1. Default is 1.

-cursor => *cursorname*
  Indicates that the cursor will change to *cursorname* when it is over the canvas.

-height => *amount*
  Sets the height of the canvas to *amount*.

-highlightbackground => *color*
  Sets the color the highlight rectangle should be when the canvas does not have the keyboard focus.

-highlightcolor => *color*
  Sets the color the highlight rectangle should be when the canvas does have the keyboard focus.

-highlightthickness => *amount*
  Sets the thickness of the highlight rectangle. Default is 2.

-insertbackground => *color*
  Sets the color of the area behind the text insert cursor.

-insertborderwidth => *amount*
  Sets the width of the borders on the insert cursor.

`-insertofftime =>` *milliseconds*
> Sets the amount of time the cursor disappears from the screen when it is blinking off.

`-insertontime =>` *milliseconds*
> Sets the amount of time the cursor appears on the screen when it is blinking on.

`-insertwidth =>` *amount*
> Sets the width of the insert cursor.

`-relief => 'flat'|'groove'|'raised'|'ridge'|'sunken'|'solid'`
> Indicates the way the edges of the canvas are drawn. Default is `'flat'`.

`-scrollregion => [` *left, top, right, bottom* `]`
> Defines the area the user is allowed to scroll.

`-selectbackground =>` *color*
> Sets the color of the area behind any selected text.

`-selectborderwidth =>` *amount*
> Sets the width of the border of the selected area.

`-selectforeground =>` *color*
> Sets the color of the selected text.

`-takefocus =>` 0 | 1 | **undef**
> Determines whether or not the canvas can get keyboard focus. Default is for the application to decide.

`-width =>` *amount*
> Sets the width of the canvas to *amount.*

`-xscrollcommand =>` *callback*
> Determines the callback used when the canvas is scrolled horizontally (automatically set to the correct callback when the **Scrolled** method is used).

`-xscrollincrement =>` *amount*
> Sets the distance the canvas contents move when the arrow on the horizontal scrollbar is clicked.

`-yscrollcommand =>` *callback*
> Determines the callback used when the canvas is scrolled vertically.

`-yscrollincrement =>` *amount*
> Sets the distance the canvas contents move when the arrow on the vertical scrollbar is clicked.

Creating Items in a Canvas

The whole point of having a canvas is to put items in it. You can create arcs, bitmaps, images, lines, rectangles, ovals (circles), polygons, text, and widgets. Each has an associated **create*XXX*** method, where the type of item you want to create replaces the *XXX*. All of the **create** methods return a unique ID, which can be used to refer to the item later. When you see a method that takes a tag or an ID as an argument, the ID is the one returned from the **create** method.

The Arc Item

When you create an arc, you specify a bounding rectangle with two sets of x and y coordinates. The arc is drawn within the confines of the bounding box. Additional options that will change how the arc is drawn in the canvas are explained shortly. The basic **createArc** statement is as follows:

```
$id = $canvas->createArc(x1, y1, x2, y2);
```

Any additional options used in the **createArc** method are specified after the coordinates:

```
$id = $canvas->createArc(x1, y1, x2, y2, option => value);
```

Each option for the arc item can be used later with the **itemcget** and **itemconfigure** canvas methods. The options are:

-extent => *degrees*

> The length of the arc is specified in degrees by using the **-extent** option. The default **-extent** (or length) is 90 degrees. The arc is drawn from the starting point (see **-start** option) counterclockwise within the rectangle defined by (*x1*, *y1*) and (*x2*, *y2*). The *degrees* value should be between –360 and 360. If it is more or less, then the value used is the specified of degrees modulo 360.
>
> Here are some examples of the **-extent** option:
>
> ```
> # This draws half of an oval
> $canvas->createArc(0,0,100,150, -extent => 180);
> # This will draw _ of an oval
> $canvas->createArc(0,0,100,150, -extent => 270);
> ```

-fill => *color*

> To fill the arc with the specified color. By default, there is no fill color for an arc.

-outline => *color*

> Normally the arc is drawn with a black outline. To change the default, use the **-outline** option. The outline color is separate from the fill color, so to make it a completely solid object, make the color for **-outline** and **-fill** the same.

-outlinestipple => *bitmap*

> To use -outlinestipple, you must also use the -outline option. Normally, the outline of the arc is drawn solid. Use a bitmap with -outlinestipple to make the outline nonsolid; the specified bitmap pattern will be used to draw the outline of the arc.

-start => *degrees*

> The value associated with the -start option determines where Perl/Tk starts drawing the arc. The default start position is at three o'clock (0 degrees). The degrees specified are added to this position, but in a counterclockwise direction. Use -start => 90 to make the arc start at the twelve o'clock position, use -start => 180 to make the arc start at the nine o'clock position, and so on.

-stipple => *bitmap*

> The -stipple option causes the arc to be filled with a bitmap pattern, but only if the -fill option has been specified as well.

-style => "pieslice" | "chord" | "arc"

> The -style of the arc determines how the arc is drawn. The default, "pieslice", draws the arc and two lines from the center of the oval ends of the arc segment. The "chord" value draws the arc and a line connecting the two end points of the arc segment. The "arc" value draws just the arc portion with no other lines. The -fill and -stipple options are ignored if "arc" is used.

-tags => *taglist*

> When you create an arc, you use the -tags option to assign tag names to it. The value associated with -tags is an anonymous list of tag names; for example:

```
$canvas->createArc(0,0,10,140,-tags => ["arc", "tall"]);
```

> You don't need to use an anonymous list if you are only specifying one tag name:

```
$canvas->createArc(0,0,10,140,-tags => "arc");
```

-width => *amount*

> The width of the outline is specified by using -width. The default -width is 1.

The Bitmap Item

A canvas widget can display a bitmap instead of text just as a button or label can. You can use createBitmap to insert a bitmap into your canvas widget:

```
$id = $canvas->createBitmap(x, y);
```

Of course, you must use the -bitmap option to specify which bitmap to display or you won't see anything. So we really create a bitmap like this:

```
$id = $canvas->createBitmap(x, y, -bitmap => bitmap);
```

Why they didn't just make the bitmap the third argument, I don't know. That's just the way it is. The other captions available for **createBitmap** are:

-anchor => **"center"** | "n" | "e" | "s" | "w" | "ne" | "nw" | "se" | "sw"

> The -anchor option determines how the bitmap is placed on the canvas rela-tive to the x,y coordinates indicated. The default for -anchor is "center", which puts the center of the image at the x,y coordinates. Using a single cardi-nal direction (for example, "e") would place the center of that edge at the x,y coordinates.

-background => *color*

> The -background option specifies the color to use for all the 0 (zero) bitmap pixels. If you don't specify a background color or use an empty string (""), the 0 pixels will be transparent.

-bitmap => *bitmapname*

> You must use the -bitmap option to tell the canvas which bitmap to display. You can use the built-in bitmaps such as 'info' or 'warning' just as you can with the button widget, or you can specify a filename. Remember, to specify a bitmap file, use an @ sign in front of the bitmap filename.

-foreground => *color*

> The foreground color of a bitmap is the opposite of the background color. (By definition, bitmaps can only have two colors.) The -foreground option will color all the 1 pixels with this color. The default for -foreground is black.

-tags => *taglist*

> When you create a bitmap, you can assign tag names to it by using the -tags option. The value associated with -tags is an anonymous list of tag names; for example:

```
$canvas->createBitmap(0,0, -bitmap => 'info',
                       -tags => ["info", "bitmap"]);
```

> You don't need to use the list if you are only specifying one tag name:

```
$canvas->createBitmap(0,0, -bitmap => 'info', -tags => "bitmap");
```

The Image Item

If we can create a bitmap on a canvas, it makes sense that we can create an image as well. We can do so with the **createImage** method:

```
$id = $canvas->createImage(x, y, -image => image);
```

Again, you have to specify an image to display or you won't see anything. The other options available for `createImage` are:

`-anchor => "center" | "n" | "e" | "s" | "w" | "ne" | "nw" | "se" | "sw"`

> The −anchor option for an image works the same as it does for a bitmap. The −anchor option is how the image is positioned around the x,y coordinates. The default for −anchor is `'center'`.

`-image => $image`

> The −image option indicates which image to display. The image value is actually a reference to an image created with `Photo` or `Bitmap` methods. (See Chapter 3 for more information on how to specify an image file.)

`-tags => ` *taglist*

> Use the −tags option to assign tag names to an image. The value associated with −tags is an anonymous list of tag names; for example:

```
$canvas->createImage(0,0, -image => $imgptr,
                     -tags => ["image", "blue"]);
```

> You don't need to use the list if you are only specifying one tag name:

```
$canvas->createImage(0,0, -image => $imgptr, -tags => "image");
```

The Line Item

The `createLine` method can actually create multiple connected lines, not just one. The first two coordinate sets you supply create the first line, and any additional coordinates will continue the line to that point:

```
$id = $canvas->createLine(0,0, 400,400);          # creates one line
$id = $canvas->createLine(0,0, 400,400, -50, 240); # creates two lines
```

After the coordinates, you can specify any options and values you wish to configure the line(s); the options and values are as follows:

`-arrow => "none" | "first" | "last" | "both"`

> You can place arrowheads at either end of the line (or both) by using the −arrow option. If you have more than one line in your `createLine` method, only the first and/or last point can be made into an arrow. If you want each line to have an arrowhead, then use multiple `createLine` statements.

`-arrowshape => [ ` *dist1, dist2, dist3* ` ]`

> The −arrowshape option only applies if you use the −arrow option as well. Figure 9-3 shows what the distance values mean.

> Specify the three distances by using an anonymous list such as this:

```
$canvas->createLine(10, 10, 200, -40, -arrow => "both",
               -arrowshape => [ 20, 20, 20]);
```

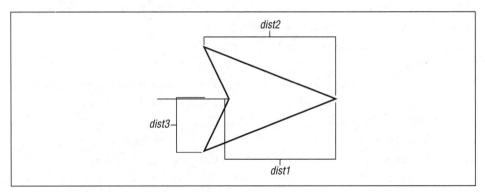

Figure 9-3. Definition of arrowhead

-capstyle => "**butt**" | "projecting" | "round"
Instead of arrowheads, you can make the ends of the line have one of these styles.

-fill => *color*
The -fill option is misnamed because it isn't actually filling anything. The line is simply drawn with this color instead of black.

-joinstyle => "bevel" | "**miter**" | "round"
The -joinstyle option affects how multiple lines are joined together. The default is "**miter**". If there is only one line created, this option has no effect.

-smooth => 1 | **0**
If -smooth has a value of 1, then, using Bezier spline(s), the line(s) will be drawn as a curve. The first two lines make the first spline, the second and third line make up the second spline, and so on. To make a straight line, repeat the end points of the desired straight line (or use createLine again to make a separate line).

-splinesteps => *count*
When you use the -smooth option, the more -splinesteps you use, the smoother the curve. To find out how many steps create the desired effect, you'll have to experiment with different values.

-stipple => *bitmap*
To have the line drawn with a bitmap pattern (1s in the bitmap have color, 0s are transparent), use the -stipple option. The bitmap can be a default bitmap name or a filename. The wider the line (see -width), the more the stipple design will show up.

-tags => *taglist*

> When you create a line (or lines), assign tag names to them by using the -tags option. The value associated with -tags is an anonymous list of tag names; for example:
>
> ```
> $canvas->createLine(0,0, 100,100, -tags => ["line", "blue"]);
> ```
>
> You don't need to use a list if you are only specifying one tag name:
>
> ```
> $canvas->createLine(0,0, 100, 100, -tags => "line");
> ```

-width => *amount*

> You can make the line(s) thicker by using the -width option. Normally the line is drawn only 1 pixel wide. The amount can be any valid screen distance (e.g., centimeters, inches).

The Oval Item

An oval can be a circle if you draw it just right. To create a circle/oval, use the createOval method and specify two sets of points that indicate a rectangle (or square) in which to draw the circle/oval. Here is a simple example:

```
$id = $canvas->createOval(0,0, 50, 50);  # creates a circle
$id = $canvas->createOval(0,0, 50, 100); # creates an oval
```

The options for the oval will be familiar, so we'll just cover them briefly:

-fill => *color*

> The oval will be filled in with the specified color. This color is different than the outline color. By default, the oval is not filled.

-outline => *color*

> The outline is the line drawn around the outside of the circle. Normally the outline is black, but it can be changed by using the -outline option. If you make the outline and the fill color the same, the oval appears solid.

-stipple => *bitmap*

> To fill the oval with a bitmap pattern (1 values in bitmap are colored, 0 values are transparent), use the -stipple option. If the -fill option isn't used, -stipple has no effect. -stipple takes a default bitmap name or a file with a bitmap in it.

-tags => *taglist*

> When you create an oval, use the -tags option to assign tag names to them. The value associated with -tags is an anonymous list of tag names; for example:
>
> ```
> $canvas->createOval(0,0, 100,100, -tags => ["oval", "blue"]);
> ```

You don't need to use a list if you are only specifying one tag name:

```
$canvas->createOval(0,0, 100, 100, -tags => "oval");
```

-width => *amount*

The -width option changes how wide the outline of the oval is drawn. The default for -width is 1 pixel.

The Polygon Item

A polygon is merely a bunch of lines where the first point is connected to the last point automatically to create an enclosed area. The createPolygon method requires at least three x,y coordinate pairs. For instance, the following piece of code will create a three-sided polygon:

```
$id = $canvas->createPolygon(1000,1000, 850,950, 30,40);
```

Additional x,y coordinate pairs can be specified as well; for example:

```
$id = $canvas->createPolygon(1000,1000, 850,950, 30,40, 500,500);
```

The options you can specify with createPolygon are the same as those you use with createLine: -fill, -outline, -smooth, -splinesteps, -stipple, -tags, and -width. Just remember that createPolygon connects the first point to the last point to enclose the area.

The Rectangle Item

As if being able to create a rectangle using createLine or createPolygon weren't enough, we also have the createRectangle method. It only takes two x y coordinate sets, which are the opposite corners of the rectangular area:

```
$id = $canvas->createRectangle(10, 10, 50, 150);
```

Again, we have seen the options available for createRectangle with the other create methods: -fill, -outline, -stipple, -tags, and -width. Although I've covered these options already, here are a few examples:

```
# A blue rectangle with black outline:
$canvas->createRectangle(10,10, 50, 150, -fill => 'blue');
# A blue rectangle with a thicker outline:
$canvas->createRectangle(10,10, 50, 150, -fill => 'blue', -width => 10);
```

The Text Item

Finally, an item type that doesn't have lines in it! You can add text to a canvas widget by using the createText method. It requires an x,y coordinate pair, which determines where you place the text in the canvas, and the text to be displayed:

```
$id = $canvas->createText(0,0, -text => "origin");
```

The -text option is actually optional, but then you wouldn't see any text on the screen. Because there is no point in that, we will assume that you will always specify -text with a text value to display. The other options available for text items are as follows:

-anchor => **"center"** | "n" | "e" | "s" | "w" | "ne" | "nw" | "se" | "sw"

> The -anchor option determines where the text is placed in relation to the x,y coordinate. The default is centered: The text will be centered over that point no matter how large the piece of text is.

-fill => *color*

> The text is normally drawn in black; you can change this by using the -fill option. The name of this option doesn't make much sense when you think about it in terms of text (normally our widgets use -foreground to change the color of the text). For example, -fill => 'blue' will draw blue text.

-font => *fontname*

> You can change the font for the displayed text by using the -font option.

-justify => **"left"** | "right" | "center"

> If the displayed text has more than one line, the -justify option will cause it to be justified as specified. The default justification is to the left.

-stipple => *bitmap*

> This option is a bit strange, but here it is anyway. If you specify a bitmap name (or file) with the -stipple option, the text will be drawn by using the bitmap pattern. Most of the time, this will make the text unreadable, so don't use it unless you're using a large font.

-tags => *taglist*

> The taglist is a single tag name or an anonymous list of tag names to be assigned to this item.

-text => *string*

> This option is not optional. The specified string is displayed in the canvas widget at the x,y coordinate.

-width => *amount*

> This is another misnamed option because it does not change the width of each text character. It determines the maximum length of each line of text. If the text is longer than this length, the line will automatically wrap to a second line. The default value for *amount* is 0, which will only break lines at newline characters. Lines are always broken at spaces so words won't be cut in half.

Text item indexes

Methods that affect text items will sometimes ask for an index value. Text indexes for the regular text widget were covered in Chapter 8, and the index values for a canvas text item are similar. The only difference is that each item is considered only one line (even if it has "\n" characters in it). Index values are as follows:

n

A number value: for example, 0 or 12. 0 is the first character, 1 is the second, and so on.

"end"

The character directly after the last one. Often used with the **insert** method to add to the end of the string.

"insert"

The character directly before the insertion cursor.

"sel.first"

The first character of the selected text. Only valid if there is a selection.

"sel.last"

The last character of the selected text. Only valid if there is a selection.

"@*x,y*"

The character closest to the point *x,y* of the canvas (not screen coordinates).

Deleting characters

To delete characters from within a text item, use the **dchars** method: $canvas-> dchars (*tag/id, first [, last]*). Specify a tag or ID to match the text item(s) and the index at which to start deleting. If the end index isn't specified, all the characters to the end of the string will be deleted (including any "\n" characters).

Positioning the cursor

You can specifically place the blinking text cursor by using **icursor**: $canvas-> icursor (*tag/id, index*). The cursor will only show up immediately if the specified item has the current keyboard focus. You can still set the position of the cursor if it doesn't, it just won't display until the item does get the keyboard focus.

Index information

You can find out an index based on another index by using the **index** method. Don't get confused yet; here's an example:

```
$index = $canvas->index("textitem", "sel.first");
```

This will return the numerical index associated with the first selected character in the text item. If more than one item will match the tag or ID indicated (in this case it's a tag named `"textitem"`), then the first one found will be used.

Adding text

To add more text to a text item, use the `insert` method: `$canvas->insert(`*tag/id, index, string*`)`. The first argument is the tag or ID, which can match multiple items. The second argument is the index before which to insert the new string, and the last argument is the actual string to insert into the text item.

Selecting text

There are several methods you can use to programmatically select portions of the text. To clear the selection (any selection; there are no tags or IDs sent with this command), use `$canvas->selectClear()`. To select a portion of text, use `selectFrom` and `selectTo`. The following two lines of code select the text from beginning to end for the first item that matches the tag `"texttag"`:

```
$canvas->selectFrom("texttag", 0);
$canvas->selectTo("texttag", "end");
```

You can add to the selection by using `selectAdjust`: `$canvas->selectAdjust("adjust",` *tag/id, index*`)`. You can get the ID of the item that currently has the selection in it by using `$id = $canvas->selectItem()`.

The Widget Item

You can put any type of widget inside a canvas—buttons, checkbuttons, text widgets, or even another canvas widget (if you are a little crazy)—by using the `createWindow` method. Before calling `createWindow`, you must create the widget to put into the canvas. Here's an example:

```
$bttn = $canvas->Button(-text => "Button",
                        -command => sub { print "Button in canvas\n"; });
$id = $canvas->createWindow(0, 0, -window => $bttn);
```

There are a few things you should note about this example (which is fairly typical except the subroutine associated with the button doesn't do anything useful):

* The button is a child of the canvas widget. The button could be a child of an ancestor of the canvas (the button could be a child of the main window if the canvas is also a child of the main window). However, the button should not be a child of a different toplevel widget that has nothing to with the canvas.

* The `createWindow` method doesn't actually create the widget; it just puts it in the canvas. The button is placed at the specified coordinates inside the canvas and has not been placed on the screen with `pack()`, `grid()`, or `place()`.

- The widget must be created before you call `createWindow`.

- You can click the button and the callback associated with it will be invoked, just as with any other button.

- When you create the widget, you can use any of that widget's options to configure it. You can continue to configure the widget by using the reference to it (e.g., `$bttn`).

The following options which you can use when you call `createWindow` are more like options you use with `pack()` than widget options:

`-anchor => "center" | "n" | "e" | "s" | "w" | "ne" | "nw" | "se" | "sw"`

The widget will be placed at the x,y coordinates according to the `-anchor` value. The default is `"center"`, which means that the widget will have its center point placed on x,y.

`-height => amount`

The widget will be given this height. If you don't use `-height`, the widget will have the height it was created with (usually the natural size of the widget).

`-tags => taglist`

The *taglist* associates a tag with the widget. You can specify either a single tag string, or an anonymous list of tag names.

`-width => amount`

The widget will be given this width. If you don't use the `-width` option, the widget will have the width it was created with (the natural size of the widget).

`-window => $widget`

This is a nonoptional option. If you don't specify `-window`, there will be no widget put in the canvas. The `$widget` is a reference to a widget item. You can create the widget beforehand or inline as follows:

```
$canvas->createWindow(0,0, -window => $canvas->Button(-text => "Button",
    -command => sub { print "Button!\"; }));
```

It makes sense to create the widget inline if you don't need to do anything fancy with it.

Configuring the Canvas Widget

As usual, to configure or get information about the canvas widget, you can use the `configure` and `cget` methods, explained in detail in Appendix A, *Configuring Widgets with configure and cget*. Remember, `configure` and `cget` operate on the entire canvas widget (possibly affecting the items within it).

Configuring Items in the Canvas Widget

To change the configuration options of any of the items within the canvas, you only need to know the tag name or the ID for that item. You can then use the `itemcget` and `itemconfigure` methods. They behave just like the `cget` and `configure` methods, except as a first argument, they take the tag or ID of the item(s). I use the term "item(s)" because a tag can refer to more than one item. Here are some examples:

```
$color = $canvas->itemcget("circle", -fill);
$canvas->itemconfigure($id_number, -fill => "yellow", -outline => 5);
```

Make sure the options you use with `itemconfigure` and `itemcget` are valid. Each item type has a list of valid options; they are listed earlier in this chapter with each `create` method.

When you set the `-tags` option, the `itemconfigure` method will replace any currently set tags for the item. The *taglist* associated with `-tags` can also be empty, which will essentially remove all tags.

Tags

Each item can also have a tag (or more than one tag) associated with it. We have seen tags used before in the text widget, where sections of text could be assigned a tag. A tag can be assigned when the item is created, or you can use the `addtag` method to assign a tag after the item has been created.

There are two special tags that are automatically assigned and maintained: the `"current"` and `"all"` tag. The `"all"` tag refers to all the items in the canvas. The `"current"` tag refers to the topmost item that the mouse cursor is over. If the mouse cursor is outside of the canvas widget or not over an item, then the `"current"` tag does not exist.

You can use tags to make changes to many different items at once. For instance, if you want all circles to have the same color, but you want to be able to change it from time to time, then give all circles a `"circle"` tag when you create them. Using the `itemconfigure` method to change the configuration options of the items with the `"circle"` tag.

The following are some sample syntax lines for creating tags.

`$canvas->addtag("newtag", "above", ` *tag/id*`);`
> The `"newtag"` tag is added to the item that is above the tag/ID item. If there is more than one match for tag/ID, the last item found will be used so the `"newtag"` is directly above the tag/ID item in the display list. The display list

is created as you add items to the canvas and can be manipulated with the
`raise` and `lower` methods.

`$canvas->addtag("newtag", "all");`

The keyword `"all"` is a special tag that includes every item currently in the
canvas. Items added to the canvas after the call to addtag will not contain
`"newtag"` in their taglist.

`$canvas->addtag("newtag", "below", *tag/id*);`

The `"newtag"` tag is added to the item that is directly below the tag/ID item.
If more than one item matches the below tag/ID search, the lowest item in the
list will be used.

`$canvas->addtag("newtag", "closest", *x, y*);`

Use the `"closest"` tag to select the item closest to the x,y coordinates (in
canvas coordinates). If more than one item matches, the last one found is
used.

There are two more possible arguments for this form of **addtag**. You can
specify a number that indicates how far out from the x,y coordinates items are
to be considered. For instance, if you want an item that is within 10 pixels to
be considered `"closest"`, make the call as follows:

```
$canvas->addtag("newtag", "closest", 50, 100, 10);
```

You can also specify a starting tag/ID to start a search. The call would then
look like this:

```
$canvas->addtag("newtag", "closest", x, y, 10, $tag_or_id);
```

By using this form, you can loop through all the closest items.

`$canvas->addtag("newtag", "enclosed", *x1, y1, x2, y2*);`

You can assign the same tag to several items within the area bounded by
(*x1,y1*) to (*x2,y2*) by using the `"enclosed"` form of **addtag**. Items will only
be given `"newtag"` if they are completely within the area. The coordinates
must make sense when you specify them: *x1* < *x2* and *y1* < *y2*.

`$canvas->addtag("newtag", "overlapping", *x1, y1, x2, y2*);`

To assign tags to any item that has any part inside a bounded region, use
`"overlapping"` instead of `"enclosed"`. Even if the item has only one pixel
inside this area, it will still count. All other rules for the bounding area are the
same as for `"enclosed"`.

`$canvas->addtag("newtag", "withtag", *tag/id*);`

Assigns `"newtag"` to all the items with the tag or ID specified.

Binding Items Using Tags

Each item in a canvas can have an event sequence bound to it so that a callback will be invoked when that event sequence happens. This is similar to adding an event sequence binding for widgets except item tags or item IDs are used. (Remember, if you want to add a normal binding to the canvas widget itself, you must use `Tk::bind` (or `canvasBind` for Tk8.0 users) instead of just `bind`.)

The general form of `bind` is as follows:

```
$canvas->Tk::bind(tag/id [ , sequence, command ] );
```

The *sequence* would be similar to `"<Button-1>"` or `"<Double-1>"`. A complete definition and explanation of event sequences is available in Chapter 14, *Binding Events*.

When you create item bindings, keep in mind that only mouse and keyboard bindings are valid for items. You can't do any of the weird esoteric bindings that are available for all widgets.

Here is an example that changes the color of any items tagged with `"blue"` when the mouse is over it:

```
# When the mouse is over the item, color it blue
$c->Tk::bind("blue", "<Enter>",
        sub { $c->itemconfigure("blue", -fill => "blue"); });
# When the mouse is not over, color it black.
$c->Tk::bind("blue", "<Leave>",
        sub { $c->itemconfigure("blue", -fill => "black"); });
```

Finding Tags

You can use the `find` command to determine which items have a certain tag. The possible ways to call `find` are the same as those of `addtag` (except for the newtag argument). Here are the basic formats (see "Tags" earlier in this chapter for more details on what they mean and how they work):

```
$canvas->find("above", tag/id);
$canvas->find("all");
$canvas->find("below", tag/id);
$canvas->find("closest", x, y [ , additional_area ] [ , tag/id ]);
$canvas->find("enclosed", x1, y1, x2, y2);
$canvas->find("overlapping", x1, y1, x2, y2);
$canvas->find("withtag", tag/id);
```

Getting Tags from a Specific Item

To get a list of all the tags associated with an item, use:

```
@list = $canvas->gettags(tag/id);
```

If the *tag/ID* matches more than one item, then the first item found is used. If the *tag/ID* doesn't match anything, an empty string is returned.

Retrieving Bounding Box Coordinates

When we talked about the scrolling region of a canvas, we saw an example of the
bbox method. The **bbox** method returns a list with four elements that define the
area in which all the specified tags exist. The example used the special **"all"** tag,
which refers to every item in the canvas. This was how we used it to define our
scrolling region. You can specify more than one tag/ID to search for as follows:

```
($l, $r, $t, $b) = $canvas->bbox("blue", "red");
```

Assuming that you have been assigning the tags **"blue"** and **"red"** to appropri-
ately color items, this code would return the region in the canvas that encloses all
blue and red items.

Translating Coordinates

When you set up a callback and use the **Ev('x')** and/or **Ev('y')** arguments to
find out where the user clicked, you must translate that information into canvas
coordinates (**Ev** is explained in Chapter 14). To do this, use the **canvasx** and
canvasy methods:

```
$x = $canvas->canvasx(screenx [, gridspacing ]);
$y = $canvas->canvasy(screeny [, gridspacing ]);
```

Each method takes an optional gridspacing argument; then the canvas coordinate
value will be rounded to the nearest value to fit the grid.

Moving Items Around

Once an item has been created on the canvas, you can move it by using one of
two methods: **move** or **coords**. The **move** method takes a tag or ID to indicate
which items to move and the amounts to add to the x and y coordinates:

```
$canvas->move(tag/id, xdistance, ydistance);
```

For instance, the following code will move items with the **"blue"** tag 100 pixels in
the x direction and 100 pixels in the y direction:

```
$canvas->move("blue", 100, 100);
```

To move an item in the negative direction, simply specify a negative value for the
xdistance and/or *ydistance*. The other method, **coords**, allows you to explicitly
specify a new x and y location for the first item found that is identified by the tag
or ID:

```
$canvas->coords(tag/id, newx, newy);
```

If the item requires more than one set of x,y coordinates, you simply continue to specify them:

```
$canvas->coords(tag/id,  newx1,  newy1,  newx2,  newy2...);
```

You can also find out where an item currently is in the canvas by using **coords** and not specifying the x or y coordinates:

```
@coords_list = $canvas->coords(tag/id);
```

Remember, the **coords** method only applies to the first item it finds that matches the given tag or ID.

Changing the Display List

Every time a method looks through all the items in the canvas for a specific tag or ID, it looks through the display list. The display list is created as items are added to the canvas. The first item added to the canvas is the first item in the display list, and items are added in order as they are created. Also, items created later are drawn above the ones created earlier if they overlap at all. To change the display order, use the **raise** and **lower** methods:

```
$canvas->raise(tag/id,  abovetag/id);
$canvas->lower(tag/id,  belowtag/id);
```

The first argument for each method is the tag or ID of the item(s) you want to move in the display list. The second is the tag or ID next to which the first item should be placed (either above or below). If the first tag or ID matches more than one item, they are all moved.

Note that if you use the **Scrolled** method to create the canvas, you can't use the item returned by that method to invoke either **raise** or **lower**; you'll get a nasty error about the wrong argument types because **Scrolled** is not invoking this version of **raise** or **lower**, but another one. Use the subwidget to get the actual canvas reference and the call to **raise** and **lower** will work.

Deleting Items

To remove an item (or more than one item) from the canvas completely, use the **delete** method. It takes a list of tag or IDs to remove from the canvas. It will delete all matches it finds for the tag names, so be careful that you aren't deleting something you don't want to delete. Here is an example that uses three separate tag/IDs:

```
$canvas->delete("blue", "circle", $id_num);
```

You can specify only one tag/ID or as many as you want.

Deleting Tags

You can remove tags from items by using the **dtag** method. There are two forms:

```
$canvas->dtag(tag);
$canvas->dtag(tag/id, deltag);
```

The first one will search for items with the specified tag and then delete the tag. The second will search for items that match the tag or ID and then delete the **deltag** (if it exists) from that item. This allows you to delete a subset of the tabs, rather than every single tag.

Determining Item Type

To determine an item's type, call the **type** method:

```
$canvas->type(tag/id);
```

If the tag or ID matches more than one item, only the type of the first item is returned. The returned value will be a string describing the item type: **"oval"**, **"text"**, **"rectangle"**, and so on.

Set Keyboard Focus

To assign the keyboard focus to an item, use the **focus** method:

```
$canvas->focus(tag/id);
```

If the item doesn't know what to do with the keyboard focus, nothing will happen. You'll use this to change the focus to a widget within the canvas.

Rendering the Canvas as PostScript

You can get a copy of the canvas as postscript by using the **postscript** method. It will either return the PostScript output or, if the **-file** option is specified, put it in a file:

```
$postscript = $canvas->postscript();
$canvas->postscript(-file => "ps.out");
```

The following options allow you to control the output of the PostScript.

-colormap => \@array

Specifies that each element in *@array* must be a valid postscript command for setting color values; e.g., **"1.0 1.0 0.0 setrgbcolor"**.

-colormode => "color" | "gray" | "mono"

Creates the postscript in full color, grayscale (**"gray"**), or black and white (**"mono"**).

`-file =>` *filename*
: Specifies the file in which to put the PostScript output.

`-fontmap => \@array`
: Each element in *@array* is a two-element array that contains a fontname and a point size. The fontname should be a complete font name so Tk will parse it correctly (e.g., `"-*-Helvetica-Bold-O-Normal--*-140-*"`).

`-height =>` *size*
: Sets the height of the area to print. The default height is the canvas height.

`-pageanchor => "n" | "e" | "s" | "w" | "center"`
: Indicates where the page should be placed over the positioning point specified by `-pagex` and `-pagey` options. Default is `"center"`.

`-pageheight =>` *height*
: Sets the height of the printed page. The canvas image will be scaled to fit. *height* is any valid screen distance.

`-pagewidth =>` *width*
: Sets the width of the printed page. The canvas image will be scaled to fit.

`-pagex =>` *x*
: Sets the coordinate for the x positioning point. Can be any valid screen distance.

`-pagey =>` *y*
: Sets the coordinate for the y positioning point. Can be any valid screen distance.

`-rotate => 0 | 1`
: If 1, the page is rotated into a landscape orientation. Default is portrait orientation.

`-width =>` *size*
: Sets the width of the canvas area to be printed. Defaults to the width of the canvas.

`-x =>` *x*
: Sets the left edge of the area to be printed (in canvas coordinates). Default is the left edge of the window.

`-y =>` *y*
: Sets the top edge of the area to be printed (in canvas coordinates). Default is the left edge of the window.

Scaling the Canvas

When you put a large number of items on the canvas, it's sometimes hard to see them all without scrolling all over the place. It's possible to scale the canvas, for example, so it will shrink everything in half or explode it to twice the original size. The usage for **scale** is as follows:

```
$canvas->scale(tag/id, xorigin, yorigin, xscale, yscale);
```

The scaling is centered around the *xorigin* and *yorigin*. I suggest using the real origin (0, 0) unless you can come up with a good reason not to. Both *xscale* and *yscale* are the scaling factors used on each coordinate in each item. Here are some examples:

```
$canvas->scale("all", 0, 0, 1, 1);   # no change!
$canvas->scale("all", 0, 0, .5, .5); # make all 1/2 size
$canvas->scale("all", 0, 0, 2, 2);   # double everything
$canvas->scale("all", 0, 0, 3, 3);   # triple everything!
```

It's a great idea to add a Zoom In and Zoom Out button that takes care of the scaling for you. Keep track of the scaling factor in a variable (**$scale**, for instance); set it to 1 to start with. Multiply it by .5 to zoom out and by 2 to zoom in. The last thing you'll need to do is make sure that, if you insert any new items into the canvas, you multiply those coordinates by the scale factor as well (otherwise they will look either too large or too small compared to the rest of the canvas items).

Scanning

Use the **scan** method to implement scanning of the canvas:

```
$canvas->scanMark(x, y);
$canvas->scanDragto(x, y);
```

The first call, **$canvas->scanMark(x, y)**, records the x and y coordinates and the current canvas view. The second call, **$canvas->scanDragto(x, y)**, causes the view in the canvas to be adjusted by 10 times the difference between these coordinates and the previous ones sent with **scanMark**. This makes the canvas look as if it was moved at high speed.

Scrolling Methods

The canvas widget can be scrolled both horizontally and vertically. The methods **xview** and **yview** are used to communicate with the scrollbars. See Chapter 6 for more information on how these methods work.

A Drawing Program Example

The canvas widget is very versatile and can be useful for displaying different types of items. One of the first things that comes to mind when people think of a canvas is a drawing program. To save you the trouble, I've written a rudimentary drawing program called Quick Draw you can use to draw rectangles, ovals, and lines. You can also change the thickness of the objects before you draw them. It only requires a tiny bit of error-checking to make it a slicker program. Here's the code:

```perl
use Tk;

$mw = MainWindow->new;
$mw->title("Quick Draw");

$f = $mw->Frame(-relief => 'groove',
                -bd => 2,
                -label => "Draw:")->pack(-side => 'left', -fill => 'y');
$draw_item = "rectangle";
$f->Radiobutton(-variable => \$draw_item,
                -text => "Rectangle",
                -value => "rectangle",
                -command => \&bind_start)->pack(-anchor => 'w');
$f->Radiobutton(-variable => \$draw_item,
                -text => "Oval",
                -value => "oval",
                -command => \&bind_start)->pack(-anchor => 'w');
$f->Radiobutton(-variable => \$draw_item,
                -text => "Line",
                -value => "line",
                -command => \&bind_start)->pack(-anchor => 'w');
$f->Label(-text => "Line Width:")->pack(-anchor => 'w');
$thickness = 1;
$f->Entry(-textvariable => \$thickness)->pack(-anchor => 'w');

$c = $mw->Scrolled("Canvas", -cursor => "crosshair")->pack(
                -side => "left", -fill => 'both', -expand => 1);
$canvas = $c->Subwidget("canvas");

&bind_start();

MainLoop;

sub bind_start {
    # If there is a "Motion" binding, we need to allow the user
    # to finish drawing the item before rebinding Button-1
    # this fcn gets called when the finish drawing the item again
    @bindings = $canvas->Tk::bind("<Motion>");
    return if ($#bindings >= 0);

    if ($draw_item eq "rectangle"||$draw_item eq "oval"||$draw_item eq "line") {
        $canvas->Tk::bind("<Button-1>", [\&start_drawing, Ev('x'), Ev('y')]);
    }
}
```

```perl
sub start_drawing {
  my ($canv, $x, $y) = @_;
  $x = $canv->canvasx($x);
  $y = $canv->canvasy($y);

  # Do a little error checking
  $thickness = 1 if ($thickness !~ /[0-9]+/);

  if ($draw_item eq "rectangle") {
    $canvas->createRectangle($x, $y, $x, $y,
      -width => $thickness, -tags => "drawmenow");
  } elsif ($draw_item eq "oval") {
    $canvas->createOval($x, $y, $x, $y,
      -width => $thickness, -tags => "drawmenow");
  } elsif ($draw_item eq "line") {
    $canvas->createLine($x, $y, $x, $y,
      -width => $thickness, -tags => "drawmenow");
  }

  $startx = $x; $starty = $y;
  # Map the Button-1 binding to &end_drawing instead of start drawing
  $canvas->Tk::bind("<Motion>", [\&size_item, Ev('x'), Ev('y')]);
  $canvas->Tk::bind("<Button-1>", [\&end_drawing, Ev('x'), Ev('y')]);
}

sub size_item {
  my ($canv, $x, $y) = @_;
  $x = $canv->canvasx($x);
  $y = $canv->canvasy($y);

  $canvas->coords("drawmenow", $startx, $starty, $x, $y);
}

sub end_drawing {
  my ($canv, $x, $y) = @_;
  $x = $canv->canvasx($x);
  $y = $canv->canvasy($y);

  # finalize the size of the item, and remove the tag from the item
  $canvas->coords("drawmenow", $startx, $starty, $x, $y);
  $canvas->dtag("drawmenow");

  # remove motion binding.
  $canvas->Tk::bind("<Motion>", "");
  &bind_start();
}
```

Note that I didn't set the **-scrollregion** at all because I wanted to create a limitless drawing space for the user. (This was the easiest way to provide this functionality: Do nothing!) It's a cute little program that demonstrates how to use **bind** and a few of the canvas methods. Figure 9-4 shows a screen shot of the application after a few items have been drawn on it.

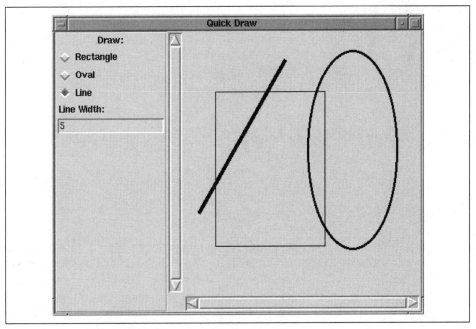

Figure 9-4. Quick Draw application screen

Fun Things to Try

The Quick Draw application doesn't do much that is useful, but here are some ideas for features to add to the application:

- Add the capability to print to a PostScript file.

- Create a Save Drawing feature that will loop through all the items and write out their types and coordinates to a text file. Of course, you'll need a Load Drawing feature as well.

- Allow the user to create text items.

- Add an entry widget that lets you change the color (by typing in a color-name) with which to draw the items.

10

The Scale Widget

 A scale widget is a strange little widget. It's similar to a scrollbar because it is long and skinny with a button in the middle of it, but it doesn't scroll anything other than itself. It does keep track of something though—a number. When you change the position of the button in the scale, the value associated with the scale changes. Here are some things you can do with a scale widget:

- Create a widget from which a user can select a number between 1 and 100.

- Create three scales, each representing a value in an RGB (red, green, blue) number.

- Create four sliders, each representing a portion of an IP address. Each scale can go from 0 to 255, and it would probably be smart to start them at 255. Use a label widget to show the completed IP address, periods and all.

- Create a temperature scale that starts at –50 and goes to 130 degrees.

- Show the amount of rainfall so far this year. The scale can be marked to show every five inches.

The scale widget can be placed horizontally or vertically, depending on where you have the most room in your application window.

Creating a Scale

As with other widgets, you can create a scale by using a parent widget and passing options to the scale to change its configuration:

```
$parent->Scale( [ option => value ] )->pack;
```

Use one of the geometry managers discussed in Chapter 2, *Geometry Management*, to place it on the screen (such as **pack**, as shown in the preceding code).

Most of the options associated with the scale widget are the standard options that used with all other widgets. All of the possible options are in the following list. A discussion of special options that have a slightly different meaning for the scale and options that are specific to the scale widget follows the list.

`-activebackground =>` *color*

Sets the color the slider's background should be when the cursor is over the slider (the `-state` is `'active'`).

`-background =>` *color*

Sets the color the slider's background should be when the cursor is not over the slider (`-state` is `'normal'`).

`-bigincrement =>` *amount*

Sets the amount by which the slider will change value when required to do so in large increments. Default is 0, causing the value to change by 1/10 the top value of the scale.

`-borderwidth =>` *amount*

Sets the width of the edges of the widget. Default is 2.

`-command =>` *callback*

Sets the callback invoked when the slider is moved.

`-cursor =>` *cursorname*

Determines the cursor to display when the mouse is over the scale.

`-digits =>` *amount*

Indicates how many significant digits to retain when conversion from a number to a string takes place.

`-font =>` *fontname*

Sets the font used to display any text in the scale.

`-foreground =>` *color*

Sets the color of the text displayed in the scale.

`-from =>` *value*

Indicates the low end of the scale values. Default is 0.

`-highlightbackground =>` *color*

Sets the color of the highlight rectangle displayed around the scale when it does not have the keyboard focus.

`-highlightcolor =>` *color*

Sets the color of the highlight rectangle displayed around the scale when it has the keyboard focus.

`-highlightthickness =>` *amount*

Sets the thickness of the highlight rectangle displayed around the scale.

`-label` => *labelstring*

    Describes a label for the scale. Default is no label.

`-length` => *amount*

    Sets the length of the slider (the long direction, regardless of the value of `-orient`) in a valid screen distance.

`-orient` => `'`**`vertical`**`'` | `'horizontal'`

    Sets the direction the scale is drawn. Default is `'vertical'`.

`-relief` => `'raised'`|`'sunken'`|`'`**`flat`**`'`|`'ridge'`|`'groove'`|`'solid'`

    Determines how the edges of the widget are drawn. Default is `'flat'`.

`-repeatdelay` => *milliseconds*

    Sets the number of milliseconds the widget waits before repeating.

`-repeatinterval` => *milliseconds*

    Sets the number of milliseconds the widget delays between repeats.

`-resolution` => *value*

    Sets the increments by which the value in the scale will change. Default is 1.

`-showvalue` => `0` | **`1`**

    If set to 0, the value of the slider setting is not shown at all. Default is 1.

`-sliderlength` => *value*

    Sets the size of the slider (inside the widget). Default is 25.

`-state` => `'`**`normal`**`'` | `'active'` | `'disabled'`

    Determines the state of the widget and whether or not the user can interact with it. Default is `'normal'`.

`-takefocus` => `1` | `0` | **`undef`**

    Determines whether or not the widget can receive keyboard focus. Default is to let the program decide.

`-tickinterval` => *value*

    Describes the labels drawn by the right (or on the bottom) of the scale. Labels are drawn for every value. A value of 0 means no labels will be drawn at all. Default is 0.

`-to` => *value*

    Sets the top value of the scale. Default is 100.

`-troughcolor`=> *color*

    Sets the color of the area behind the slider button (same as a scrollbar).

`-variable` => `\`*$variable*

    Sets the variable in which the slider value is stored.

`-width` => *amount*

    Sets the width of the skinny part of the slider (regardless of the value associated with `-orient`).

Assigning a Callback

As usual, use the -command option to assign a callback for the widget. The callback is invoked every time the scale value is changed. So if you change the value from 50 to 100 and the scale increment is 1, the callback will be invoked 50 times. The callback is also called when the widget is created. My recommendation is not to use -command unless you have a small number of possible values.

Orientation

To change the orientation of the scale, use the -orient option. It takes a string value that should contain either "horizontal" or "vertical". The default for this option is "vertical". Figure 10-1 shows both a horizontal scale and a vertical scale.

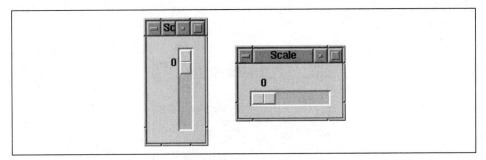

Figure 10-1. Vertical scale (the default orientation) and horizontal scale

Minimum and Maximum Values

Use the -from and -to options to change the possible range of values for the scale. Usually the value associated with -from is smaller than the value associated with -to. If you happen to switch them, the scale will still display with the higher value on the right and the lower value on the left. Either or both values can be negative. Here are some examples:

```
$mw->Scale(-from => -10, -to => 10)->pack;
$mw->Scale(-from => 10, -to => -100)->pack;
$mw->Scale(-from => -100, -to => -50)->pack;
$mw->Scale(-from => -0.5, -to => 0.5, -resolution => 0.1)->pack;
```

As you can see, the values assigned to -from and -to also don't need to be whole integers.

Displayed Versus Stored Value

Sometimes the value you are searching for resides between two numbers that are very far apart, such as 0 and 1,000,000. Stepping through each of those values one by one would be tedious. You can change the step value of the displayed number using the **-resolution** option. The default for **-resolution** is 1, but it can be changed to any value that is less or greater than that.

Note that if the resolution is larger than 1, it is possible for the slider to have a value (set by the program, for example) that is smaller or larger than the displayed value.

Adding a Label

You can add a label to your scale by using the **-label** option. The label is placed in a different location depending on the value associated with **-orient** (see Figure 10-2).

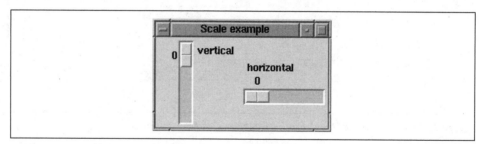

Figure 10-2. Two scales with labels

Displaying Value Increments

The scale displays its current value above or to the left of itself (depending on the value associated with **-orient**). Suppose you want to display labels (such as 0, 10, 20, ... 100) that show the user approximately where the button needs to be to select those values. If you want to display them underneath or to the left of the scale, you can use the **-tickinterval** option. By default, it is set to 0 and no numbers are displayed. To show the values every 10 numbers, use **-tickinterval => 10**. The larger the range of values from which the scale can select, the larger the value this should be, or you'll end up with a bunch of numbers so close together that you won't be able to tell what they are. See Figure 10-3.

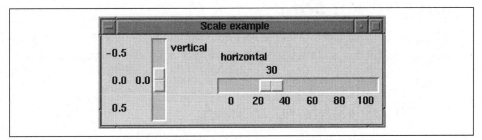

Figure 10-3. Using -tickinterval with both horizontal and vertical scales

Changing the Size of the Scale

You can change the size of the scale by using the `-length` and `-width` options. You can also change the size of the button displayed in the slider widget; to do so, use the `-sliderlength` option. It takes a value specified in screen units and will change the length of the slider button. See Figure 10-4.

```
$mw->Scale(-sliderlength => 100); # make the button 100 pixels.
```

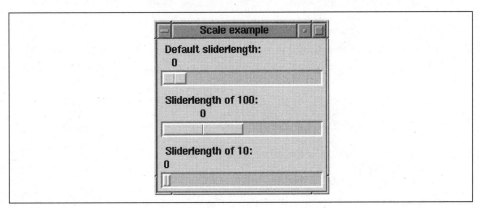

Figure 10-4. Different -sliderlength values

Options You'll Probably Never Need

The two final options for the `Scale` widget creation method are `-bigincrement` and `-digits`. The `-bigincrement` option specifies the size of jumps when using really large numbers. The default for `-bigincrement` is 0, which means it will jump in increments that are 1/10 the total range.

The `-digits` option represents how many digits will be used when converting from a number to a string. The default (0) forces the scale to use a precision that allows for a different string for every possible value on the scale.

Configuring a Scale

As usual, the scale has both `configure` and `cget` methods, which let you query and set options for the scale widget. See Appendix A for more details on how to use these methods.

Getting the Value of a Scale

The `get` method will return the current value of the scale:

```
$value = $scale->get( );
```

You can also specify x and y coordinates and retrieve the value of the scale at that point:

```
$value = $scale->get(x, y);
```

Setting the Value of a Scale

You can force the value associated with the scale by using the `set` method:

```
$scale->set(value);
```

This method is great for setting an initial value if you aren't using the `-variable` option at all. If you were using `-variable`, just set that variable to the desired starting value.

Determining Coordinates

The `coords` method returns a list containing x and y coordinates:

```
($x, $y) = $scale->coords();
```

The coordinates indicate the position in which the current value is located in the scale. You can also pass in a value to find the coordinates of:

```
($x, $y) = $scale->coords(value);
```

Identifying Parts of a Scale

You can find out what part of the scale a coordinate resides in by using the `identify` method:

```
$value = $scale->identify(x, y);
```

The `identify` method returns a string containing one of the following values: `"slider"`, `"trough1"`, `"trough2"`, or an empty string (if the coordinates don't refer to any of these parts).

Fun Things to Try

- Create a survey form that contains scale widgets for user information. Items such as age (0–150 would be a safe range), income, and number of children in the household can all be entered into a scale. Make good use of the **-resolution**, **-to**, and **-from** options to make the job easier for the user.

- Create a *ping* application that uses scale widgets (one for each portion of the IP address) to request an IP address from the user.

11

Menus

Different Types of Menus

There are several ways to create and utilize a menu from within your Perl/Tk application. Here are some examples of how you can use a menu-type widget:[*]

- Create File, Edit, and Help menus across the top of your application.

- Display a list of fonts from which the user can choose (the selected font can be marked with a checkmark).

- Display a list of editing commands that become available when the user right-clicks on another object (such as a listbox or entry widget) in your window.

You can build each of these different types of menus with the basic menu widget. The menu widget itself is a list of items that are displayed one item per line in a box. Each item can have an associated callback that is called when the menu item is invoked or selected. Unlike the other widgets we have seen so far, you cannot use any of the geometry managers on a menu. Instead, you must use a method called post to display your menu widget (post will be discussed later in this chapter).

Figure 11-1 shows the contents of a typical menu widget. It contains several items, a separator, and a few more items. Separators are useful for grouping together related commands and providing a visual break if one menu contains a number of commands.

---

[*] Typically, a menu contains commands that aren't used frequently, such as configuration options, File Open, File Close, Help, and so on. You would be wise to put frequently accessed commands in the window to provide easier access for the user.

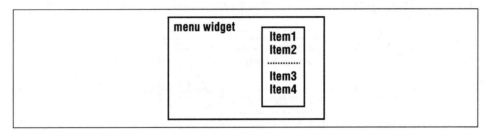

Figure 11-1. Simple menu widget with five items: Item1, Item2, Separator, Item3, and Item4

Menus are a great way to replace checkbuttons and radiobuttons. If you have five radiobuttons, you can place them on a menu and save a ton of screen space for more important widgets.

A menubutton widget is based on the menu widget and has a button that controls when the menu is displayed. When the button is pressed, the menu is displayed directly below the button. The button contains a text string that describes the items in the menu. A menubutton is the type of menu you'll use 90% of the time. Figure 11-2 shows a block diagram of a menubutton after the button has been pressed. The button part of the menubutton is the where the word "File" appears.

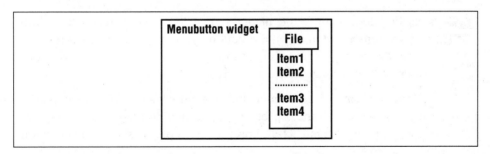

Figure 11-2. A menubutton widget that uses a menu widget

The main advantage of using a menubutton widget is that it handles the display functions of the menu. Because this is the most frequently used menu-related widget, it will be covered first.

The last menu-related widget covered is the optionmenu, which behaves differently than the other type of menus. The optionmenu allows the user to select one item from a list of items. For example, you can use an optionmenu to add the following options to your program:

- Allow users to select a favorite color from a list of colors.

- Allow users to select the country in which they live.

- Allow users to choose how verbose they would like the application to be: Silent, Semi-Verbose, and Verbose.

Figure 11-3 shows a block diagram of an optionmenu with Item3 selected.

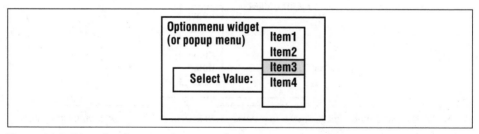

Figure 11-3. Example of an optionmenu widget

Menus simply give you a way to group related tasks together, and the optionmenu allows you to group several choices together. There is a callback associated with each menu item, much like the callbacks associated with button widgets. Instead of using 10 separate buttons, you can create 2 menus that each contain 5 menu items. This saves on display space and helps users understand that those items have a similar purpose and have been grouped together for their convenience.

The Menubutton Widget

As described earlier, the menubutton widget has a menu that drops down from a button when the button is pressed. The menu is removed from the window when an item from the menu is selected or when the user clicks elsewhere in the application.

Many applications use a menubutton-type construct. The menubuttons are normally grouped across the top of the application and have names like File, Edit, Options, and Help. Figure 11-4 shows an example of several menubuttons grouped together in a frame.*

Creating a Menubutton

When you create a menubutton widget, use the parent widget to invoke the **Menubutton** method, which then creates a menubutton widget reference. The options you send with the **Menubutton** method can configure both the button that is initially displayed on the screen and the actual menu items:

```
$mbutton = $parent->Menubutton( [ options... ] )->pack;
```

---

* You can accomplish this same look in a window by using a menubar widget. However, the additional functionality that it provides is minimal, so we won't be covering it in this book. To get this look, create a frame widget with a relief of "ridge" and borderwidth of 2. Pack the menubuttons with -side => "left" for all but the help menu, which has -side => "right".

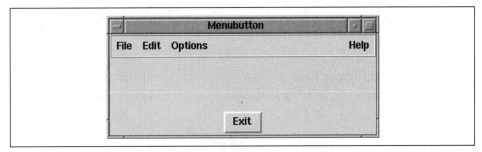

Figure 11-4. Example of window with several menubuttons across the top

When it is first displayed with one of the geometry managers, you will only see the button part of the menubutton, which is a button with "flat" relief. The menu part of the menubutton won't appear until you press the button. Figure 11-5 shows the menubutton widget before and after the button is pressed. Notice how the relief of the button changes after it is pressed.

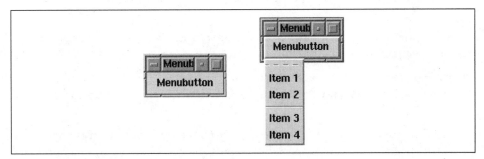

Figure 11-5. Menubutton before and after the button is pressed

Menubutton Options

The options specified with the **Menubutton** command (or via the **configure** method) can affect only the button part of the menubutton, both the button and the menu, or just the menu.* The options that affect the menu are valid for the menu widget as well as the menubutton widget. We will cover the available options briefly (and some not so briefly) in order to discuss the effects of each. The brief synopsis of all the options and their effects appears first.

When the description says "Affects the button only," the behavior is the same as it would be for a button widget.

---

* The menubutton widget comprises other widgets (in this case, button and menu) to provide the overall functionality.

-activebackground => *color*
> Affects the background color of the button and the currently highlighted menu item.

-activeforeground => *color*
> Affects the text color of the button and the currently highlighted menu item.

-anchor => 'n' | 'ne' | 'e' | 'se' | 's' | 'sw' | 'w' | 'nw' | **'center'**
> Affects the button only. Changes the position of the text within the button.

-background => *color*
> Affects the button and the menu. All the background color changes to *color* when the state of the button and menuitems is 'normal'.

-bitmap => *bitmapname*
> Affects the button only. Displays bitmap instead of text.

-borderwidth => *amount*
> Affects the button only. Changes the width of the button edges.

-cursor => *cursorname*
> Affects the button only. Changes the cursor when it's over the button part of the menubutton.

-disabledforeground => *color*
> Affects the button and the menu item text when the -state for either is 'disabled'.

-direction => "above" | "below" | "left" | "right" | "flush"
> Tk8.0 option only. The value "above" puts the menu above the menubutton, "below" puts it below the button, and "left" and "right" puts it on the appropriate side of the button. "flush" puts the menu directly over the button.

-font => *fontname*
> Affects the button only. Changes the font of any text displayed in the button.

-foreground => *color*
> Affects the button only. Changes the color of any text or bitmap to *color.*

-height => *amount*
> Affects the button only. Changes the height of the button.

-highlightbackground => *color*
> Affects the button only. Changes the color of the highlight rectangle displayed around the button when the button does not have the keyboard focus.

-highlightcolor => *color*
> Affects the button only. Changes the color of the highlight rectangle displayed around the button when the button does have the keyboard focus.

`-highlightthickness` => *amount*
> Affects the button only. Default is 0. Changes the width of the highlight rectangle around all edges of the button.

`-image` => *imgptr*
> Affects the button only. Displays an image instead of text.

`-indicatoron` => **0** | 1
> Affects the button; indirectly affects the display mechanism for the menu. When set to 1, a small bar appears on the right side of the button next to any text, bitmap, or image.

`-justify` => 'left' | 'right' | **'center'**
> Affects the button only. Changes the justification of the text within the button.

`-menu` => $menu
> Tells the menubutton to display the menu associated with $menu instead of anything specified via the `-menuitems` option.

`-menuitems` => *list*
> Causes the menu to display a list of items to create.

`-padx` => *amount*
> Affects the button only. Adds extra space to the left and right of the button inside the button edge.

`-pady` => *amount*
> Affects the button only. Adds extra space to the top and bottom of the button inside the button edge.

`-relief` => **'flat'** | 'groove' | 'raised' | 'ridge' | 'sunken'
> Affects the button only. Default is 'flat'. The relief of the button changes to 'raised' when the button is pressed.

`-state` => **'normal'** | 'active' | 'disabled'
> Affects the button; indirectly affects menu (menu cannot be displayed if state is 'disabled').

`-takefocus` => **0** | 1 | undef
> Affects the button only. Default is 0. Determines whether or not the button can have the keyboard focus.

`-tearoff` => 0 | **1**
> Affects the menu only. Default is 1. If set to 0, does not display the tear-off dashed line in the menu.

`-text` => *text string*
> Affects the button only. Displays the specified string on the button (ignored if the `-bitmap` or `-image` option is used).

`-textvariable => \$variable`

> Affects the button only. The information displayed in `$variable` is displayed on the button.

`-underline =>` *charpos*

> Affects the button only. The character at the integer *charpos* is underlined. If the button has the keyboard focus, pressing the key causes the button that corresponds to the underlined character to be pressed.

`-width =>` *amount*

> Affects the button only. Changes width of the button to *amount*.

`-wraplength =>` *pos*

> Affects the button only. Default is 0. Determines the screen distance for the maximum amount of text displayed on one line.

Button-Only Options

The following options affect only the button portion of the menubutton, and behave exactly as described in Chapter 3: `-cursor`, `-anchor`, `-bitmap`, `-border-width`, `-font`, `-foreground`, `-height`, `-highlightbackground`, `-highlight-color`, `-highlightthickness`, `-image`, `-justify`, `-padx`, `-pady`, `-relief`, `-state`, `-takefocus`, `-text`, `-textvariable`, `-underline`, `-width`, and `-wraplength`.

Tear-off Items

Each menu you create can be "torn off" from its window. The first item on the menu is a dashed line (see Figure 11-6); when you select this item, the menu widget becomes its own window and remains present until you close it with the window manager.

You can move the menu around on the screen, but you can't resize it. The other menu items will behave normally when they are selected. Be careful; you can tear off the same menu multiple times. Torn-off menus won't be updated when other events in the program are updated, so it is a good idea to limit your use of tear-off menus.

To remove the tear-off ability, use `-tearoff => 0` with your list of arguments when you create the menu and the dashed line will no longer appear.

The tear-off line in the menu actually counts as an item. It uses index 0 if it exists, so your menu items will then number from 1 and up. If you use `-tearoff=>0`, then your menu items will number from 0 and up.

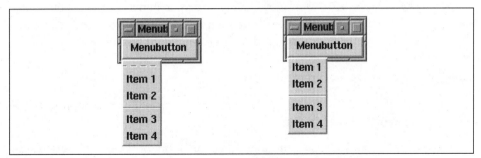

Figure 11-6. Menu with tear-off item and menu without tear-off item

Color Options

Several options that determine color affect both the button and the menu: -activebackground, -activeforeground, -background, and -disabledforeground.

Both -activebackground and -activeforeground affect the text/bitmap displayed in the button and the currently active menu item in the menu. The currently active menu item is the one that the mouse cursor is currently over. The menu item becomes slightly raised and might change color depending on these options. The effect of these options on the button is the same as it is for a normal button widget.

The -background option affects the entire menu and button background. The -disabledforeground option changes the color of the text of any menu items that have their own -state of 'disabled'; it also changes the text/bitmap color of the button if its -state is 'disabled'.

Button Indicator

In Chapter 4, we saw how the radiobutton and checkbutton widgets each have their own type of indicator. The button part of a menubutton also has an indicator that can be displayed on it. The indicator is a small 3D bar displayed to the right of the text, bitmap, or image on the button (see Figure 11-7). Usually the indicator is used to show that something different will happen when you press the button. The option to display the indicator is -indicatoron, the same option used to display the indicator for the radiobutton and checkbutton widgets.

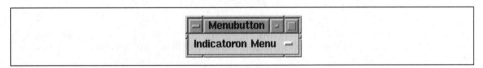

Figure 11-7. Menubutton with indicator shown

Setting –indicatoron to 1 does not change the appearance of the menu at all. Usually, you would not use the –indicatoron option unless you were using the menubutton as a type of option menu or in a non-standard fashion.

Specifying Items for the Menu

Everything in this section will also apply to using the –menuitems option with the menu widget in addition to the menubutton widget.

The easiest way to add items to the menu in a menubutton is to use the –menuitems option. The value sent with the –menuitems option is a list of lists* that indicates not only the order of items in the menu but also any possible configuration options for that menu item. The best way to illustrate this is with an example.

```
$menub = $mw->Menubutton(-text => "Menubutton",
                  -menuitems => [[ 'command' => "Item 1"],
                                 [ 'command' => "Item 2"],
                                 "-",
                                 [ 'command' => "Item 3"],
                                 [ 'command' => "Item 4"]]);
```

In this snippet of code, we are creating the same menu that we displayed in Figure 11-5.

Here's a breakdown of the elements of the list and what they mean. The –menuitems option expects a list of lists. It is the sub-lists that contain information about each menu item. Each list that configures a menu item has a specified order to it. The first thing in the list is a string that will determine what type of menu item is created. The available types of menu items are "command", "radiobutton", "checkbutton", and "cascade". The second thing in the item list is a string that is displayed on the menu. After that, the options that affect that menu item type can be specified. To create a separator, use a string in place of an anonymous list.

As you can see, after –menuitems, I didn't assign any callbacks for any of the menu items. If you selected one, nothing would happen. To assign callbacks, we would change the statement to look like this:

```
$menub = $mw->Menubutton(-text => "Menubutton",
                  -menuitems => [[ 'command' => "Item 1",
                                   -command => \&do_item1 ],
                                 [ 'command' => "Item 2",
                                   -command => \&do_item2 ],
                                 "-",
```

---

* If you don't know what I mean by "list of lists," you'll find that the Camel book (*Programming Perl*) is a useful reference. The new version contains more information than you'll ever need to know about lists, hashes, and creating anonymous lists.

```
[ 'command' => "Item 3",
  -command => \&do_item3 ],
[ 'command' => "Item 4",
  -command => \&do_item4 ]]);
```

I used the `-command` option to add the callbacks, and I used a different subroutine for each menu item. It doesn't make any sense to specify a callback for the separator item.

The first two items for each item list must be the item type string followed immediately by a text string that will be displayed in the menu. Even if you plan to display a different text string by using the `-label` option or to display an image, the second argument in this list must be a string.

It might be confusing that we use both `"command"` and `-command`. The first is the item type string and the second is the option (which should be followed by a callback).

You can also use the `AddItems()` method to add items to the menu: `$menub->AddItems("command", -label => "Item1", -command => \&do_item1);`. The argument list is slightly different (you send only the type, and then you must use the `-label` option to specify the text to appear on the menu, but all the options for each menu item type are exactly the same).

Certain options only apply to certain menu item types, which are discussed in the following sections.

Command item type

So far, each example of a menu has had only `"command"` and `"separator"` types of items. Usually, you'll also use the `-command` option so that something will happen when the menu item is selected.

Radiobutton item type

It is possible to put radiobuttons in a menu rather than inside the window where they take up space. They look and act just like a radiobutton would in the window except they are listed in the menu instead. The same radiobutton rules apply: You should always have at least two radiobuttons and they should be grouped logically by using the same `-variable => $variable` option for each group. Figure 11-8 shows an example of the placement of radiobuttons in a menu.

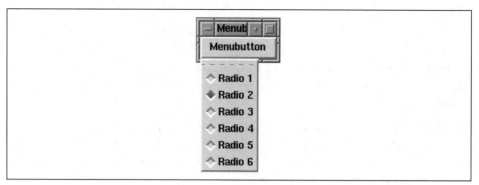

Figure 11-8. Radiobuttons as menu items

In an example in Chapter 4, *Checkbuttons and Radiobuttons*, we used radiobuttons to select the background color of the window. We could also use those radiobuttons in a menu and save space in our application:

```perl
#!/usr/bin/perl -w

use Tk;
my $mw = MainWindow->new;
$mw->title("Menubutton");
$menub = $mw->Menubutton(-text => "Color")->pack(-side => 'left',
                                                 -anchor => 'n');
foreach (qw/red yellow green blue grey/) {
  $menub->radiobutton(-label => $_,
                      -command => \&set_bg,
                      -variable => \$background_color,
                      -value => $_);
}

MainLoop;

sub set_bg {
  print "Background value is now: $background_color\n";
  $mw->configure(-background => $background_color);
}
```

Figure 11-9 shows what the window looks like after it has been resized and the menu has been posted.

Checkbutton item type

You can also put checkbuttons in a menu to keep them out of the way. Use the -command option to configure the checkbutton to perform an action when it is selected. Figure 11-10 shows what checkbuttons look like in a menu.

Remember the checkbutton guidelines: each checkbutton should have its own -variable, because each can be selected or not.

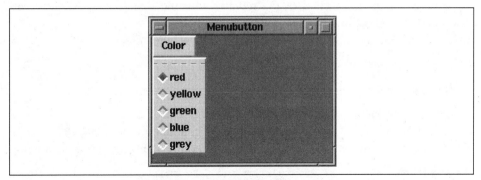

Figure 11-9. Using radiobuttons in a menu to set background color

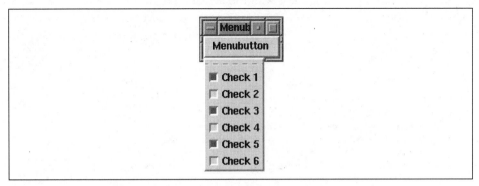

Figure 11-10. Checkbuttons in a menu (1, 3, and 5 selected manually)

Cascade item type

A cascade menu item points to another menu. When you select this type of menu item, another menu will pop up to the right of the current menu. This is the most complicated item type to implement because you have to create another entire menu to display (the next major section in this chapter covers the menu widget). Figure 11-11 shows what a cascade menu item looks like.

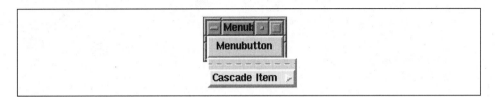

Figure 11-11. Cascade menu item inside a menubutton widget

The submenu must be a child of the menu within the menubutton widget. This allows Perl/Tk to keep track of the correct hierarchy of the menus. The best way to create a submenu is to create the menubutton first and then create the submenu.

```
$menub = $mw->Menubutton(-text => "My Menu",
                         -menuitems => [["cascade" => "Submenu"]]);
$submenu = $menub->menu->Menu(-menuitems => [ ... ]);
```

We can use the menubutton widget's **menu()** method to return the actual menu item and then create the new menu as a child of the menu item. Now we can add the cascade item to the menubutton and configure it to point to the new submenu:

```
$menub->entryconfigure("Submenu", -menu => $submenu);
```

Because of some problems with cascade menus, it is necessary to first create the cascade entry and then configure it with the actual menu it will display. Here is an entire Perl program for you to play around with so you can get the feel of cascade menus. It creates two submenus, one with numbers and one with letters:

```perl
#!/usr/bin/perl -w

use Tk;
my $mw = MainWindow->new;
$mw->title("Menubutton");
# Create menubutton and put on the screen
$menub = $mw->Menubutton(-text => "Menubutton")->pack;

# make our sub menu to be cascaded a child of upper menu.
$menu1 = $menub->menu->Menu;
foreach (qw/one two three four/) {
  $menu1->add('command', -label => $_);
}

# make second sub menu also a child of the upper menu
$menu2 = $menub->menu->Menu;
foreach (qw/A B C D/) {
  $menu2->radiobutton(-label => $_);
}

# now add the cascade items to the main menu
$menub->cascade(-label => "Numbers");
$menub->cascade(-label => "Letters");

# now configure those cascade entries to point to correct submenu
$menub->entryconfigure("Numbers", -menu => $menu1);
$menub->entryconfigure("Letters", -menu => $menu2);

MainLoop;
```

You can also create cascade menu items on a menu that cascades from another menu, but remember to create it as a child of that menu's menu.

Separator item type

Separators are noninteractive portions of a menu. They do nothing except provide a visual break between menu items. To create one, either call the `separator` method on the menubutton widget or use a string in the `-menuitems` list instead of another list.

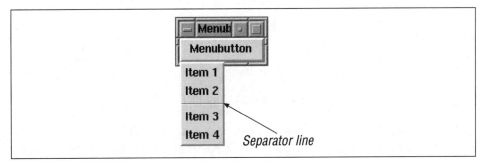

Figure 11-12. Separator in a menubutton widget

Figure 11-12 shows the separator line. It is a solid line, unlike the tear-off menu, which is a dashed line (not shown in Figure 11-12). The following code was used to create the menubutton shown in Figure 11-12:

```
$mw->Menubutton(-tearoff => 0, -menuitems => [ ['command' => "Item 1"],
                                               ['command' => "Item 2"],
                                               "-",
                                               ['command' => "Item 3"],
                                               ['command' => "Item 4"] ])->pack;
```

We could have used any string at all in place of the `"-"` line. However, it is good style to always use the same string so it is easy to recognize when a separator item is created.

Accelerators

The `-accelerator` option allows you to place a text string to the right of the text or image displayed in the menu. The string usually contains a clue to a quick-key combination that will execute the command associated with the menu item. In Figure 11-13, Item 1 has the accelerator string Alt+1 next to it. The menuitem was created by using this list in the `-menuitems` option: [`'command'` => `'Item 1'`, `-accelerator` => `"Alt+1"`]. To make the Alt-1 key combination actually perform an action, you'll need to use **bind** (see Chapter 14, *Binding Events*).

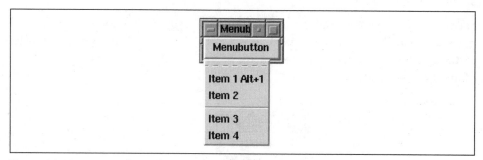

Figure 11-13. Menu with accelerator next to Item 1

Displaying an Image in a Menu Item

Each menu item is a type of button, so it makes sense that you can display an image instead of text. Figure 11-14 shows what happens when you also specify the **-image** option. The code that created the menu is as follows:

```
$img1 = $mw->Bitmap(-file =>
    "/usr/X11R6/include/X11/bitmaps/lineOp.xbm");
$mw->Menubutton(-text => "Menubutton",
                -menuitems => [[ 'command' => "Item 1"],
                               [ 'command' => "Item 2",
                                 -image => $img1],
                               '-',
                               [ 'command' => "Item 3"],
                               [ 'command' => "Item 4"]
                              ])->pack(-side => 'left');
```

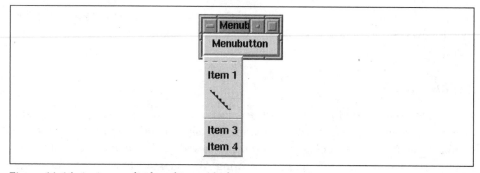

Figure 11-14. An image displayed instead of text

In Chapter 4, I discussed using icons and how they can make options easier to understand. Try to use good judgement and not go crazy with the picture menu items. Too many vague icons (such as the one displayed in Figure 11-14) can make an application confusing.

Assigning a Different Menu

By default, when you use the -menuitems option, a menu is created. You can create your own menu widget and tell the menubutton widget to use it instead. But there is a trick involved. It's a chicken-before-the-egg problem. You need to create the menubutton and then create the menu widget as a child of the menubutton. Use configure to assign the new menu to the menubutton. Here is a code example:

```
# create menubutton w/ some fake menu items
$m1 = $mw->Menubutton(-text => "Text Menu1",
                    -menuitems => [[ 'command' => "Item 1"],
                                   [ 'command' => "Item 2"],
                                   "-",
                                   [ 'command' => "Item 3"],
                                   [ 'command' => "Item 4"]
                                   ])->pack(-side => "left",
                                            -expand => 'y',
                                            -fill => 'both');

# Create a Menu as a child of the Menubutton $m1
$menu = $m1->Menu(-menuitems => [[ 'command' => "Item 1"],
                                 [ 'command' => "Item 2"],
                                 [ 'command' => "Item 3"]]);

# Now use the $menu with the Menubutton
$m1->configure(-menu => $menu);

MainLoop;
```

As mentioned, you need to create the menubutton first and make it a child of $mw (the MainWindow). I created some menu items that will be different on the new menu so you can tell which menu the menubutton is using.

Configuring a Menubutton

The cget method allows you to get configuration information about any of the options associated with a menubutton. You can use configure to query or change any of the options. Both configure and cget are explained fully in Appendix A, *Configuring Widgets with configure and cget.*

Configuring Menubutton Items

The menubutton widget has an entrycget method that is the same as the menu widget's entrycget method.

```
$value = $menub->entrycget(index, option);
```

The arguments are an index and the option to query. Valid index values are discussed in "The Menu Widget" later in this chapter.

The `entryconfigure` method is also provided by the menubutton widget. It performs the same function the menu widget's `entryconfigure` method performs:

```
$menub->entryconfigure(index, [ option ]);
```

Adding Items to a Menubutton

The `AddItems` method gives you another way to put new items in the menu. It will always add the new item(s) to the end of the menu in the order they appear in the list. Similar to the arguments sent to the `-menuitems` option, the arguments sent to `AddItems` are included in several lists. There is no need to enclose the item lists inside another list level because the only thing you send to `AddItems` is item lists. Here is an example:

```
$menub = $mw->Menubutton(-text => "File")->pack;
$menub->AddItems(["command" => "Open", -command => \&do_open],
                 ["command" => "Close", -command => \&do_close],
                 "-",
                 ["command" => "Exit", -command => sub { exit } ]);
```

This use of `AddItems` is just another way of saying the following:

```
$menub = $mw->Menubutton(-text => "File", -menuitems =>
          [ ["command" => "Open", -command => \&do_open],
            ["command" => "Close", -command => \&do_close],
            "-",
            ["command" => "Exit", -command => sub { exit } ]
          ])->pack;
```

Notice the extra set of [ ] around the lists containing the menu item information. All the information in between the [ ] is exactly the same as it was when it was sent to `AddItems`.

The `command` method adds a command item to the end of the menu. When you use `command`, you must use the `-label` option to specify the text to be displayed in the menu. This code creates the same menu `AddItems()` example created:

```
$menub = $mw->Menubutton(-text => "File")->pack;
$menub->command(-label => "Open", -command => \&do_open);
$menub->command(-label => "Close", -command => \&do_close);
$menub->separator;
$menub->command(-label => "Exit", -command => sub { exit });
```

Creating a Checkbutton

The `checkbutton` method adds a checkbutton item to the end of the menu. Like the `command` method, you are required to use the `-label` option to specify the text string to display in the menu with the checkbutton. All other checkbutton item options are the same as those listed in "Specifying Items for the Menu" earlier in this chapter. Here's an example:

```
$menub = $mw->Menubutton(-text => "Options");
$menub->checkbutton(-label => "Confirm Quit?",
                    -variable => \$confirm_quit);
```

checkbutton is really a menu widget method, but it also works on a menubutton widget. The same is true of radiobutton, separator, and cascade.

Creating a Radiobutton

The radiobutton method adds a radiobutton item to the end of the menu. You must specify the text to be displayed in the menu by using the -label option.

```
$menub->radiobutton(-label=>"Radio item");
```

Creating a Separator

The separator method adds a separator line to the end of the menu. It does not take any arguments:

```
$menub->separator();
```

Adding a Cascade Menu

The cascade method adds a cascade item to the end of the menu. You must specify the text to be displayed by using the -label option. Use $menub-> entryconfigure(-menu => $submenu) to assign the menu to be cascaded.

```
# assume we already created $menu_more
$menub->cascade(label => "More menu...");
$menub->entryconfigure("More menu...", -menu => $menu_move);
```

Getting a Reference to the Menu Item

The menu method returns a reference to the menu used within the menubutton widget. This allows us to create cascade entries with the actual menu as the parent of the cascaded menu; it also allows us access to all of the menu widget methods. For example, we could delete a menu item from our menu by using $menub->menu->delete(1), which would delete the second item in the menu. For more information on the menu widget methods, see "The Menu Widget" later in this chapter.

Complete Menubutton Examples

Menus are a more complicated widget than we've seen before because you don't always add items to them the same way. Sometimes you can use the simple `-menuitems` option, and other times you'll want to add to them dynamically. This section contains some full-length Perl scripts that create some useful menus.

Creating a Menubar

Here is the code that was used to create the window and menubar in Figure 11-4:

```
#!/usr/bin/perl -w
use Tk;
my $mw = MainWindow->new;
$mw->title("Menubutton");

$mw->Button(-text => "Exit",
            -command => sub { exit; })->pack(-side => "bottom");

my $f = $mw->Frame(-relief => 'ridge', -borderwidth => 2);
$f->pack(-side => 'top', -anchor => 'n', -expand => 1, -fill => 'x');

foreach (qw/File Edit Options Help/) {
  push (@menus, $f->Menubutton(-text => $_));
}

$menus[3]->pack(-side => 'right');
$menus[0]->pack(-side => 'left');
$menus[1]->pack(-side => 'left');
$menus[2]->pack(-side => 'left');

MainLoop;
```

First a frame was created across the top of the window and packed so it will resize itself dynamically when the window gets larger or smaller. Then the menubuttons were created and packed into the frame. Each of the menus has no items. We'll leave that as an exercise for the reader.

Dynamic Document List

In certain cases, you'll want to add and remove items from a menu dynamically. Many applications remember which documents you've most recently opened and keep them attached to the File menu for easier access later. This example does something similar, but I've simplified the problem—we'll just have a button that creates a new document name, and we'll display that document name in an entry widget so we know which one we are editing. Using our menubutton and a few select methods from the menu widget, we can create a solution like this:

```perl
#!/usr/bin/perl -w

use Tk;
$mw = MainWindow->new;
$mw->title("Documents");

# Create a frame for our menubar across the top of the window
$f = $mw->Frame(-relief => 'ridge', -borderwidth => 2)
  ->pack(-side => 'top', -anchor => 'n', -expand => 1, -fill => 'x');

# Create the menubutton, with two items: New Doc and a separator
$filem = $f->Menubutton(-text => "File",
                        -tearoff => 0,
                        -menuitems => [ ["command" => "New Document",
                                         -command => \&new_document],
                                        "-"
                                      ])->pack(-side => 'left');
# We will open document 1 to begin with, and we want to limit the number
# of documents in our list to 0-9 (leaves 10 docs max in menu)
$doc_num = 1;
$doc_list_limit = 9;

# Create button that will do the same thing as the New Document menu item
$mw->Button(-text => "New Document",
            -command => \&new_document)->pack(-side => 'bottom',
                                              -anchor => 'e');
# The entry will display the current doc we are "editing".
$entry = $mw->Entry(-width => 80)->pack(-expand => 1, -fill => 'both');

MainLoop;

# Creates the next doc in line, incs the doc counter
# Adds the new doc to the menu, and removes any docs from the
# menu that are over the limit (oldest out first)
sub new_document {
  my $name = "Document $doc_num";
  $doc_num++;

  push (@current, $name);
  $filem->command(-label => "$name",
                  -command => [ \&select_document, $name ]);

  &select_document($name);

  if ($#current > $doc_list_limit) {
    $filem->menu->delete(2);
    shift(@current);
  }
}
```

```
sub select_document {
  my ($selected) = @_;

  $entry->delete(0, 'end');
  $entry->insert('end', "SELECTED DOCUMENT: $selected");
}
```

Figure 11-15 shows what our window looks like after we've created three documents:

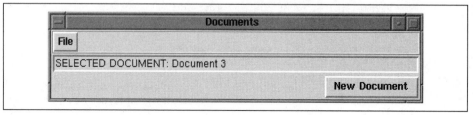

Figure 11-15. Example of Document History window

The Menu Widget

There are times when you won't want to use a menubutton widget. Perhaps you need to create some menus that will cascade from your menubutton. You still need to create the menus. You might also think of a way to use a menu that doesn't involve a button. For example, you could set up your application so the user right-clicks on a widget* and a related menu pops up, allowing the user to change configuration options.

It is also a good idea to be familiar with the methods for manipulating a menu, whether it's a menu widget by itself or the menu attached to a menubutton.

Creating the Basic Menu

To create a menu widget, invoke **Menu** from the desired parent of the menu:

```
$menu = $parent->Menu(options);
```

The menu widget is the only widget on which one of the geometry managers is not used directly. The menu is displayed to the user via a **post** directive:

```
$menu->post( ... );
```

Different arguments sent to **post** will determine how the menu is displayed. This method is discussed later in this chapter.

---

* Use "<Button-3>" with bind.

Menu Creation Options

As with any widget, there are options that affect how the menu widget looks and behaves. Many of the options for the menu widget were discussed in the menubutton widget portion of the chapter, so I'll only cover those that perform actions that aren't available with the menubutton widget or whose actions are different.

The following is a list of the options available for the menu widget:

-activebackground => *color*
> Sets the color of the background behind the active menu item.

-activeborderwidth => *amount*
> Sets the width of the edges of the active menu item's border.

-activeforeground => *color*
> Sets the color of the text in the active menu item.

-background => *color*
> Sets the color of the background of the entire menu.

-borderwidth => *amount*
> Sets the width of the menu's edge.

-cursor => *cursorname*
> Sets the cursor displayed when the mouse cursor is over the menu.

-disabledforeground => *color*
> Sets the color of the text of any disabled menu items.

-font => *font*
> Sets the font of the text displayed in the menu.

-foreground => *color*
> Sets the color of the text in the menu.

-menuitems => *list*
> Defines a list of items to create in the menu.

-postcommand => *callback*
> Sets the callback that is invoked before the menu is posted to the screen.

-relief => 'flat' | 'groove' | **'raised'** | 'ridge' | 'sunken'
> Sets the relief of the edges of the menu.

-selectcolor => *color*
> Sets the color of the selection box in checkbutton or radiobutton items.

-takefocus => **0** | 1| undef
> Controls the ability to use the keyboard to traverse the menu. Default is 0.

-tearoff => 0 | **1**
> Determines whether or not the menu will contain the tear-off item as the first item. Default is 1.

Menu Style

The edges of the menu default to 'raised' with a -borderwidth of 2. This makes the menu look like a large button with multiple items of text listed in it. We can change the look of the menu edges by using the -relief option:

```
-relief => 'flat' | 'groove' | 'raised' | 'ridge' | 'sunken'
```

The menus in Figure 11-16 were created and then torn off so they are left on the screen. The actual menu edge is inside the window manager's decoration.

Figure 11-16. Different relief options with menu widget

The width of the menu's edges (regardless of the -relief) are changed by using the -borderwidth option:

```
-borderwidth => amount
```

Changing the -borderwidth always makes the different relief types stand out more, as shown in Figure 11-17.

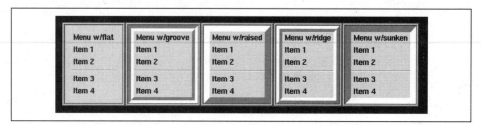

Figure 11-17. Menus with different relief options and -borderwidth set to 4

The -activeborderwidth option affects the active menu item (the one with the mouse cursor over it):

```
-activeborderwidth => amount
```

Menu Fonts and Cursors

The font of the text displayed in the entire menu is controlled with the -font option:

```
-font => font
```

Figure 11-18 shows a menu with a different font, `"lucidasans-14"`. Fonts that can be used for the value of `-font` were covered in Chapter 3.

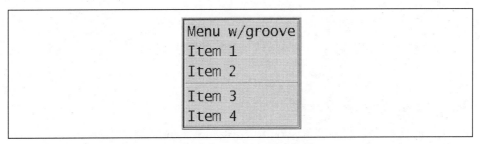

Figure 11-18. Menu with a different font

To change the cursor displayed when the mouse cursor is over a menu widget, use the **-cursor** option:

```
-cursor => cursorname
```

The default cursor for a menu widget is different than the window's default cursor. The default cursor for a menu is **'arrow'**, whereas the window cursor is an arrow that points the other way.

Calling a Subroutine Before Displaying the Menu

Before displaying the menu (via the **post** command or a menubutton), you can use the **-postcommand** option to specify a subroutine to call:

```
-postcommand => callback
```

The form for the callback is the same as the one used in a button widget (described in Chapter 2). One of the best uses of the **-postcommand** option is to update the state of each menu item if needed. Here is an example that uses a menubutton widget but uses **-postcommand** to perform an update of the menu before it is drawn:

```
# Create the menubutton
$menub = $mw->Menubutton(-text => "File", -tearoff => 0,
    -menuitems => [[ 'command' => "Open", -command => \&do_something],
                   [ 'command' => "Save", -command => \&do_something],
                   [ 'command' => "Close", -command => \&do_something],
                   "-",
                   [ 'command' => "Exit", -command => sub { exit }]]
    )->pack();

# A flag we use to see if the document has been saved yet.
$unsaved = 0;

# We have to wait until after we've created the menubutton to
# access the menu widget part of it:
$menub->menu()->configure(-postcommand => \&update_menu);
```

```
# This looks at some flags in our program and determines if the items
# should be updated or not
sub update_menu {
  if ($unsaved) {
    $menub->menu->entryconfigure(1, -state => "normal");
  } else {
    $menub->menu->entryconfigure(1, -state => "disabled");
  }
}
```

Specifying Menu Items

The -menuitems option allows you to create the menu and the menu items at the same time. The format for doing so is the same as the format for the menubutton's -menuitems option.

There is no AddItems method for a menu widget. The AddItems method is only available with the menubutton widget. You can use either the -menuitems option or the add method with a menu widget. add is described in the next section.

Menu Indexes

Like entry and text widgets, menu widgets have their own indexing scheme, as follows.

n

> The items in a menu are numbered from 0 to *n*; 0 is the first item at the top of the menu, and *n* is the last item in the menu. (The tear-off item in a menu counts as index 0 if it is present. Use -tearoff => 0 to turn it off.)

"active"

> The menu item that is currently active (the mouse is over it and it is highlighted). If there are no menu items active, then "active" means the same as 'none'.

"end"

> The last menu item in the menu. If there are no items in the menu, then 'end' means the same as "none".

"last"

> Another way to say "end".

"none"

> No item.

"@*y*"

> The number is a y coordinate in the window. This form of index specification will resolve to the menu item closest to the y coordinate. "@0" means the same as 0.

"pattern"

> The pattern is text to match the menu items against. The first menu item (starting with 0) it matches is used.

There aren't really that many menu widget methods. The most important methods are probably entryconfigure and delete because you'll use them more often than you'll use the others. Remember, if you are using a menubutton widget, you can invoke the menu widget method directly by using $menubutton->menu-> *method*().

Configuring the Menu Widget

The cget method returns the current value of an option. It only affects the options for the entire menu; there is an entrycget method that will return information about specific menu items. Both the configure and cget methods are discussed in detail in Appendix A.

Configuring Menu Items

The entrycget method queries a specific menu item and returns the information about that configuration option:

```
$menu->entrycget(index, -option);
```

The index determines which menu item entrycget affects. Any of the options that can be sent with the add method (covered in the following section) are valid.

The entryconfigure method returns or alters the configuration options of the menu item at *index* just as configure does for the entire menu widget:

```
$menu->entryconfigure(index, [-option, value, ...]);
```

You can specify no options to get the current configurations for all of the options at that index. You can specify a single option to get the value of only that option for that index. You can also specify multiple option/value pairs to set the values of those options for that index.

Adding Items

In addition to the -menuitems option, you can use the add method to add items to the end of a menu. The first argument to add is the type of menu item to be added. It should be one of the following: "command", "radiobutton", "checkbutton", "separator", or "cascade". Here is a usage statement:

```
$menu->add(type [ , options... ]);
```

The options that affect each menu item are the same as those for the -menuitems option: -activebackground, -activeforeground, -accelerator,

-background, -bitmap, -command, -font, -foreground, -image, -indica-
toron, -label, -menu, -offvalue, -onvalue, -selectcolor, -selectimage,
-state, -underline, -value, and -variable.

The results of the following two code snippets are identical:

```
# Snippet 1
# Using add for menu items
$menu = $mw->Menu;
$menu->add("command", -label => "Open",
          -command => \&open_file);
$menu->add("command", -label => "Close",
          -command => \&close_file);


#Snippet 2
# Sending a list intially using -menuitems option
$menu = $mw->Menu(-menuitems => [ ["command" => "Open",
                                   -command => \&open_file],
                                  ["command" => "Close",
                                   -command => \&close_file]
                                ]);
```

Each additional call to **add** will add another item to the end of the menu. To add a
menu item to somewhere other than the end of the menu, see the **insert** method
(covered in the next section).

Instead of -text or -textvariable options, we use -label to indicate the text
shown on the menu item. You should notice that we don't have a -labelvari-
able option. If you need to change the text shown in the menu item, you will
need to use the entryconfigure method (discussed later in this chapter).

Inserting Menu Items

The insert method works exactly the same way the add method works, except
the new menu item will be inserted right before the menu item at *index*. You cannot insert a menu item before the tear-off menu item because the tear-off must
always be the first item in the menu:

```
$menu->insert(index, type [, options ... ]);
```

Here is an example:

```
$menu->insert("end", "radiobutton",-label=>"red");
```

Deleting Menu Items

To remove menu items from your menu, use the delete method:

```
$menu->delete(index);
# or..
$menu->delete(index1, index2);
```

You can delete one item by specifying only one index. You can delete more than one by specifying a range of indexes. Here are some examples:

```
$menu->delete('last');    # deletes the last menu item
$menu->delete(0, 'end');  # deletes every menu item (except tearoff)
$menu->delete("Open");    # deletes the item that matches "Open"
```

Invoking Menu Items

The invoke method will try to invoke the menu item at the specified index (as if you clicked on it with the mouse):

```
$menu->invoke(index);
```

The specific result of the invocation depends on what type of menu item is at *index*. The result from any -command callback associated with that index will be returned by the invoke method.

```
$menu->invoke("red");
```

Determining Item Type

The type method returns a string that indicates the type of menu item located at *index*:

```
$type = $menu->type(index);
```

The string returned will be one of the following: "command", "radiobutton", "checkbutton", "cascade", "separator", or "tearoff".

```
$type = $menu->type(0); # look at index 0
```

Translating Index Values

The index method returns the numerical index of the menu item at *index*:

```
$menu->index(index);
```

The code $menu->index('end') returns 9 if there are 10 menu items in the menu. The code $menu->index("Open") returns the index number of the menu item that matches "Open".

Displaying a Menu

If you aren't using a menubutton widget to display your menu, you need a way to display it. You can use the post method or the Popup method.

The post method displays the menu for you, but the menu only goes away after you select a menu item or specifically call unpost. The Popup displays the menu only while the mouse button is depressed.

The `post` method requires x and y coordinates to tell it where to place the menu on the screen. Typically, you call it wherever the user clicked (unless you want it to display in the same place all the time). Here is an example that displays the menu when the user clicks the right mouse button in a listbox:

```
# Create a menu with two items for our example
$menu = $mw->Menu(-tearoff => 0,
                    -menuitems => [['command' => "A"],
                                   ['command' => "B"]]);
$lb = $mw->Listbox()->pack();
# create a binding on the listbox that will display our menu
# when we click with the right mouse button
$lb->bind("<Button-3>", [ \&display_menu(), Ev('X'), Ev('Y')]);

sub display_menu {
  my ($lb, $x, $y) = @_;
  $menu->post($x,$y);
}
```

I created a simple menu so we can get through the example quickly. I removed the tear-off item from the menu because I don't like tear-off menus all over the place (but some users do, so keep this in mind). The `bind` is where I mapped the right mouse button to display the menu. I used `Ev("X")` and `Ev("Y")` to send the coordinates of the location in which the user clicked (see Chapter 14 for more information about `Ev("X")` and `Ev("Y")`). The subroutine simply calls `post` with the correct arguments.

The menu will be displayed even when the user lets go of the mouse button. It will `unpost` itself automatically when the user selects a menu item.

Another way to display a menu is to use `Popup`. This causes the menu to be displayed only while the user holds down the mouse button. To select a menu item, you must click down the mouse button, slide the cursor to the desired item, and then let go of the mouse button. The `Popup` method can be called with no arguments or with one or two options. The options that affect `Popup` are `-popover` and `-popanchor`. Calling `Popup` like this

```
$menu->Popup();
```

displays the menu at the very center of your entire screen. This isn't very useful, so I recommend that you at least use the `-popover` option. The `-popover` option will take either the string `"cursor"` or a widget reference. The menu will be centered under the cursor or centered over the widget; for example:

```
$menu->Popup(-popover => "cursor");  # Center menu under cursor
$menu->Popup(-popover => $button);   # Center menu over $button
$menu->Popup(-popover => $listbox);  # Center menu over $listbox
```

Notice that we are not using the syntax `\$listbox`. Because our scalars already contain a reference to a widget, we don't need to reference it again.

The second option, –popanchor, affects how the menu gets positioned relative to the –popover argument (or the entire screen if –popover isn't specified). The –popanchor option takes a string argument where the string is one of the following: "nw", "ne", "sw", or "se". For instance, if you would like to display the menu's upper-left corner where the user clicks, use this code:

```
$menu->Popup(-popover => "cursor", -popanchor => "nw");
```

This is how I like to create right-click menus that are associated with widgets. See the complete example in the "Right-Click Menu Example."

Displaying a Cascading Menu

If your menu has a cascading menu associated with it, use postcascade to display it:

```
$menu->postcascade(index);
```

The postcascade method will unpost any other submenu and then post any cascade menu associated with the menu item located at *index.* If the menu item at *index* is not a cascade item type, then the only thing that happens is that any other submenus are unposted.

```
$menu->postcascade("submenu");
```

Undisplaying a Menu

If you have displayed the menu on the screen using post, you can use unpost to remove it from the screen:

```
$menu->unpost();
```

This will unmap $menu from the window. If any cascaded menus of this menu are also displayed, they will be unmapped as well.

Getting the Position of an Item

The yposition method returns a decimal string that gives the y coordinate of the topmost pixel of the menu item at index:

```
$location = $menu->yposition(index);
```

Right-Click Menu Example

There are times you'll want to use a right-click menu, which is a menu that appears when you right-click on a particular widget or location in the application. A canvas is a perfect place to use a right-click menu; there are often so many different possible actions to take that associating different menus with different types of objects in the canvas is advantageous.

To create a right-click menu, simply create a menu widget, add the items to it as desired, and use the **-command** option to make the items perform useful tasks. To display the menu when the user right-clicks on the desired object, use the **bind** command:

```
$object->bind("<Button-3>", sub { $menu->Popup(-popover => 'cursor'); });
```

You can use a right-click menu with a listbox to allow users to delete or edit the currently selected item.

Optionmenu Widget

The optionmenu is a specific implementation of a menubutton widget. The difference between the two is that the optionmenu automatically sets the **-indicatoron** option to 1, removes the tear-off menu item, and handles the display of the menu in a slightly different way.

You can use an optionmenu when you want to give the user a choice between several different items but don't want to waste space with a listbox and scrollbar or with several radiobuttons. To add items, use the **-options** command instead of **-menuitems** or the other methods that allowed you to add to a menu or menubutton.

Creating and Configuring an Optionmenu

The optionmenu is created by using the **Optionmenu** method:

```
$optionmenu = $mw->Optionmenu( ... );
```

All the options that are available with a menubutton widget are also available for the optionmenu widget. The following options are specific to the optionmenu: **-textvariable**, **-options**, **-variable**, and **-command**.

Instead of using a **-menuitems** option or other methods to add items to an optionmenu, use the **-options** option. It takes an anonymous list that can contain either strings or other anonymous lists. The idea behind an optionmenu is to select one item from a list of items. The text displayed is the currently selected menu item. The **-textvariable** option determines where the displayed text is stored. There is also a **-variable** option, which you can use to store a value that is different than the one shown on the menu. Specify the displayed value and the stored value by using the **-options** option. If the displayed value is the same as the stored value, use a simple list:

```
-options => [1, 2, 3, 4, 5, 6], -textvariable => $number
```

To store a value other than the one shown, use this code:

```
-options => [["one",1], ["two",2], ["three",3],
             ["four",4], ["five",5], ["six",6]],
-textvariable => $displayed,
-variable => $number
```

In this example, the written words are displayed in the menu (and are stored in $displayed), and the stored value (in $number) are the integers. The nondisplayed value can be any scalar value.

The -command option assigns a callback that will be executed when a selection has been made. The default arguments to the callback are the variables assigned with -textvariable and then -variable (if it exists). You can use callbacks to perform an action based on the item selected from the optionmenu.

Here's a complete script that will allow you to see most of the optionmenu's useful features:

```
#!/usr/bin/perl -w

use Tk;

$mw = MainWindow->new;
$mw->title("Optionmenu");

$display_var = "ten";
$mw->Optionmenu(-command =>
  sub { print "ARGS: @_\n"; print "in optionmenu\n"; },
                -textvariable => \$display_var,
                -variable => \$stored_var,
                -options => [["ten", 10],
                             ["twenty",20],
                             ["thirty",30]]
                )->pack();
MainLoop;
```

It's a good idea to also create a label widget so the user is aware of the optionmenu's purpose (shown in Figure 11-19).

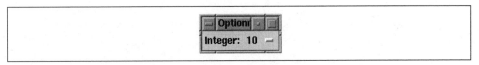

Figure 11-19. Optionmenu with a label widget to the left

The only methods available with the optionmenu are the cget and configure methods. The cget method returns information about an option in the optionmenu. The configure method can get or set option values for the optionmenu widget. Both cget and configure are covered in detail in Appendix A.

Fun Things to Try

- Create one menu that has two items: Disabled and Normal. When you right-click on a widget, the menu will pop up. If you select 'Disabled', that widget will be disabled. Selecting 'Normal' reenables that widget.

- Create an application with two menubuttons. Have the items on the first add and delete different types of menu items to the second menu.

- Take all the fun things from previous chapters and add menus to them. Add at least a File menu, with an Exit item. Be inventive!

12

Frames

A frame widget is a boring widget at first glance. All it does is provide a place for other widgets to sit. This doesn't seem important, but it is. The geometry managers provided with Perl/Tk have some limitations (see Chapter 2, *Geometry Management*), and we can use frames to help them do their jobs better. We'll use **pack** as our example geometry manager throughout this chapter because it seems to be the most popular, but remember that the basic rules for using a frame apply to the other geometry managers as well.

A frame widget's job is to contain other widgets, accommodating the size of the widgets within. If you don't have any widgets packed into the frame, you won't see the frame. If the widgets inside the frame are resized for any reason, the frame will try to resize as well (either larger or smaller).[*]

Creating a Frame

Use the parent widget of the frame to invoke the **Frame()** method:

```
$frame = $parent->Frame( [ option => value, ... ])->pack();
```

The **$parent** can be a MainWindow, a toplevel, or another frame widget.[†] After the frame is created, it can become a parent to other widgets. You must have created the frame but not necessarily packed it on the screen for it to be the parent

---

[*] You can change this behavior by using **packPropagate()** or **gridPropagate()**.

[†] Technically, any widget can be a parent of another widget, but I like to make my life easier when it comes to placing the widget inside the window. If I made a frame the child of a **$button**, I wouldn't be able to pack it inside the button. I would then have to use the **-in** option with **pack**, confusing myself even further. Keep it simple, and you'll be much happier.

of other widgets. Keep in mind that, even if you pack other widgets inside your frame, if you don't pack the frame as well, the other widgets won't show on the screen.

Just as with all the other widgets in Perl/Tk, the options specified in the `Frame` method will change how the frame looks inside the window. There are few options available with the frame widget, and they aren't complicated at all. This section covers all the options and what they do.

`-background =>` *color*

> Sets the color of the frame's background area (there is no foreground area).

`-borderwidth =>` *amount*

> Sets the width of the frame's edges. Default is 0.

`-class =>` *classname*

> Indicates the class associated with the frame in the option database. This option can actually be used on any widget, not just a frame.

`-colormap => "new" | $window`

> Specifies whether to use a new colormap or share one with another widget in the application. Default is `undef`.

`-container => 0 | 1`

> Tk8.0 only. If true, this frame will be used to contain another embedded application.

`-cursor =>` *cursorname*

> Changes the cursor to use when the mouse pointer is over the frame.

`-height =>` *amount*

> Sets the starting height of the frame in a valid screen distance.

`-highlightbackground =>` *color*

> Sets the color the highlight rectangle should be when the frame does not have keyboard focus.

`-highlightcolor =>` *color*

> Sets the color the highlight rectangle should be when the frame does have the keyboard focus. Default color is black.

`-highlightthickness =>` *amount*

> Sets the thickness of the highlight rectangle. Default is 0.

`-label =>` *labelstring*

> Adds a label to the Frame with the text *"labelstring"*.

`-labelPack => [` *pack options* `]`

> Specifies pack options for the label.

`-labelVariable => \$variable`
  Specifies a variable that contains the text for the label.

`-relief => `**`'flat'`**`|'groove'|'raised'|'ridge'|'sunken'|'solid'`
  Changes the appearance of the edges of the widget. Default is `'flat'`.

`-takefocus => `**`0`**` | 1 | undef`
  Specifies whether the frame should take the focus. Default is 0.

`-visual => "`*type #*`"`
  When used on an X Windows system, changes the depth of colors available to
  your application. Does nothing on Win32 systems.

`-width => `*amount*
  Sets the starting width of the frame in a valid screen distance.

Frame Style

As with all widgets, you can use the `-relief` and `-borderwidth` options to
change how the edges of a frame widget are drawn. The default `-relief` is
`'flat'`, and the default `-borderwidth` is 0. If you want the frame to have any
edges at all, make sure you change `-borderwidth` to something higher than 0.
Unless you put something in a frame, you'll never see it. So, for the examples in
Figure 12-1, I have inserted a label widget and an entry widget that state the relief
of that frame. Note that I actually created a label widget by using `Label()` and did
not use the `-label` option (see the next section).

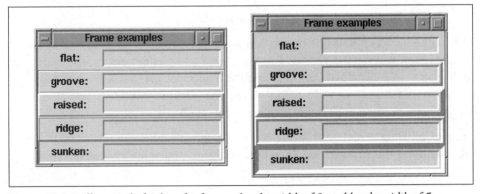

Figure 12-1. Different relief values for frames; borderwidth of 2 and borderwidth of 5

Using `-relief` and `-borderwidth` is a great way to find out where your frame is
in the window. If you have a complicated window, it's confusing to remember
which frame is where. I'll often add `-borderwidth => 5`, `-relief =>`
`"groove"` to my `Frame` command to find that frame in the window.

Adding a Label to a Frame

With Perl/Tk, you can add a label to your frame by using the `-label` option, which takes a text string as an argument:

```
$mw->Frame(-label => "My Frame:")->pack;
...
# configure label in frame later :
$frame->configure(-label => "My Frame:")->pack;
```

By default, the label is placed at the top of the frame, centered across the width (see Figure 12-2). Again, I put something in the frame so you can see the frame as well as the item in the frame. In this case, I placed a button with the default pack options in the frame. I also created the frame with `-relief => 'groove'`, `-borderwidth => 2` options so you can see the edge.

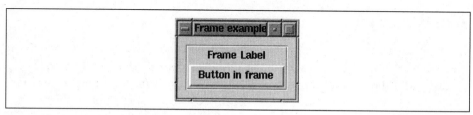

Figure 12-2. Frame with label in default position

You can change the location of the label inside the frame by using the `-labelPack` option. It takes an anonymous array as an argument, where the array contains any pack options for the label:

```
-labelPack => [ -side => 'left', -anchor => 'w']
```

Be careful to notice that this option has an uppercase letter in it. If you try to use `-labelPack` without the capital "P," you'll get a compilation error. Also notice that there isn't a `-labelGrid` option available. You must use `pack()` to put widgets inside your frame if you are going to use the `-label` option. If you don't, bad things happen (your application might not run at all).

Instead of using a static text string with your frame's label, you can assign a variable by using the `-labelVariable` option (again, notice the capital V):

```
-labelVariable => \$label_text
```

When you change the contents of the variable `$label_text`, the label in the frame will change as well.

The instant you use the `-label` or `-labelVariable` option, a label is created and placed inside the frame. You can use these options either in the initial `Frame()` call or later with `$frame->configure( ... )`. If you use them later, the label is placed above all other widgets inside the frame.

Frames Aren't Interactive

The frame widget itself is not interactive; by default, it can't accept input from the user. The widgets inside it can, but the frame cannot. As always, the focus ability is controlled by the -takefocus option:

```
-takefocus => 0
```

With a frame widget, it is set to 0. If for some reason you need to get input from the user on your frame, you will need to change it to -takefocus => 1.

Colormap Complications

When you are running several applications at once and you start a web browser, you'll sometimes notice that the colors become corrupted. When you switch from an application to the browser, the colors in your other applications suddenly change. If you switch back from your browser to an application, the browser colors change. This is happening because the web browser is a color hog. It has requested more colors than the operating system can allocate at once. The OS must alter the colormap between applications to allow the active application to use the colors it wants to use. The colormap simply gives the operating system a way to keep track of who is using which colors.

Perl/Tk applications can have many colors too—you can get color-happy and make each button a different color of the rainbow. This can cause problems if there are other applications running that want a lot of different colors too. If other applications are color hogs, Perl/Tk will switch to black-and-white mode. If you don't like this behavior, you can use the -colormap option to override it. -colormap takes either the word "new" or a reference to another window. If given "new", it will create its own colormap. When you use -colormap with another window, the two windows will share the colormap. But there is one catch, and that is the -visual option.

The -visual option takes as an argument a string that contains a keyword and a number; for example:

```
-visual => "staticgrey 2"
```

The keyword can be any one of the following: staticgrey, greyscale, static-color, pseudocolor, truecolor, or directcolor. The number indicates the depth of color used (2 = black/white).

When you use -colormap to share the colormap between two windows, the -visual option for both must be the same. This means that -visual must be undef for both (the default) or it must have the same value. Neither -colormap nor -visual can be altered by using the configure method.

You will see both -colormap and -visual options in Chapter 13, *Toplevel Widgets*, also. We covered it here first because this is where we see it first. To be honest, you'll probably never use either option in either widget.

The Magical Class Option

You can force your frame to be in another class (besides frame) by using the -class option. Simply give it a string that is a unique class identifier;

```
-class => "Myframe"
```

For more information on using classes (and what good they can do you), see Chapter 13.

Frame Methods

The only methods available with the frame widget are cget and configure. These are described in detail in Appendix A, *Configuring Widgets with configure and cget.*

Fun Things to Try

When you use the Scrolled method, you are using frames without even knowing it. The newly scrolled widget is placed inside a frame with its scrollbars so that it behaves as one contained widget. Here are some other ways you can use frames:

- Create several lines of labels with entry widgets. Each 'line' needs to be in its own frame so it will look right.

- Place an image along one side of your application window. Put the widgets in a frame (on the left or on the right) and place the image on the other side of them.

- Place a scrolled listbox in your application window, a frame containing three buttons (OK, Cancel, Apply) along the bottom of the window, and a frame along the right containing two buttons (Delete, Add) that manipulate the listbox. By using frames, you can keep the buttons that belong together in one area instead of grouping them with other buttons that serve a different purpose.

13

Toplevel Widgets

Any Perl/Tk application includes at least one toplevel widget. When you call the new method from the **MainWindow** class, you are creating a toplevel widget without even knowing it. You can create other toplevel widgets to be used in your application in addition to the MainWindow toplevel widget. The MainWindow is special because it automatically displays when you call **MainLoop()**. Other toplevel widgets in your program must be explicitly displayed somewhere in the code.

Here are some examples of how you can use toplevel widgets:

- Display informational text with a Close button.*
- Provide data gathering that is triggered by something the user does (for example, clicking a button).

All toplevel widgets have the same behavior: Each has decoration that is consistent with the system on which your application is run. Each toplevel can contain other widgets and/or multiple groups of widgets (for example, they can be grouped in a frame widget).

The rest of the chapter will cover how to use toplevel widgets and what options allow you to change their behavior.

Creating a Toplevel Widget

To create a toplevel, call **Toplevel** from the desired parent widget, usually the MainWindow widget (you already know that to create a main window, you must

---

* Look at Tk::Dialog. It is designed to do this and uses a toplevel widget.

use `MainWindow->new()`). The returned item is a reference to the toplevel widget; the reference allows you to configure the widget, call methods on it, and place items within it. Here is a simple example:

```
use Tk;
$mw = MainWindow->new;
$mw->title("MainWindow");
$mw->Button(-text => "Toplevel", -command => \&do_toplevel)->pack();

MainLoop;
sub do_toplevel {
  if (! Exists($tl)) {
    $tl = $mw->Toplevel();
    $tl->title("Toplevel");
    $tl->Button(-text => "Close",
                -command => sub { $tl->withdraw })->pack;
  } else {
    $tl->deiconify();
    $tl->raise();
  }
}
```

When you run this program, clicking on the Toplevel button in the main window creates the toplevel widget (if it needs to) and displays it. Clicking Close hides the toplevel from view. You need to test for the existence of the toplevel before you show it because you don't want to re-create it if it already exists and you don't want to try to show something that doesn't exist.

When the Close button is clicked, the toplevel is withdrawn. It still exists; it is just not visible to the user. This saves time the next time around by redisplaying the same window. You can also use `withdraw` if you don't want to show the toplevel while you are filling it with widgets. Simply use the `withdraw` method, place the interior widgets, and then redisplay the widget by using `deiconify` and `raise`.

These options can be specified in the call to `Toplevel` or by using the `configure` method.

`-background` => *color*

Sets the background color of the toplevel widget. Note that the background may be hidden by widgets placed in the toplevel if the toplevel is completely covered by widgets.

`-borderwidth` => *amount*

Sets the width of the border around the toplevel. Default is 0.

`-class` => *classname*

Sets the classname used with the option database for this toplevel widget.

`-colormap => "new" | $window`

Specifies whether to use a new colormap or share one with another widget in the application. Default is **undef**.

`-container => 0 | 1`

Tk8.0 only. If true, this window will contain an embedded application (see the `-use` option).

`-cursor => ` *cursorname*

Sets the type of cursor used over the toplevel widget.

`-height => ` *amount*

Sets the height of the toplevel.

`-highlightbackground => ` *color*

Sets the color the highlight rectangle should be when the toplevel does not have focus.

`-highlightcolor => ` *color*

Sets the color the highlight rectangle should be when the toplevel does have focus.

`-highlightthickness => ` *amount*

Sets the thickness of the highlight rectangle. Default is 0.

`-menu => $menu`

Tk8.0 only. Indicates that the toplevel uses the menu in $menu across the top of the window.

`-relief => 'flat'|'groove'|'raised'|'ridge'|'sunken'|'solid'`

Changes the appearance of the edges of the toplevel. Default is `'flat'`.

`-screen => ` *screenname*

Sets the screen on which to place the toplevel. Cannot be changed by configure method.

`-takefocus => 0 | 1 | undef`

Determines if toplevel can have keyboard focus. Default is 0, meaning it cannot have keyboard focus.

`-use => $windowid`

Tk8.0 only. $windowid must contain a hex string of the window to embed in the toplevel. The `-container` option must have the value 1 to use this option.

`-visual => "`*type #*`"`

When used on an X Window System, changes the depth of colors available to your application. Does nothing on Win32 systems.

`-width => ` *amount*

Sets the desired width of the toplevel.

Toplevel Methods

The methods available with the toplevel widget are listed and explained in the following sections (it is important to note that all of these methods apply to a Main-Window as well; a MainWindow is just a specialized toplevel widget). You haven't seen many of them before because toplevel is a different sort of widget than the others covered so far in this book. Also keep in mind that a lot of these methods were designed originally for use with a Unix windowing environment, and quite a few of them will state "No effect in Win32 system." Many of these functions serve no useful purpose to the typical ordinary Perl/Tk application, but I'll document them here for thoroughness.

Several of the methods here alter *window manager properties*, which often look like WM_PROPERTY_THING. These properties are also traditionally associated with the X Window system on Unix, but some still apply in Win32 systems as well. If a specific method doesn't say anything about which system it applies to, it will apply to both. If it only applies to one or the other (or only half-works in one system), this will be mentioned as well.

Configuring a Toplevel

Both `cget` and `configure` methods are used to set and get option values for a toplevel widget. See Appendix A for more detailed information on how to use these methods.

Sizing a Toplevel

You can use the `geometry` method to define or retrieve a geometry string. A *geometry string* determines the size and placement of a window on the screen. The geometry string is a concept that originated on Unix systems, and at first glance, it is a bit cryptic. Here is a regular expression that describes a complete geometry string:

```
=^?(\d+x\d+)?([+-]\d+[+-]\d+)?$
```

The equal sign can be omitted completely (and usually is). The first portion (\ d+)x(\d+) is the width and height (in that order) separated by an x. Both width and height are specified in pixels by default and in grid units if the window is gridded with the `grid` method (described later). The last portion of the geometry string represents the x and y coordinates of the location in which the toplevel should be placed on the screen. Both x and y are always in pixels. Here are a few examples of what some geometry strings look like:

```
300x300        # width and height both = 300
300x450        # width = 300, height = 450
300x450+0+0    # width = 300, height = 450 placed in upper left corner
300x450-0-0    # width = 300, height = 450 placed in lower right corner
```

```
300x450+10+10 # width = 300, height = 450
              # placed 10 pixels out from upper left corner
+0+0          # window is 'natural' size, placed in upper left corner
```

When `geometry` is called with no arguments, the current geometry string is returned. You can also specify a new geometry by using `geometry` with the new geometry string as the argument. To set the size and position of the window immediately, you would do this:

```
$mw = MainWindow->new();
$mw->geometry("300x450+0+0");
```

If you specify only the width and height, the placement of the window is determined by the window manager. If you specify only the positioning, then the size of the window will be determined by the widgets placed within the toplevel, but the window will be placed at those x and y coordinates.

You can force the window back to its natural size by calling `geometry()` with an empty geometry string:

```
$toplevel->geometry("");
```

Maximum Size

You can use `maxsize` to restrict the largest size of the window. It takes two integers as arguments, as follows:

```
$toplevel->maxsize(300,300);
```

If you call `maxsize` without any arguments, you'll get an empty string or a list with two items in it representing the current values. Calling `maxsize` with two empty strings cancels the limitation.

Minimum Size

You can also restrict the smallest size of the window by using `minsize`. The window will always be at least the size specified:

```
$toplevel->minsize(100,100);
```

Calling `minsize` without arguments will return an empty string or a list containing the width and height respectively. Calling `minsize` with two empty strings will eliminate the minimum size restriction.

Limiting Resizing

You can control whether a window can be resized in width and/or height by using `resizable`:

```
$toplevel->resizable(1, 0);
($canwidth, $canheight) = $toplevel->resizable();
```

Specifying 1 means it is resizable, and 0 means it is nonresizable in the specified direction. If you don't specify any arguments, `resizable` returns a list with two items. The first item is a 1 or 0 and indicates whether the width is resizable. The second item is a 1 or 0 and indicates whether if the height is resizable. By default, a window is resizable in both directions.

Using a Size Aspect

You can use the **aspect** method to force the window to stay a certain width and height:

```
$toplevel->aspect( [ minN, minD, maxN, maxD ]);
```

The **aspect** method does some very subtle things, and you'll probably never use it. If you do, play around with different values (starting with the example below) to get the effect you want.

When you use the **aspect** method with no arguments, it returns either an empty string (if there are no constraints to the aspect of the window) or an array containing four elements:

```
($minN, $minD, $maxN, $maxD) = $toplevel->aspect;
```

Using these values, you can see how **aspect** controls the window:

```
($minN/$minD) < width/height < ($maxN/$maxD)
```

You can also send four empty strings to unset the aspect restrictions on the window. Try using `$toplevel->aspect(1,2,3,1)`; the effect is subtle.

Setting the Title

You can change the text across the top of the window by using the `title` method:

```
$toplevel->title("This will be the title");
```

Pass a string in with `title` and the new title will appear immediately in the window, assuming the window is currently visible. If you don't pass an argument with `title`, the current title string is returned. For the X Window System, the default title of a window is the name used to run the program, and the first character of the name is uppercase. For Microsoft Windows, the title always starts out as Toplevel.

Showing the Toplevel

The `deiconify` method causes the toplevel to be displayed noniconified or deiconifies it immediately if the window has already been displayed once. If the window has been withdrawn, a `$toplevel->raise()` must also be done to correctly display the window.

The **raise** method brings the toplevel to the front of all the other toplevel windows in the application if you call it with no arguments:

```
$toplevel->raise();
```

You can also put the toplevel in front of another toplevel:

```
$toplevel->raise($other_toplevel);
```

It is sometimes necessary to use both **deiconify** and **raise** to get the window to show up on the screen.

Withdrawing the Toplevel

When you create a window, it is a good idea to make it invisible while you fill it with widgets. You can do so by using the **withdraw** method:

```
$toplevel->withdraw();
```

If the window is already visible, **withdraw** will make the window manager forget about the window until it has been deiconified.

Iconifying the Toplevel

The **iconify** method forces the toplevel into iconified form:

```
$toplevel->iconify();
```

Iconifying is not the same as withdrawing the window; withdrawing the window will not show an icon on the desktop.

Specifying the Icon Bitmap

In the Unix X Window System, when you iconify your application, it is represented on the screen with a bitmap. You use the **iconbitmap** method to specify this bitmap:

```
$toplevel->iconbitmap();
$toplevel->iconbitmap("bitmap");
```

It takes a bitmap in the same form the **-bitmap** option supported by the button widget (see Chapter 3, *The Basic Button*). Calling **iconbitmap** with no arguments returns the current bitmap or an empty string. Calling **iconbitmap** with an empty string removes the current bitmap.

On Win32 systems, the application is kept in the Start taskbar with an unchangeable Tk icon and the name of the application. Using the **iconbitmap** method on a Win32 system does nothing.

Specifying the Icon Mask

A mask for the icon bitmap can be specified by using the `iconmask` method (remember, this will only work with X Window Systems). It also takes a bitmap specified from a file or a default bitmap name (see `-bitmap` documentation in Chapter 3). Where the bitmap mask has zeroes, no part of the normal icon bitmap will be displayed. Where the mask has ones, normal icon bitmaps will be displayed.

Calling `iconmask` with no arguments returns the current bitmap mask or an empty string if no bitmap is being used. Calling `iconmask` with an empty string unsets the mask:

```
$currentmask = $toplevel->iconmask();    # get the mask
$toplevel->iconmask("bitmapname");       # set the mask
$toplevel->iconmask("");                 # unset the mask
```

Setting the Name of the Icon

The `iconname` method sets or returns the current text associated with the icon that is displayed when the application is iconified. You can pass in a new string or an empty string:

```
$toplevel->iconname("newname");
$current_name = $toplevel->iconname();
```

If you don't specify an argument at all, `iconname` returns the current iconname or an empty string. You can query and set the iconname on a Win32 system, but it doesn't do anything. This is a method that is used on the X Window System only.

Setting the Icon Position

The `iconposition` method suggests to the X Window System manager where the icon should be placed on the desktop when the application is iconified:

```
($x, $y) = $toplevel->iconposition();
$toplevel->iconposition($x, $y);
```

If x and y aren't specified, a list is returned containing only two items, the current x and y. If you call `iconposition` with two empty strings (one for each x and y), the suggestion to the window manager is cancelled.

Using a Window Instead of an Icon

Some systems (not Win32) support the idea of using a widget (or window) instead of a bitmap for an icon. Specify the widget by using the `iconwindow` method. To find out what the current widget is, call `iconwindow` with no arguments (an empty string is returned if there is no associated $widget). You can specify an empty string instead of $widget to cancel by using a widget for the icon:

```
$currentwindow = $toplevel->iconwindow();  # get
$toplevel->iconwindow($window);            # set
$toplevel->iconwindow("");                 # unset
```

Determining the State

The state method returns one of three strings: "normal", "iconic", or "withdrawn".

```
$state = $toplevel->state();
```

The string indicates the state of the window when state is called.

Assigning an Application Name

The client method returns an empty string if your application doesn't have a name assigned to it.

```
$name = $toplevel->client( );
$toplevel->client("name");
```

To assign a name, send a string to the client method after you create your toplevel widget. You can use this in an *.Xdefaults* file in the X Window System to assign colors to your application.

Window Properties

The protocol method controls the following window properties: WM_DELETE_ WINDOW, WM_SAVE_YOURSELF, and WM_TAKE_FOCUS. The callback (if any) associated with each property will be invoked when the window manager recognizes the event associated with the property:

```
$toplevel->protocol ( [ property_name] [, callback ] );
```

The WM_DELETE_WINDOW property callback is invoked when the window has been deleted by the window manager. By default, there is a callback assigned by Perl/Tk that destroys the window. If you assign a new callback, your callback will be invoked instead of the default callback. If you need to save data associated with that window, do so in the callback and then invoke $toplevel->destroy() to mimic the correct behavior afterward.

The other two properties, WM_SAVE_YOURSELF and WM_TAKE_FOCUS, are much less commonly used. For instance, WM_TAKE_FOCUS is used in Unix systems but not in Win32. The presence of these properties is dependent on the window system you are running. If your application will be running on multiple systems, don't expect these properties to always be available. To find out if they are available, assign each one a callback that does a `print` and then run the application to see if the `print` is ever invoked.

If you leave out the callback when you use `protocol`, the current callback assigned to that property will be returned (or an empty string if there isn't a current callback assigned). You can remove the callback by sending an empty string instead of the callback. If neither argument is specified, the method returns a list of all properties that have callbacks assigned to them.

Colormap Property

The `colormapwindows` method affects the WM_COLORMAP_WINDOWS property. This property is used to talk to the window manager about windows that have private colormaps. Using `colormapwindows` with no arguments returns a list of windows. The list contains windows (in order of priority) that have a different colormap than their parents:

```
@list = $toplevel->colormapwindows();
```

You can pass a list of windows to `colormapwindows` as well:

```
$toplevel->colormapwindows(@list);
```

If you don't use this function at all, Perl/Tk will take care of everything for you, although the order of the windows might be different.

The Command Property

The `command` method (not to be confused with the `-command` option used with most of the widgets) controls the WM_COMMAND property. When used with no arguments, `command` returns a list reference:

```
$listref = $toplevel->command();
```

The list holds the words of the command used to start the application. Use this bit of code to determine what your application command was (which is sometimes nothing):

```
$listptr = $mw->command();
foreach (@$listptr) {
  print "$_\n";
}
```

You can unset the WM_COMMAND property by sending an empty string:

```
$toplevel->command("");
```

The Focus Model

The `focusmodel` method controls whether or not the toplevel widget will give up the keyboard focus when another application or window should have it:

```
$toplevel->focusmodel( [ "active" | "passive" ] );
```

The default is **"passive"**, meaning it will give up the keyboard focus. The changes present in your application depend completely on the type of window manager you are running your application under. My testing revealed no changes under Win32 or the X Window System.

Getting the Parent of the Toplevel

The `frame` method returns a hexadecimal string that is the "ID" of the parent of the toplevel widget:

```
$id = $toplevel->frame();
```

You can use `$widget->id()` to get the same ID from any widget in your application.

The Application Grid

There are a few complications with the `grid` method. Remember way back in Chapter 2 there was a `grid` there also which controlled geometry management. To resolve this little problem, we have to call this `grid` method in a funny way:

```
$mw->wm('grid', ... );
```

We must use the `wm` (stands for window manager) method to invoke `grid` indirectly.

Now that we have that cleared up, we can get into what `wm('grid', ...)` does. When you tell the window to `grid`, you are restricting the size it can be. The size must always snap to the grid as defined in `grid`. We have to remember the listbox widget and the `-setgrid` option back in Chapter 7, *The Listbox Widget*. Once you use `-setgrid => 1` on a listbox, you can use `@list = $toplevel-> wm('grid');` to determine the values used in the grid. The values I got on my system were 10, 10, 7, and 17. This means the base width and height were each 10 pixels and each grid unit incremented by 7 pixels in width and 17 pixels in height. You can change the grid size and increments by calling `wm('grid', ...)` with new values if you desire, but if you don't, Tk manages everything quite nicely for any of the gridded widgets.

You should also know that you can unset the grid values by using empty strings for each instead of new values.

Being the Leader

This is another method you'll never use, but it's good to know what you're not using it for. The `group` method makes a widget the group leader of related windows. For each toplevel that you want to be in `$widget`'s group, call `$toplevel->group($widget)`. If `$widget` isn't specified, it will return the current group leader of `$toplevel`, or it will return an empty string if `$toplevel` isn't part of a group.

You can send an empty string to cancel toplevel's association with that group. That is, to remove a toplevel from the group, call `$toplevel->group("")`.

Removing Decorations

To make a window with none of the normal window decorations (titlebar, borders, and so on) you can use the `overrideredirect` method with a true value:

```
$toplevel->overrideredirect(1);   # Remove all decorations
```

Be careful though; you won't be able to move the window on the screen once it is drawn. If you forgot to put an exit button on it, you won't be able to quit the application gracefully (doing a CTRL-C in the window that started the script will kill it).

This is a way to make a splash screen—a screen that shows up as your application is loading. Remember that you must call `MainLoop` for it to show up at all.

Calling `overrideredirect` with no argument returns the current value (1 or 0):

```
$current_value = $toplevel->overrideredirect();
```

Calling `overrideredirect` again with a 0 value will not turn decorations back on once the window has been displayed.

Who Placed the Window?

When the toplevel widget is placed on the window, either the window manager tells the program where to be or the program tells the window manager where it wants to be. In some cases, the user positions the window manually when it comes up.

```
$who = $toplevel->positionfrom();
$toplevel->positionfrom("program");   # Try and force it
```

When called without argument, the `positionfrom` method returns information on which one happened. If it returns the string `"program"`, an empty string, or a `$widget`, it means either the window manager or the program requested the position. If `positionfrom` returns the string `"user"`, the user manually placed the window when it was created.

You can try to force which will happen by calling `positionfrom` with the "pro-gram" or "user" string, but it will only work if your window manager agrees with you.

Who Sized It?

The `sizefrom` method does the same thing `positionfrom` does except it returns information regarding the size of the window.

```
$who = $toplevel->sizefrom(); # "program" or "user"?
$toplevel->sizefrom("user");  # Try and force it
```

Not a Real Window

A transient window is one that isn't quite a real window (such as a pull-down menu). You can indicate to the window manager that the toplevel (for example, the pulldown menu) is related to its master (the window in which it is displayed) by using the `transient` method:

```
$mymaster = $toplevel->transient();
$toplevel->transient($master);
```

If you don't use any arguments with `transient`, it returns either the current master or an empty string.

Review

It is a good idea to use another toplevel widget instead of the MainWindow if there is too much information to fit in one window. Using toplevels to group information is also sometimes a good idea. When to use an additional toplevel is a design decision that you'll have to make. You don't want to have too many windows for the user to navigate, but a well-designed application might be able to make use of one or two. For instance, the Tk module comes with a Tk::Dialog module that lets you easily display messages to the user. Check out the documentation included with the *Dialog.pm* file for more information on how to use it.

Fun Things to Try

Take the Dynamic Document List example from the last chapter and make it create a new toplevel every time the user hits the New Document button. (Advanced: actually create or load a file.)

14

Binding Events

Perl/Tk is an event-driven programming language. You design your program to respond to events generated by the program. Event sequences can be pushing a button, moving the mouse, or typing some characters with a keyboard. The relationship between the event sequence and the widget is called a *binding*.

Each widget provided with Perl/Tk has its own default bindings. For example, the button widget changes color when the mouse pointer is over the button and it invokes a callback that you specified when it is clicked. These are default bindings, ones that are created when you create the widget itself.

You can have your program respond to additional events by using the `bind` command to assign callbacks to different event sequences; the basic format is:

```
$widget->bind(sequence, callback);
```

In addition, you can override the default bindings by creating your own or just removing them.

The bind Method

To use the `bind` method, invoke it from the widget to which you would like to add the binding. For instance, if you want to add a binding to a button in $button, use $button->bind. In certain instances, you would use the main window of your application: `$mw->bind(...)`. There are several different sets of valid arguments you can send to `bind`. The following list explains them all:

`$widget->bind();`

> Calling `bind` with no arguments returns a list of bind sequences (e.g. `<Button-1>`, `<Key-D>`) that have been created for that widget. It will not return any of the default bindings. Here's an example:

```
$button = $mw->Button( ... )->pack;
$button->bind("<Button-3>", sub { ... } );

@bindings = $button->bind();
print "Bindings for button: @bindings\n";
# would print:
# Bindings for button: <Button-3>
```

> This function will return an empty string if there are no additional bindings for that widget.

`$widget->bind(`*sequence*`);`

> You can determine what callback is associated with a bind sequence. Pass in the bind sequence (for example, `"<Button-3>"`) as the first argument and the currently assigned callback will be returned. Expanding the preceding example, we can use the information in **@bindings** to see what callbacks are associated with them:

```
foreach (@bindings) {
  print "$_ is assigned callback ", $button->bind($_), "\n";
}
# <Button-3> is assigned callback Tk::Callback=CODE(0x91fdcc)
```

> If you send a bind sequence that doesn't exist for that widget, you'll simply get an empty string as the result. Also, if you use a sequence that is considered a default binding (for example, `"<Button-1>"` on a button widget), you'll get an empty string as well (unless you've added another binding to it with `bind`).

`$widget->bind(`*sequence, callback*`);`

> To have a callback invoked when a sequence happens, specify it after the sequence in the `bind` call. It can be any of the valid forms for callbacks discussed in Chapter 3. Here are a few examples:

```
$button->bind("<Button-3>", sub { print "Right clicked\n" });
$entry->bind("<Return>", sub { print "Hit return in entry widget\n" });
$button->bind("<Button-1>", \&b1_addtl_action());
$canvas->Tk::bind("<Button-1>", [ \&draw_rectangle, Ev("X"), Ev("Y") ]);
```

> To remove a binding for a specific sequence, send an empty string for the callback.

```
$widget->bind(tag [ , sequence, callback ] );
```

A tag is a way to refer to a widget class. You use tags if you wanted every widget of a certain type to have the same behavior. For instance, if you want a search menu to pop up when you right-click in the text widget, you can do this:

```
$t1 = $mw->Scrolled("Text")->pack(-expand => 1, -fill => 'both');
$t2 = $mw->Scrolled("Text")->pack(-expand => 1, -fill => 'both');

$menu = $mw->Menu(-menuitems => [ ["command" => "Search",
                                   -command => \&search_file],
                                  ["command" => "Search Again",
                                   -command => \&search_again]
                                ],
                      -tearoff => 0);
$mw->bind(Tk::Text, "<Button-3>",
          sub { $menu->Popup(-popover => 'cursor',
                             -popanchor => "nw") });
```

Any text widgets you create inside the application would then have the search menu pop up over it. You would have to do a little work in the search routines to determine which text widget triggered the function, but you wouldn't have to recode the same bind sequence for each text widget you create.

In the preceding example, we specified the sequence ("<Button-3>") to be bound. If we didn't, we would get a list of the current callbacks associated with that event sequence.

The special tag 'all' can be used to refer to every widget and window in the application. But be careful; you'll get much more activity in your callback than you would think!

Arguments Sent to the Callback

The first argument to a callback assigned with **bind** is always a reference to the calling widget. This is true even when you bind to a widget class. You can use the reference passed in to retrieve information about the widget from which the sequence was invoked.

Here's an example of using a single entry widget:

```
$entry = $mw->Entry()->pack;
$entry->bind("<Return>", \&hit_return);
sub hit_return {
  my ($e) = @_;
  print "Entry contained: ", $e->get, "\n";
}
```

When you use **bind** to invoke a callback on an entire widget class, it makes the job of determining which widget was the subject of the event much easier:

```
$mw->Scrolled("Text")->pack(-expand => 1, -fill => 'both');
$mw->Scrolled("Text")->pack(-expand => 1, -fill => 'both');

$menu = $mw->Menu(-menuitems => [ ["command" => "Save",
                                   -command => \&save_file],
                                  ["command" => "Open",
                                   -command => \&open_file]
                                ],
                       -tearoff => 0);
$mw->bind(Tk::Text, "<Button-3>",
          sub { $menu->Popup(-popover => 'cursor') });
sub save_file {
  my ($text) = @_;
  open(FH, ">outfile") || die "Couldn't open outfile for writing";
  print FH $text->get("1.0", "end");
  close (FH);
}
```

The call to **bind** uses **Tk::Text** as the first argument. This will cause the bind to be applied to every text widget in the application. In this example, no matter which text widget is clicked, its contents will be written to **"outfile"**. The application might also prompt the user for a different filename at that point, allowing it to actually do something useful.

Defining Event Sequences

So far, you've seen several different event sequences—<Button-3>, <Button-1>, and <Return>—but I haven't yet explained the format for building them. Although the examples you've seen may seem obvious and simple, event sequences can get much more complicated.

The event sequence is built from an optional modifier, an event, and an optional detail. They are separated by dashes and then placed between angle brackets:

```
<modifier-event-detail>
```

As we discuss all the possible bindings, keep in mind that it is possible for more than one event sequence to match. The more detailed matches will invoke their callbacks first. If a binding has been created on a specific button, and then another binding is created on all of the buttons, the specific-button bind callback will be invoked first, and then the more general all-button bind callback will be invoked.

Modifiers

A modifier is an event that happens at the same time the main event happens, such as holding down the Control key and clicking the mouse. The modifying event must happen first in order for the entire event sequence to match (e.g., pressing the Control key and then pressing the mouse button).

The possible modifiers and their meanings are as follows:

Control

The Control key must be pressed down as the main event is happening (e.g., `<Control-Button-1>`).

Shift

The Shift key must be pressed down as the main event happens (e.g., `<Shift-Button-3>`).

Lock

The Caps Lock key must be pressed to turn on caps lock (e.g., `<Lock-Key-a>`).

Alt

Causes the main event to match only if either of the Alt keys is pressed down while the main event happens (e.g., `<Alt-Key-x>`).

Microsoft Windows users should be aware that sometimes MS Windows doesn't allow the event notifier to notify applications that the left Alt key has been pressed. The left Alt key is normally the Alt key people use when switching between applications by using ALT-Tab. If the left Alt key doesn't work, try the right one before giving up. This warning also applies if you are using an X Window server (e.g., Exceed) on MS Windows to access a Unix system.

Button# where # is 1, 2, 3, 4, or 5. You could also use B# as a shortcut.

These modifiers indicate that, before the rest of the event happens, the specified mouse-button number must be depressed. For instance, if you want to trigger an event when the user clicks mouse button 1 and then mouse button 3, you can use the event `<Button1-Button-3>` (or `<B1-Button-3>`). The same event would not be triggered if you clicked mouse button 3 and then mouse button 1. The events are order dependent.

It is not valid to use only `<Button#>` because, without the dash between `"Button"` and the number, you are indicating a modifier to another event type.

Double

Double is a special type of modifier that indicates the main event should happen twice. Double puts a constraint on the minimum amount of time between the repetitions of the main event. Double is most often used to indicate a double-click of a mouse button.

It is important to note that `<Double-Button-1>` is *not* equivalent to `<Button-1><Button-1>`. Although they sort of mean the same thing, there is no time constraint with the `<Button-1><Button-1>` event. The second means "You clicked button 1, and then at some later point, you clicked button 1 again." The `<Double-Button-1>` event means "You clicked button 1, and within a certain time period, you clicked button 1 again."

Triple

Similar to Double, Triple is another special modifier type. It requires that the main event occur three times in rapid succession.

Another interesting thing to consider with Double and Triple modifiers is that they are cumulative. If you click five times quickly on a button, the first click would match at `<Button-1>` event, the second click would match a `<Double-Button-1>` event, the third click would match `<Triple-Button-1>` event, and the fourth click would also match a `<Triple-Button-1>` event, and so on. This is true only if the `<Triple-Button-1>` event is defined. If only `<Double-Button-1>` is defined, the third click would reactivate that binding instead of the `<Triple >` binding. The timeline in Figure 14-1 shows when the events are generated.

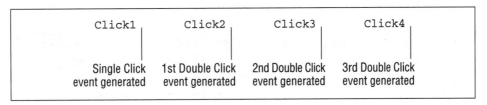

Figure 14-1. Cumulative double-clicking example

Meta (or M)

Requires that the Meta key be pressed during the main event. The Meta key is usually used on X Window Systems only.

Mod# or M#

This is also only used on X Window Systems. There are several modifiers (1–5); use `Ev('K')` to determine where they are on your keyboard.

Event Types (with Optional Details)

The event portion of the event string is the event we are looking for. It can have a modifier or not (as specified in the preceding section). When the information says an event is triggered or generated, it means that the event has happened. If there is no callback associated with the event, it will look as if nothing has actually happened. The following is a list of event types and the optional details where applicable.

ButtonPress (or Button)

A ButtonPress happens when a mouse button is pressed down. The Button event also refers to a ButtonPress; it's just a shorter way to write it. If you use the event `<Button>`, it refers to any mouse button, but you can specify a specific button by adding a detail: `<Button-1>`, `<Button-2>`, and so on.

ButtonRelease

A ButtonRelease event happens when the mouse button is released. You can have different things happen based on the button being pressed down (Button or ButtonPress) and let up (ButtonRelease). You can specify a detail to indicate a different button: `<ButtonRelease-1>`, `<ButtonRelease-2>`, and so on. If a specific button isn't specified, any button will match the event.

Circulate

The Circulate event is generated when your application has more than one window and the stacking order is switched around.

Colormap

The Colormap event happens when the colormap for the widget (usually a toplevel) has changed.

Configure

The Configure event happens when a widget is configured. If you map a callback to this one, be careful; it can be called quite often. Every time the application window is resized, each widget within the window is configured, resulting in a Configure event being generated for those widgets. When the widget is first created, it also generates a Configure event.

Destroy

When the widget is destroyed, the Destroy event is generated. You can forcefully destroy a widget by using `$widget->destroy()`.

Enter

The Enter event happens when the mouse cursor enters the area occupied by the widget. It is important to remember that this is not the "user-presses-the-RETURN/Enter-keyboard-key" event.

Expose

The Expose event happens when the window has been exposed.

FocusIn

When the widget receives the keyboard focus because the user has tabbed to it (or `$widget->focus()` happens in the program), the FocusIn event happens.

FocusOut

The FocusOut event is the opposite of FocusIn. When the keyboard focus leaves the widget, FocusOut is triggered.

Gravity

> The Gravity event happens when the widget moves because the widget's parent changed size.

KeyPress (or Key)

> When a key on the keyboard is pressed, the KeyPress (or Key) event is generated. It is possible to narrow this down to the specific key such as the "a" key by using a detail with the event: **<Key-a>**. If you want to determine which key was pressed to trigger the event, you can use **Ev('K')** as an argument with your callback:

```
$mw->bind("<Key>", [ \&check_key, Ev('K') ]);
```

> This has the effect of sending the key symbol for the key pressed as an argument to **check_key**. To find out which key symbols are for which keys, use this piece of code:

```
use Tk;
$mw = MainWindow->new;
$mw->bind("<Key>", [ sub { print "Key: $_[1]\n"; }, Ev('K')] );
MainLoop;
```

> As you press keys on the keyboard, you'll see their key symbols printed out on the screen. Notice that the shift characters above the numbers (such as $, %, ^, and so on) come out as named ("dollar," "percent," "caret," and so on).

KeyRelease

> The KeyRelease event is the companion event to KeyPress. It is invoked when the key is released. Sometimes it is preferable to wait until the key has been released before doing anything.

Leave

> The Leave event happens when the mouse cursor leaves the area occupied by the widget. Use Enter and Leave events to create two bindings for the same widget and you can do neat things such as change the mouse cursor while the mouse is in the widget (look into using **-cursor** first if it's available for that widget).

Map

> The Map event happens when window has been mapped or opened (deiconified).

Motion

> When the mouse moves around on the screen above your application, it generates a Motion event. This is another event that you don't want to bind to lightly because your callback will be triggered all the time. Granted, if you bind to just a single widget, you'll only get Motion events when you are passing over that widget, but that is still a lot of invocations of the callback. I suggest having a very good reason for binding to the Motion event.

Reparent

The Reparent event happens when parent of the bound widget has changed.

Unmap

The Unmap event happens when the bound window has been iconified.

Visibility

When a widget first becomes visible, it triggers the Visibility event. There are several ways a widget becomes visible in your application:

- When the application first starts up, and the widget is placed on the screen, it triggers a Visibility event. Note that if you create a widget and don't pack it onto the screen, a Visibility event will not be generated.

- When the widget is unpacked by using `pack('forget')` and then repacked.

- When the window is resized and the widget suddenly comes into view (usually after the window has been made smaller and then resized larger).

- When the widget is inside another widget (such as a text or canvas widget) and scrolls back on the screen.

Event Information

You can find out information about an event by using the **Ev** method. There are many values you can use in a call to **Ev**, and they are thoroughly documented on the Perl/Tk documentation web site at *http://w4.lns.cornell.edu/~pvhp/ptk/ doc/bind.htm*, which is maintained by Peter Prymmer, and *http://www.perl.com/ ptk/pod/bind.pod*. I'll cover the values that you would want to use 99.9 percent of the time. Remember that certain values used with **Ev** are only valid for certain events. If you use an **Ev** value that doesn't apply, you'll get an undefined value.

Coordinates

To determine the coordinates at which the event happened, use `Ev('x')` and `Ev('y')`. They return coordinates relative to the window in which the event happened. If you want coordinates relative to the root of your window system (desktop in Windows, Xroot in X), use uppercase X and Y: `Ev('X')` and `Ev('Y')`.

`Ev('X')` and `Ev('Y')` are valid only for ButtonPress, ButtonRelease, KeyPress, KeyRelease, or Motion events.

Button Number

To find out which button number on the mouse was pressed, use `Ev('b')`. It is valid only for ButtonPress or ButtonRelease events. If you use `Ev('b')` with a `<Button-1>` event, you would obviously get 1 back.

Height and Width

Use an `'h'` to return the height and a `'w'` to return the width associated with the event. The width and height returned indicate how large the widget is. For instance, if you want to find out the new size of a button after the window has been manually resized by the user, you can do this:

```
$button->bind("<Configure>", [ sub { print "H: $_[1], W: $_[2]\n"; },
                                Ev('h'), Ev('w') ]);
```

The callback will only be invoked when the widget has been configured. This happens when the widget is first created and any time the widget is resized.

`Ev('h')` and `Ev('w')` are valid only for Configure, Expose, and GraphicsExpose events.

Keyboard Information

There are several ways to find out which keys the user has pressed on the keyboard. Use `'K'` to print out the value associated with that key called a keysym. If you use lowercase `'k'`, you'll get the ASCII value associated with the key. Try this bit of code to see the difference:

```
$b->bind("<Key>", [ sub { print "ARGS: @_\n"; }, Ev('k'), Ev('K') ]);
```

`Ev('k')` and `Ev('K')` are valid only for KeyPress and KeyRelease events.

You can also get the keysym as a decimal number rather than a string by using `Ev('N')`.

Event Type

You can find out what type of event the callback is responding to by using `Ev('T')`. When responding to a KeyPress event, the string will be `"KeyPress"`. It's pretty obvious, but sometimes it's useful if you are using the same callback to respond to several different events.

Bailing Out of a Callback Created with bind

To stop the processing within your callback, you can use a **return** statement to return control. This will not stop any further bound callbacks from being processed. To halt the processing of any and all callbacks bound to a widget/event combination, you can use **Tk::break** instead of the milder **return**.

The bindtags Method

To find out the tags associated with a widget, use the `bindtags` method; for example:

```
print join(' ', $button->bindtags());
# prints this: Tk::Button .button . all
print join(' ', $mw->bindtags());
# prints this: MainWindow . all
```

This tells us the order in which the widget will respond to binding callbacks. The first response is always to the class that the widget belongs to; Tk::Button in the first example and MainWindow in the second.

The information returned from `bindtags` isn't nearly as interesting as what you can do with arguments sent to it. To remove all specific bindings from a widget except those that apply to `'all'`:

```
$button->bindtags(['all']);
```

Now the button will not respond to being pressed, mouse movements, or the default bindings associated with the widget. As demonstrated in the Perl/Tk web page for `bindtags`, you can reverse the order in which the widget responds to events like this:

```
$b->bindtags(['all',$b->toplevel,ref($b),$b]);
```

We already know that `'all'` means any bindings associated with the special `'all'` bindtag. Using `$b->toplevel` returns the window `$b` lives in: MainWindow=HASH(0x9798d8). Using `ref($b)` gives the package `$b` belongs to: Tk::Button. Finally, `$b` means the specific instance of `$b`: Tk::Button=HASH(0x99c0cc).

HASH(0x99c0cc) is a what we see when we print the value out. The hex number in parentheses is just the physical memory location of that widget. HASH means that it is stored in a hash structure.

Ways to Use bind

Using `bind` is a powerful way to make your application do things easily. You can add a binding to a listbox widget so it will display a menu when you right-click on it. Use `bind` with text tags to create a pseudo-html document. Add a double-click binding to the listbox so that something happens when a user double-clicks on an item in the listbox. There are more ways you can use `bind` than I could ever cover here. Just make sure you don't do anything that the user can't figure out (for example, triple-clicking while holding down the Control key is a bit obscure).

15

Composite Widgets

So far, we have only discussed each basic widget separately. The Perl/Tk distribution also includes several *composite widgets*. Composite widgets are combinations of widgets that do something specific when they are combined. Here are some examples of composite widgets:

Optionmenu

Based on menubutton widget; it allows the user to select from a list of items on the menu.

LabEntry

Based on frame widget; it is an entry widget with a configurable label.

Dialog

Based on toplevel widget; it displays a bitmap and a message to the user.

I chose these examples because they demonstrate a good point about composite widgets. They can be based on a widget (in this case, menubutton), on a frame that contains widgets, or on a toplevel widget that contains other widgets and is a complete window.

When I first started learning about composite widgets, I always felt like I was missing something. If I looked at the code out of the corner of my eye, it made sense. Yet if I looked at it head on, I was suddenly utterly confused and wasn't sure what it was doing. The important thing to remember is that there is quite a bit that goes on behind the scenes that we take advantage of when we are creating a composite widget.

My goal with this chapter isn't for you to write the most complex type of composite widget you can think of. Simply understanding how composite widgets work is more than enough. You can build up slowly from there. The best thing to do is read through this chapter and then look at the examples already included with the distribution of Perl/Tk. The composite widgets included with the Tk module are complete, have been reviewed by many different people, and will do something when you run them (plus they are usually documented with pod documentation). Rather than show a do-nothing example in this chapter, I will refer you to real code.

Looking at an Example Sideways

I admit it. I like examples. They give me a starting point to come back to when I'm getting into the nitty-gritty. Since there is quite a bit of nitty-gritty with composite widgets, we'll start simple and work up from there.

If you look at the code for these composite widgets, the LabEntry has the smallest amount of code. Here is the *LabEntry.pm* widget code:

```
# Copyright (c) 1995-1997 Nick Ing-Simmons. All rights reserved.
# This program is free software; you can redistribute it and/or
# modify it under the same terms as Perl itself.
# Class LabeledEntry

package Tk::LabEntry;
require Tk::Frame;
@ISA = qw(Tk::Frame);

Construct Tk::Widget 'LabEntry';

sub Populate
{
 require Tk::Entry;
 # LabeledEntry constructor.
 #
 my($cw, $args) = @_;
 $cw->SUPER::Populate($args);
 # Advertised subwidgets:  entry.
 my $e = $cw->Entry();
 $e->pack(-expand => 1, -fill => 'both');
 $cw->Advertise('entry' => $e);
 $cw->ConfigSpecs(DEFAULT => [$e]);
 $cw->Delegates(DEFAULT => $e);
 $cw->AddScrollbars($e) if (exists $args->{-scrollbars});
}

1;
```

That's the complete set of code, comments and all. You can tell it's a frame-based composite widget because of the line `@ISA = qw(Tk::Frame)`. We can look in *Programming Perl* (O'Reilly, 1997) to find out what the `@ISA` array is for: "Within each package a special array called `@ISA` tells Perl where else to look for a method if it can't find the method in that package." There's a lot more there about how this implements inheritance, but I wouldn't want to overuse their words just to explain a simple concept: To have your composite widget work, you need this line in your code.* All the other explanation is nitty-gritty.†

Next step—how does the entry widget come into play? We know it gets created because if we use a LabEntry, we see one on the screen. You'll notice there's only one subroutine in the whole file; that subroutine is called `Populate`. You never call it directly, but it does get called. The arguments to `Populate` are two scalars. The first is a reference to the frame itself, and the second is a reference to a hash that contains all the argument pairs you would have used to create the widget. Here's an example of creating a LabEntry widget:

```
$label_entry = $mw->LabEntry(-textvariable => \$text,
                             -label => "Enter Name:",
                             -labelPack => [ -side => 'left' ])->pack();
```

As you glance through the code, you know an entry widget is created because you see this line: `my $e = $cw->Entry()`. Then a bunch of weird stuff happens with Advertising, ConfigSpecs, and Delegates. For now let's just say that these functions allow the entry widget to behave as you would expect an entry widget to behave.

The LabEntry's label is created automatically because we use the `-label` option when we create it. If we look back to Chapter 12, *Frames*, we know that if we use the `-label` option with a frame, a label will be created for us. So what makes this a simple composite widget is that it takes advantage of the label already included with a frame widget.

Location of Files

When you create your own composite widgets, you create a file that has the same name (including capitalization) of your widget and has a *.pm* suffix. For instance, if you wanted to create a new composite widget called ListButton, you would place the code for it in a file called *ListButton.pm*.

In the code that uses your new widget, include `use ListButton` after the `use Tk` at the top of your code, assuming you keep your composite widget files (such as *ListButton.pm*) in the same directory as the rest of your application code. If not, before any `use` or `require` statements, add:

```
use lib ("dir1", "dir2");
```

pointing to whatever directory you're using for *ListButton.pm*.

---

* You really don't need to inherit from a frame, but most people do, and it makes things a little simpler because you have an automatic container for your composite widget.

† The nitty-gritty would involve tracing through all the Perl/Tk code to see what gets called where, but we don't need that level of detail here.

Creating a Composite Widget Based on Frame

There are slight differences between creating a composite widget based on a frame and creating one based on a toplevel. I will include a short example for each to give you an idea of what you can do.

Assuming you're making a composite widget called MyWidget, the first five lines you absolutely must have in your new composite widget file are:

```
package MyWidget;
require Tk::Frame;
@ISA = qw(Tk::Frame);

Construct Tk::Widget 'MyWidget';

sub Populate
{
  ...
}
```

You must declare your new widget as its own package, hence the package MyWidget line. (If you were going to have a subdirectory for your widgets, you would use DirName::MyWidget.)

The next two lines are simple: require Tk::Frame to make sure you have loaded the information necessary to use a frame widget, and then add Tk::Frame to the @ISA variable. The next line calls the Construct method from Tk::Widget (you could also write this as Tk::Widget->Construct("MyWidget")) with the name of your widget. In this call to Construct you do not add the name of the directory in which your widget resides.

By calling Construct, you create a constructor method for your new MyWidget widget. This allows you to create a new MyWidget by calling the MyWidget method:

```
$newwidget = $mw->MyWidget(...);
```

You are creating a composite widget based on a frame, so you need to use Populate to create your subwidgets and do any other necessary configuration.

Inside Populate

It is a good idea to add a require statement for any other widgets you want to create in your composite widget. In the LabEntry code, we saw a require Tk::Entry because LabEntry creates an entry widget.

`Populate` is called with two arguments: a reference to the composite widget and a reference to a hash. Assign these arguments to variables so you can use them later:

```
my ($cw, $args) = @_;
```

The next thing you should do is deal with any specific options that apply to your entire composite widget. Do this by getting them out of the `$args` hash reference and then seeing if the value was defined:

```
$option_value = delete $args->{"-flag"};
if (defined $option_value) {
  ...
}
```

Let's say you want to use the option `-filename`, which will get the value associated with the `-filename` option into `$filename`:

```
$filename = delete $args->{"-filename"};
if (defined $filename) {
  # Open file...
  ...
}
```

After dealing with all the arguments that you want to pull out directly, it is a good idea to call `SUPER::Populate` like this:

```
$cw->SUPER::Populate($args);
```

Next you should create the widgets you want in your composite widget. For instance, if you want to create a listbox with several buttons, call the appropriate methods for each one. If you want the user to be able to manipulate those widgets, you should call `Advertise` for each one.

Calling Advertise

The `Advertise` method allows you to use the **subwidget** method to get directly at that widget later on in the program. For example, after you create the LabEntry, you can get a reference to the entry widget:

```
$label_entry = $mw->LabEntry(-textvariable => \$text,
                             -label => "Enter Name:",
                             -labelPack => [ -side => 'left' ])->pack();
$entry = $label_entry->Subwidget("entry");
$entered = $entry->get();
```

When you create a composite widget remember to add another call to `Advertise` for each widget. For example, if you create an entry and a button, you'll have two calls to `Advertise`:

```
$cw->Advertise('entry' => $e);
$cw->Advertise('button' => $button);
```

Calling Delegates

When you create a composite widget, you are essentially combining two or three widgets into one. When you invoke methods on the composite widget, you have to define what methods are actually called. Do so by using the *Delegates* method and sending it a reference to the widget you want to use:

```
$cw->Delegates(DEFAULT => $e);
```

All other subwidget methods of the composite will have to be accessed by using the subwidget method and then invoking methods from there.

You can also use Delegates to call a method on a subwidget as follows:

```
$cw->Delegates('insert' => $scrolled_listbox,
               'delete' => $scrolled_listbox,
               DEFAULT => $e);
```

In this example, if the user calls $composite->insert(...), the method call will be passed along to the $scrolled_listbox->insert method. You cannot pass along any methods that your composite already defines. If your composite uses its own insert method, you would have to manually pass control to the subwidget yourself.

Calling ConfigSpecs

When you create a composite widget, you want to be able to call configure on it. You can use ConfigSpecs to do so. There are three different ways to call ConfigSpecs: create an option and a way to handle it, alias an option to another option, or specify a default widget that will handle all of the configure calls.

A simple composite widget such as LabEntry will call ConfigSpecs just to set a default widget to handle all of the configuration. It called ConfigSpecs like this:

```
$cw->ConfigSpecs(DEFAULT => [$e]);
```

Specify DEFAULT as the first parameter, and then specify an anonymous list containing the widget to use as the second parameter. This way, anytime you call configure and use the composite widget reference, you'll be configuring the entry widget.

Creating an alias

You can use ConfigSpecs to create an alias for an option, possibly to make a short and long version of the same option. If you want to use -file and -filename to mean exactly the same thing, call ConfigSpecs like this:

```
$cw->ConfigSpecs('-file' => '-filename');
```

Specify the alias first and the equivalent option second.

Defining options

To define an option and associate some action with it, call `ConfigSpecs` like this:

```
$cw->ConfigSpecs(-newoption => [ <action>, "newOption",
                                 "NewOption", <fallbackvalue> ]);
```

The option you are creating the action for is listed first, and the second argument is an anonymous list consisting of four items. The first item is the action you want to take and should be `"DESCENDANTS"`, `"ADVERTISED"`, `"SELF"`, `"CHILDREN"`, `"PASSIVE"`, `"METHOD"`, `"CALLBACK"`, or a `$reference` to a subwidget. The second and third items in the list have to do with the option database and can be left blank if you prefer. The fourth item is the default value of that option, usually `undef` or `""` or whatever you want the default value of that option to be if the user doesn't specify it.

The action part of the list defines what happens. Each possible value is defined as follows:

DESCENDANTS

> The configure for that option will be applied recursively to all descendants.

ADVERTISED

> The configure will be applied to all advertised subwidgets.

SELF

> The configure will be applied to the base widget (in this case, a frame, but the base widget can also be another composite widget).

CHILDREN

> The configure will be applied to all children.

PASSIVE

> The value will be stored in `$args`. This is the way you would use `Config-Specs` on any options that can be used at create time or by custom methods of your composite widget.

METHOD

> The method with the same name as the option will be called. For instance, if you call `$cw->ConfigSpecs(-newoption => ["METHOD", "","", undef])` and then the user uses the `-newoption` option, the method `new-option` (which you still have to define in the file somewhere) will be invoked. When you cannot define an option with one of the other settings, you can use `METHOD`.

CALLBACK

> Invokes a method inside your composite widget if that option is configured or sent when the widget is created. For instance, `$cw->ConfigSpecs(-myopt => ["CALLBACK", "myMethod", "MyMethod", undef])` would call the

subroutine myMethod when the option -myopt is used (also see *BrowseEntry.pm*'s ConfigSpecs below for an example).

$reference

Forces a call to $reference->configure(-option => value) for that option. Usually $reference is a subwidget of the composite widget (for example, an entry widget).

ConfigSpecs example

Here is the ConfigSpecs call from the Tk8.0 version of *BrowseEntry.pm*:

```
$w->ConfigSpecs(
        -listwidth    => [qw/PASSIVE  listWidth    ListWidth/,    undef],
        -listcmd      => [qw/CALLBACK listCmd      ListCmd/,      undef],
        -browsecmd    => [qw/CALLBACK browseCmd    BrowseCmd/,    undef],
        -choices      => [qw/METHOD   choices      Choices/,      undef],
        -state        => [qw/METHOD   state        State         normal/],
        -arrowimage   => [{-image => $b},qw/arrowImage ArrowImage/,undef],
        -variable     => "-textvariable",
        DEFAULT       => [$e] );
```

As you can see, you can send multiple pairs of information to ConfigSpecs. In this example, there is one PASSIVE option, two CALLBACK options, and two METHOD options. Any other calls to configure with different options will be directed to the subwidget $e. Take a look at the complete code to see what the methods pointed to in ConfigSpecs do.

Frame-Based Widget Review

Just to sum up, here's some pseudocode to show you how to create your own frame-based composite widget:

```
$package NewWidget;
@ISA = qw(Tk::Frame);
Tk::Widget->Construct('NewWidget');

sub Populate()
{
  my ($cw, $args) = @_;

  # Handle any creation only options
  my $value = delete $args->{-option};
  if (defined $value) {
    ...
  }

  # Create any subwidgets you want to...
  $widget = $cw->Widget(...);
```

```
    $cw->Delegates();
    $cw->ConfigSpecs( ... );

}

sub myoption {
    ...
}

1;
```

Toplevel-Based Composite Widgets

There is one small difference between a composite widget based on a frame instead of a toplevel. If you want to be able to use ->new() to create your window, define InitObject instead of Populate. Most of the composite widgets included with the Tk distribution do not do this, however. Look at *ColorEditor.pm* and *DialogBox.pm* for examples of how to create a toplevel-based composite widget. All the rules for using ConfigDefaults are the same.

16

Methods for Any Widget

So far, most of the chapters in this book have concentrated on specific widgets. This chapter covers the methods that apply to all widgets. You'll probably never need most of these methods, but there are a few that you'll use frequently.

Many times, you'll use a MainWindow reference (usually $mw in our examples) to call these methods, but you can also call them from other widgets, such as $button, $checkbutton, and so on. Most of the methods are informational only, meaning you pass no arguments to them; you only get a value back.

We'll use the generic $widget here instead of a specific widget type. This will help you to remember that these are multipurpose methods.

Building a Family Tree

The following methods deal with the ancestors or children of widgets and how they were created: children, name, parent, toplevel, manager, and class.

Widget's Children

To determine the children of a widget (usually a toplevel or a frame), use the children method:

```
@kids = $widget->children();
# i.e. Tk::Button=HASH(0x85e3a0) Tk::Button=HASH(0x85e4a8)
```

The list returned contains scalars that are the children of $widget. You can then use those references to perform actions such as setting a background color or font.

Name of a Widget

To determine what the parent calls the widget use the **name** method:

```
$name = $widget->name();
```

You can combine the **name** and **children** method like this:

```
@kids = $widget->children();
foreach (@kids) {
  print "Name: ", $_->name(), "\n";
}
```

Here is example output from that code:

```
button
button1
```

Parent of a Widget

To get a reference to the parent of a widget, use the **parent** method:

```
$parent = $widget->parent();
```

The Widget's Toplevel

To get the toplevel widget that contains a widget, use **toplevel**:

```
$path = $widget->toplevel();
```

The **$path** returned is a number (that is, 8606484) that you can compare to another number that was returned from another call to **toplevel** to see if they are equal.

Widget's Manager

You can find out which geometry manager $widget used by calling **manager**:

```
$manager = $widget->manager();
```

It returns a string that describes the geometry manager; for instance, if it is a toplevel widget, it will return **"grid"**, **"pack"**, **"place"**, or **"wm"**. The **manager** method doesn't seem to work correctly on Windows 95, but it works on Unix and Windows NT.

The Widget's class

The **class** method returns a string that indicates which class it belongs to. For example, $listbox->class() returns **"Listbox"**, and $menu->class() returns **"Menu"**.

Widget's ID

You can get an ID string for a widget by using the id method:

```
$id = $widget->id();
print "$id\n";
# Prints 0x9c944c
```

The value returned is a hex value. This method does not work under Windows 95.

Widget's Path

You can get the pathname of the window by calling **pathname** and using the ID you retrieved with the id method:

```
$path = $widget->pathname($id);
```

There is also the **PathName** method:

```
$path = $mw->PathName();
```

This method prints out the path of the widget that is calling it. For example, my $mw would have a **PathName** of ".".

Color-Related Methods

There are four methods that deal with color: colormapfull, rgb, cells, and depth.

Is the Colormap Full?

To determine if the colormap for the widget is full, use colormapfull:

```
$isfull = $widget->colormapfull();
```

The colormapfull method returns a 1 if the colormap is full and 0 if it is not full.

Cell Count

The number of cells in the colormap can be obtained by using the cells method:

```
$count = $widget->cells();
```

The value returned is a number indicating the number of colors; for example, 64.

Color Depth

You can get the number of bits per pixel by using the depth method:

```
$depth = $widget->depth();
# $depth might contain "16"
```

Translate to RGB Value

You can translate a color name to the red, green, and blue values by using the rgb method. Send rgb a color name (valid color names were covered in Chapter 3) and it returns a list containing three items that represent the red, green, and blue numbers.

```
($red, $green, $blue) = $widget->rgb("color");
```

Now $red, $green, and $blue each contain an integer from 0 to 255.

Setting Colors

You can have your entire application based on one color automatically by using the setPalette method:

```
$widget->setPalette(color);
```

The background color of $widget is set to the specified color, and the colors for all other widgets are calculated based on that color. So if a button's edge is a lighter color than the background, it will show up a lighter shade of whatever color you picked. This method affects the entire application even if you only call it on a widget instead of a toplevel.

You can set colors for explicit options by specifying the name and then the color to associate with it. For instance, the following code will set all foreground items in the application to red and all backgrounds to blue:

```
$b->setPalette("background" => "blue", "foreground" => "red");
```

Predefined Color Scheme

The bisque method sets the entire application to use a bisque scheme. Calling $widget->bisque() is the same as calling $widget->setPalette("bisque").

Option Databases

Under the X Window System, a file named *.Xdefaults* in the user's home directory contains configuration information for X applications, including the colors and fonts an application should use. You can create the same type of file for Win32 systems and call it whatever you want. You might use a file like this to let your users change the application's color settings.

Typically the lines in this file look something like this:

```
screen*background: yellow
screen.button.foreground:green
screen*font: {Arial} 24 {normal}
```

The first item in each line should be the name of your application unless the options are for your application only. My test application was in a file named *screen*, so that is what I used as the first keyword in each line. The second keyword (if specified) is a widget type or name (you can specify a name for any widget by adding the -name option to the creation command of that widget). The third keyword is the "class" for which you want to set a default. You can set a default value for any of the options associated with a widget. See Appendix A to find out which class is associated with each widget type.

To read in this file, call optionReadfile with the location of the file (for example, "color_options" or "C:/.Xdefaults" or ".Xdefaults"):

```
$widget->optionReadfile("filename");
```

Make sure to include a newline on the last line of this file or you'll get an error that says, "missing newline on line 2 at *C:\PERL\lib\site/Tk/Submethods.pm* line 16." This error doesn't make much sense except that the first line number it gives you matches the number of lines in the option file you are trying to read in. If you use $widget->option("readfile", ...) to call the method, you'll get a more sensible error message.

As the second argument to optionReadfile you can specify an optional priority, which should be one of "widgetDefault", "startupFile", "userDefault", or "interactive". The default priority is "interactive", which is the highest priority.

```
$widget->optionReadfile("filename", "widgetDefault");
```

You can add an option type in the program dynamically by using the optionAdd method (whether or not you have used optionReadfile):

```
$widget->optionAdd(pattern => value);
```

For example, we can change the font for the entire program like this:

```
$widget->optionAdd("screen*font", "{Arial} 24 {normal}");
```

The optionClear method should clear out any current option settings and reread the file (or retrieve them from the resource manager):

```
$widget->optionClear();
```

To determine the current setting for the value associated with a specified name and class, call optionGet:

```
$widget->optionGet(name, class);
```

The Application's Name

The name of the application that is used in the option file discussed earlier is by default the name of the file from which the script is run. You can use the **appname** method to change the name of the file:

```
$mw->appname("newname");
```

You can find out the current name of the application by calling **appname** with no arguments:

```
$name = $mw->appname();
```

Widget Existence

To determine if a widget has been created, use `Exists($widget)`:

```
if (Exists($widget)) {
    ...
}
```

Note the uppercase "E" on this method. The `Exists` method is different from the built-in Perl `exists` method. Make sure you don't confuse the two.

Is the Widget Mapped?

To find out if the widget has been mapped to the screen, use the `ismapped` method:

```
if ($widget->ismapped())
    # Do something
} else {
    # map the widget
}
```

The `ismapped` method returns 1 if the widget is currently mapped to the screen and 0 if it is not.

Converting Screen Distances

If you prefer to use inches as a screen distance but you want to print out pixels, you can use the **pixels** method to convert any valid screen distance string into a pixel value; for example:

```
$pixels = $widget->pixels("2i");    # What is 2 inches in pixels?
$pixels = $widget->pixels("2m");    # What is 2 millimeters in pixels?
```

The `pixels` method rounds to the nearest whole pixel. You can get a fractional pixel result by using `fpixels`:

```
$pixels = $widget->fpixels("2i");    # What is 2 inches in pixels?
$pixels = $widget->fpixels("2m");    # What is 2 millimeters in pixels?
```

Size of Widget

You can use the following methods to find out the size of a widget in several different ways.

Widget's Geometry

The `geometry` method returns the geometry string for the widget in the form of *widthxheight+x+y*.

```
$geom = $widget->geometry();
```

The geometry string was discussed in detail in Chapter 13. Geometry values are specified in pixels.

Requested Height

The height of the widget is returned by the `reqheight` method:

```
$height = $widget->reqheight();
```

The widget itself determines the appropriate height.

Requested Width

The width of the widget can be determined by using the `reqwidth` method:

```
$width = $widget->reqwidth();
```

Actual Width

To get the width of the widget as it currently is drawn, use the `width` method:

```
$cur_width = $widget->width();
```

When the widget is first created, `width` will return a 1 until the application has finished drawing everything. After that, it will return the actual width of the widget.

Actual Height

To get the current height, use the `height` method:

```
$h = $widget->height();
```

Just like the `width` method, `height` returns a 1 when the widget is first created. You can use the `update` or the `afterIdle` method to force everything else to happen and then call `height` or `width` to get the finished values.

Widget Position

The methods in this section all deal with the position of a widget.

Position Relative to the Root Window

To determine which widget is at the point x,y;, use the `containing` method:

```
$which = $widget->containing($x, $y);
```

The `$x` and `$y` coordinates must be relative to the root window (or on a Microsoft Windows system, the desktop). An empty string is returned if there is no widget found at those coordinates. If there are several widgets located at those coordinates, the one closest to the front is returned.

Coordinates Relative to Parent

You can get the coordinates of the upper-left corner of a widget by using the `x` and `y` methods. The coordinates they return are relative to the parent of the widget:

```
$x = $widget->x();
$y = $widget->y();
```

Coordinates Relative to Root Window

To get the coordinates relative to the root window, you can use `rootx` and `rooty` on the widget:

```
$x = $widget->rootx();
$y = $widget->rooty();
```

The coordinates refer to the upper-left corner of the widget.

Virtual Desktop Coordinates

If you have a virtual desktop, there are special methods that will give coordinates relative to the virtual desktop. Virtual desktops are very common on the X Window System (such as the *fvwm* and *tvtwm* window managers), but they exist on Microsoft Windows as well.

To determine the height and width of the virtual desktop, use the **vrootheight** and **vrootwidth** methods:

```
$height = $widget->vrootheight();
$width = $widget->vrootwidth();
```

To get the coordinates of the widget's upper-left corner relative to the virtual desktop, use **vrootx** and **vrooty**:

```
$x = $widget->vrootx();
$y = $widget->vrooty();
```

All four of these methods return an empty string if a virtual desktop is not found.

Cursor Coordinates Relative to Desktop

You can use **pointerx**, **pointery**, and **pointerxy** to determine where the user clicked on the screen in a widget:

```
$x = $widget->pointerx();
$y = $widget->pointery();
($x, $y) = $widget->pointerxy();
```

All the coordinates returned are relative to the desktop (even if it is a virtual desktop).

Screen Information

The following methods all return information based on the screen (which can be a virtual desktop or a normal desktop) and the colors of the desktop.

Screen Name

Each screen you use has a name associated with it. To get the name, use the **screen** method:

```
$name = $widget->screen();
```

The name returned will be formatted as *"displayName.screenIndex"*. My Windows 95 machine returned **":0.0"** as the screen name.

Screen Height and Width

The screen height and width is really just the resolution of the screen. Sometimes you might need information to determine how large a window can fit on a user's display. To get the height and width of the screen in pixels, use the **screenheight** and **screenwidth** methods:

```
$height = $widget->screenheight();
$width = $widget->screenwidth();
```

If my resolution is 768x1024, then `screenheight` returns 768 and `screenwidth` returns 1024. If you prefer to get the size of the screen in millimeters, then use `screenmmheight` and `screenmmwidth`:

```
$heightmm = $widget->screenmmheight();
$widthmm = $widget->screenmmwidth();
```

The same resolution, 768x1024, returns 203 millimeters as the height and 270 millimeters as the width for my monitor.

Cell Count

The number of cells in the default colormap is retrieved by using `screencells`:

```
$count = $widget->screencells();
```

My Windows 95 machine has 64 cells in its default colormap.

Screen Depth

To determine the number of bits per pixel your screen has, use the `screendepth` method:

```
$depth = $widget->screendepth();
```

The depth of my Windows 95 machine is 16 bits per pixel.

Color Type

The type of color is defined by class, and it will be `"directcolor"`, `"gray-scale"`, `"pseudocolor"`, `"staticcolor"`, `"staticgray"`, or `"truecolor"`. To determine the class for the screen that contains the widget, use `screenvisual`:

```
$type = $widget->screenvisual();
```

To determine the class of color for the widget itself, use `visual`:

```
$type = $widget->visual();
```

To find out the entire list of classes available for the current setup, use the `visualsavailable` method:

```
@list = $widget->visualsavailable
```

Each element in `@list` describes the visual and the color depth for that visual. For instance, on my Windows 95 machine, `@list` contained only one item: `"truecolor 16"`.

Server Type

The type of server is available through the **server** method:

```
$server_type = $widget->server();
```

My Windows 95 has a server type of **"Windows 4.0 67109975 Win32"**.

Is the Widget Viewable?

A widget is determined viewable if the widget and all of its ancestors are mapped. You can ask the widget itself if it is viewable by using the **viewable** method:

```
$isviewable = $widget->viewable();
```

viewable returns 1 if the widget can be viewed and 0 if not.

Atom Methods

Each widget is assigned a name, which is called an *atom*. The atom has a string name (you can get it for each widget by using the **name** method) and a 32-bit ID. These methods are used internally to handle things such as the selection mechanism.

To get the 32-bit ID for a given widget, send the **name** of the widget to the **atom** method:

```
$id = $widget->atom($widget->name());
```

You can do the opposite and use the ID to get the name of the atom back. To do so, use the **atomname** method:

```
$name = $widget->atomname($id);
```

Ringing a Bell

To make the computer beep at the user, call **bell**:

```
$widget->bell();
```

Clipboard Methods

The following methods manipulate the internal Tk clipboard and also the Windows clipboard (either Unix or Win32).

To add data to the clipboard, use the **clipboardAppend** method:

```
$widget->clipboardAppend("data to add");
```

When you call **clipboardAppend**, you can specify a format by using the **-format** option with a value. The **-format** by default is **"STRING"**, but it can also be `"ATOM"`. Another option can be specified, `-type`, which takes a string such as `"STRING"` or `"FILE_NAME"`.

To clear out the clipboard, use `clipboardClear`:

`$widget->clipboardClear();`

Any data in the clipboard will be removed.

To find out what is in the clipboard, see the `selectionGet` method in the section entitled "Getting the Selection."

Selection Methods

Some widgets allow the user to make a selection. For example, the user can make a selection in the text, entry, and listbox widgets. You can manipulate the selection by using the following methods.

Clearing the Selection

To clear the current selection from any widget (this will also clear an X selection) use `SelectionClear`:

```
$widget->SelectionClear();
```

You can specify a `-selection` option, which takes either `"PRIMARY"` or `"CLIP-BOARD"`. The default is `"PRIMARY"`. Using `"CLIPBOARD"` clears out the clipboard as well.

Getting the Selection

To determine what the current selection for the application is, use `SelectionGet`:

```
$selection = $widget->SelectionGet();
```

You can also specify the `-selection` option with the `SelectionGet` method:

```
$clipboard = $widget->SelectionGet(-selection => "CLIPBOARD");
```

The `-selection` method takes either `"PRIMARY"` or `"CLIPBOARD"`. The default is `"PRIMARY"`, so if you don't specify `-selection`, you will get back the value that represents the current selection in the application. Using `"CLIPBOARD"` will return the value in the clipboard.

Assigning a Callback

You can call `SelectionHandle` to assign a callback that will automatically be invoked when the selection associated with `$win` changes:

```
$widget->SelectionHandle($win => \&subroutine);
```

When $win owns the selection, the callback will be invoked (in this example, subroutine). You can specify the options -format, -type, and -selection with the same possible values shown in the preceding code example. If you call SelectionHandle with an empty string as the callback, the previously assigned callback is removed.

Determining Owner

You can find out which widget on the screen currently owns the selection by calling SelectionOwner (a widget owns the selection if it has something selected in it):

```
$widget = $widget->SelectionOwner();
```

You can also specify the -selection option with either "PRIMARY" or "CLIPBOARD" as the value to determine who owns the selection, or the current clipboard value, respectively.

Setting the Owner

To force a widget to own the selection, call SelectionOwn:

```
$widget->selectionOwn();
```

You can also specify which type of selection to force by using the -selection option with "PRIMARY" or "CLIPBOARD". Finally, you can specify a -command option with an associated callback that will be invoked when that widget's selection is forced away.

Destroying a Widget

You can destroy a widget by calling destroy on the widget (using if Tk::Exists is recommended):

```
$widget->destroy() if Tk::Exists($widget);
```

If the widget is a parent of any other widgets, the other widgets are destroyed as well.

Focus Methods

When your application is running, you can force a widget to have the keyboard focus by calling focus on that widget:

```
$widget->focus();
```

You might want to do this if you have an entry widget into which the user should start typing first. Calling focus right before MainLoop causes the widget to get the focus right away. If you press the Tab key, the focus automatically changes from one widget to the next (remember that you can tell when a widget has the focus by the highlight rectangle around it). There are several methods that allow you to manipulate the focus.

To make the focus follow the mouse around, use **focusFollowsMouse**:

```
$widget->focusFollowsMouse();
```

This method is buggy under both Windows 95 and Unix. A patch just recently came out for Tk8, so if you want to use this method and it isn't working, make sure you get the patch.

To find out which widget has the focus, call **focusCurrent**:

```
$who = $widget->focusCurrent();
```

To force a widget to have the focus even if the application isn't currently active, call **focusForce**:

```
$widget->focusForce();
```

This is not a nice thing to do, so try to not use it.

To find out which widget had the focus last, call **focusLast**:

```
$which = $widget->focusLast();
```

If none of the widgets in the window has the focus, the toplevel is returned.

To find out the order in which the focus will change, you can use the **focusNext** and **focusPrev** methods:

```
$nextwidget = $widget->focusNext();
$prevwidget = $widget->focusPrev();
```

Grab Methods

When a window does a "grab" it means that it holds all of the keyboard and mouse input to itself. That window will not allow any other windows in the application to receive input. There is also a global grab, which means that no applications in the entire system can get input except the one window that has done the global grab. These methods are usually called from a toplevel widget.

To do a local grab for the widget, use **grab**:

```
$widget->grab();
```

A local grab means that you can interact with other windows in the system but not with other windows in the application. To do a global grab, use **grabGlobal**:

```
$widget->grabGlobal();
```

```
$widget->grabGlobal();
```

To "ungrab", call **grabRelease**:

```
$widget->grabRelease();
```

To find out which widget has done a grab, call **grabCurrent**:

```
$who = $widget->grabCurrent();
```

To find out the current grab state of a **$widget**, call **grabStatus**:

```
$status = $widget->grabStatus();
```

The **grabStatus** method returns a string that is **"none"**, **"local"**, or **"global"**.

To find out all the windows that are currently under the influence of grab, use **grabs** to get a list back:

```
@windows = $widget->grabs();
```

Interapplication Communication

You can use the **send** command to have Perl/Tk (and even Tcl/Tk) applications communicate back and forth. The arguments include an application to talk to and the command to execute in that application.

```
$widget->send("application" => callback);
```

You can also specify the option **-async**, which will return control immediately instead of waiting for the callback to execute.

By default, your application will return an error to another application trying to communicate with it. If you want to actually receive communications from other applications, define **Tk::Receive($widget, "command")** and be very careful with what you do with the command string. Allowing any application to send unknown commands to your application can be dangerous.

When doing interapplication communication, it is a good idea to run your Perl script with the *-T* switch, which forces taint checking.

Waiting for Events to Happen

At certain points in your application, it makes sense to wait until something happens. For instance, if you create a ColorEditor window and want it to assign the color the user selects to a variable, you can use **waitVariable** to wait until the variable is set.

To have a program wait until a variable's value is changed, call **waitVariable**:

```
$widget->waitVariable(\$var);
```

Processing will continue as soon as the value contained within $var is changed to something different. To wait until a $widget is visible, use **waitVisibility**:

```
$widget->waitVisibility();
```

To wait until a widget is destroyed, call **waitWindow**:

```
$widget->waitWindow();
```

When you call these methods, nothing will happen in your program until the requested for event has taken place.

An alternative to **waitWindow** is **OnDestroy**, where you specify a callback. The widget methods are still available when you use **OnDestory**:

```
$widget->OnDestroy(sub { ... });
```

File Events

There is a special method in Perl/Tk called **fileevent**. You can use it to watch and be notified when a file is readable or writable. Here is an example snippet of code that shows how it can be used (this code is meant to be executed on a Unix system because we use the Unix **tail** command):*

```
use Tk;
open (FH, "tail -f -n 25 text_file|") || die "Could not open file!\n";
my $mw = MainWindow->new();
my $text = $mw->Scrolled("Text",
                            -width => 80,
                            -height => 25)->pack(-expand => 1);
$mw->fileevent(FH, 'readable', [\&insert_text]);
MainLoop;

sub insert_text
{
  my $curline;
  if ($curline = <FH>)
  {
    $text->insert('end', $curline);
    $text->yview('moveto', 100);
  }
  else
  {
    $mw->fileevent(FH, 'readable', "");
  }
}
```

---

* Thanks to my friend Phivu Nguyen for sharing his code with me.

This short program sits around and waits until a file is readable and then does an insert into a text box with the newly read information. You can also use 'writable'.

```
$mw->fileevent(FH, 'writable', callback);
```

If you get rid of the callback portion, the callback will be returned. Replace the callback with an empty string ("") and the callback is removed.

Parsing Command-Line Options

In the Unix world, it is standard practice to specify command-line options when you are invoking an application, especially a graphical program. Starting your program as myscript -geometry "80x40" would not be unusual. To have Perl/Tk automatically parse and apply these command-line options for you, just call Cmd-Line immediately after you create your MainWindow.

```
$mw->CmdLine();
```

In Tk4, if you want to have CmdLine stop processing command-line arguments and leave some for you to deal with, add a double dash (--) before the arguments you want it to leave for you; for instance, myscript -geometry "80x40" -- -myopt.

In Tk8, the processing of options will stop when the first unknown option is found.

Another way to deal with command-line options is to use the Perl Getopts modules. Take a look in *Programming Perl* (O'Reilly, 1997) to find out how to use the methods available in Getopts. The methods inside Getopts don't handle the options for you; it just puts them in a structure that's easier to deal with.

Time Delays

There are times when you'll want to be able to delay the program a bit before going on, or maybe you'll want to execute the same command every minute. To have the program sleep for *x* number of milliseconds, call after with the number of milliseconds:

```
$widget->after(milliseconds);
```

To specify a callback that will be called after so many milliseconds instead of waiting, send a callback as the second argument to after:

```
$id = $widget->after(milliseconds, callback);
# i.e.
$id = $widget->after(1000, \&do_something);
```

If you want to execute a subroutine after the program has been idle for a while, call `afterIdle`:

```
$id = $widget->afterIdle(callback);
```

To cancel the call to **after** or **afterIdle**, use **afterCancel** with the $id returned by **after**:

```
$widget->afterCancel($id);
# You can also do this:
$id->cancel();
```

You can have the program repeatedly call the same callback by using the **repeat** method:

```
$widget->repeat(milliseconds, callback);
# i.e.
$widget->repeat(600, \&update_status);
```

If you destroy $widget, any calls to **after** and **repeat** are automatically canceled for you.

Configuring Widgets with configure and cget

Every widget included in the Perl/Tk distribution (and some not included, but available separately) can use the **configure** and **cget** methods. No matter the widget, the arguments to these functions are the same, and the results passed back have the same format.

The **configure** method allows you to assign or change the value of an option to the widget. It can also be used to retrieve the current value of the option. The **cget** method cannot assign values, but simply retrieves them with simpler syntax than that of **configure**.

The configure Method

The basic format of the **configure** method is as follows:

```
$widget->configure( [ option => newvalue, ... ] );
```

Depending on the arguments passed to it, the **configure** method can do three things:

- Set or change the values of the options for $widget
- Get the current value of any option for $widget
- Get the current values for all of the options for $widget

To set or change the value for an option, send the option pair exactly as it would have appeared in the widget creation command:

```
$widget->configure(-option => newvalue);
```

Whatever effect the option has will take place immediately. To see the current values for a single option, send the option you are interested in as the argument. The return value depends on whether `configure` is called in list context or scalar context. In the following line, `configure` is called in list context (since its return value is being assigned to an array):

```
@info = $widget->configure(-highlightthickness);
```

In list context, an array of scalars is returned. The results of this call look like this:

```
-highlightthickness highlightThickness HighlightThickness 2 2
```

The following five values are in the returned array:

0	Option name
1	Option name from the option database (also as it would appear in the *.Xdefaults* file)
2	Class in the option database
3	Default value of the option
4	Current value of the option

Often, all you're interested in is the current value of the option. If that's the case, call `configure` in scalar context by assigning the result to a scalar:

```
$val = $widget->configure(-highlightthickness);
print "$val\n";
```

The result would be:

```
2
```

If you want to see the list of values for all of the options the widget supports, use this format:

```
@config = $widget->configure();
```

`@config` is now an array of arrays. The easiest way to print out this information is to utilize Tk::Pretty, which will do all the hard work of traversing the arrays and then put the information into a readable form:

```
use Tk;
use Tk::Pretty;

$widget = $mw->Button;

@config = $widget->configure;
print Pretty @config;
```

The result is as follows:

```
['-activebackground',activeBackground,Foreground,'#ececec','#ececec'],
['-activeforeground',activeForeground,Background,Black,Black],['-activeimage',
activeImage,ActiveImage,undef,undef],['-anchor','anchor',Anchor,'center',
'center'],['-background','background',Background,'#d9d9d9','#d9d9d9'],['-bd',
borderWidth],['-bg','background'],['-bitmap','bitmap',Bitmap,undef,undef],
['-borderwidth',borderWidth,BorderWidth,2,2],['-command','command',Command,
undef,bless([CODE(0x8189888)],Tk::Callback)],['-cursor','cursor',Cursor,
undef,undef],['-disabledforeground',disabledForeground,DisabledForeground,
'#a3a3a3','#a3a3a3'],['-fg','foreground'],['-font','font',Font,'-Adobe
-Helvetica-Bold-R-Normal--*-120-*-*-*-*-*-*','-Adobe-Helvetica-Bold-R-Normal
--*-120-*-*-*-*-*-*'],['-foreground','foreground',Foreground,Black,Black],
['-height','height',Height,0,0],['-highlightbackground',highlightBackground,
HighlightBackground,'#d9d9d9','#d9d9d9'],['-highlightcolor',highlightColor,
HighlightColor,Black,Black],['-highlightthickness',highlightThickness,
HighlightThickness,2,2],['-image','image',Image,undef,undef],['-justify',
'justify',Justify,'center','center'],['-padx',padX,Pad,3m,9],['-pady',padY,
Pad,1m,3],['-relief','relief',Relief,'raised','raised'],['-state','state',
State,'normal','normal'],['-takefocus',takeFocus,TakeFocus,undef,undef],
['-text','text',Text,undef,Do_Something],['-textvariable',textVariable,
Variable,undef,undef],['-underline','underline',Underline,-1,-1],['-width',
'width',Width,0,0],['-wraplength',wrapLength,WrapLength,0,0]
```

Although this list may look nasty and ugly, it distinguishes between the different lists of lists for you by adding the [and] characters and the commas that separates them. Usually, you would only look at this list for debugging purposes. The default values for each widget are listed at the end of this appendix.

The cget Method

Instead of using **configure** to retrieve values, you can use the **cget** method:

```
$widget->cget(-option)
```

It only returns the current value (or address if the option stores a reference) of the option rather than the entire list that **configure** returns. Think of **cget** as standing for "configuration get." Here is an example of how to use **cget**:

```
print $b->cget(-highlightthickness), "\n";
## Prints this:
2
```

Default Values for Each Widget in Table Form

The following tables contain all of the options for each standard widget (in Tk8). The five columns represent the five values returned in the arrays for each option when **configure** is used. Note that column 5, "Current Value," will probably not mean much to you, but I've included it for completeness because you'll get it back when you run the same code.

The information in the tables was created by using this code snippet (substitute the correct widget in for `Widget`):

```
$w = $mw->Widget->pack;
@config = $w->configure();
print Pretty @config;
```

Button

Option name	Xdefault's name	Class name	Default Value	Current Value
-activebackground	activeBackground	Foreground	SystemButtonFace	SystemButtonFace
-activeforeground	activeForeground	Background	SystemButtonText	SystemButtonText
-activeimage	activeImage	ActiveImage	undef	undef
-anchor	anchor	Anchor	center	center
-background	background	Background	SystemButtonFace	SystemButtonFace
-bd	borderWidth			
-bg	background			
-bitmap	bitmap	Bitmap	undef	undef
-borderwidth	borderWidth	BorderWidth	2	2
-command	command	Command	undef	undef
-cursor	cursor	Cursor	undef	undef
-default	default	Default	disabled	disabled
-disabledforeground	disabledForeground	DisabledForeground	SystemDisabledText	SystemDisabledText
-fg	foreground			
-font	font	Font	{MS Sans Serif} 8	bless({MS Sans Serif} 8 Tk::font)
-foreground	foreground	Foreground	SystemButtonText	SystemButtonText
-height	height	Height	0	0
-highlightback-ground	highlightBackground	HighlightBackground	SystemButtonFace	SystemButtonFace
-highlightcolor	highlightColor	HighlightColor	SystemWindowFrame	SystemWindowFrame
-highlightthickness	highlightThickness	HighlightThickness	1	1
-image	image	Image	undef	undef
-justify	justify	Justify	center	center

Button (continued)

Option name	.Xdefault's name	Class name	Default Value	Current Value
-padx	padx	Pad	1	1
-pady	pady	Pad	1	1
-relief	relief	Relief	raised	raised
-state	state	State	normal	normal
-takefocus	takeFocus	TakeFocus	undef	undef
-text	text	Text		
-textvariable	textVariable	Variable	undef	undef
-underline	underline	Underline	-1	-1
-width	width	Width	0	0
-wraplength	wrapLength	WrapLength	0	0

Canvas

Option name	.Xdefault's name	Class name	Default Value	Current Value
-background	background	Background	SystemButtonFace	SystemButtonFace
-bd	borderWidth			
-bg	background			
-borderwidth	borderWidth	BorderWidth	0	0
-closeenough	closeEnough	CloseEnough	1	1
-confine	confine	Confine	1	1
-cursor	cursor	Cursor	undef	undef
-height	height	Height	7c	265
-highlightback-ground	highlightBackground	HighlightBackground	SystemButtonFace	SystemButtonFace

Canvas (continued)

Option name	.Xdefault's name	Class name	Default Value	Current Value
-highlightcolor	highlightcolor	HighlightColor	SystemWindowFrame	SystemWindowFrame
-highlightthickness	highlightthickness	HighlightThickness	2	2
-insertbackground	insertBackground	Foreground	SystemButtonText	SystemButtonText
-insertborderwidth	insertBorderWidth	BorderWidth	0	0
-insertofftime	insertOffTime	OffTime	300	300
-insertontime	insertOnTime	OnTime	600	600
-insertwidth	insertWidth	InsertWidth	2	2
-relief	relief	Relief	flat	flat
-scrollregion	scrollRegion	ScrollRegion	undef	undef
-selectbackground	selectBackground	Foreground	SystemHighlight	SystemHighlight
-selectborderwidth	selectBorderWidth	BorderWidth	1	1
-selectforeground	selectForeground	Background	SystemHighlightText	SystemHighlightText
-takefocus	takeFocus	TakeFocus	undef	undef
-width	width	Width	10c	378
-xscrollcommand	xScrollCommand	ScrollCommand	undef	undef
-xscrollincrement	xScrollIncrement	ScrollIncrement	0	0
-yscrollcommand	yScrollCommand	ScrollCommand	undef	undef
-yscrollincrement	yScrollIncrement	ScrollIncrement	0	0

Checkbutton

Option name	.Xdefault's name	Class name	Default Value	Current Value
-activebackground	activeBackground	Foreground	SystemButtonFace	SystemButtonFace
-activeforeground	activeForeground	Background	SystemWindowText	SystemWindowText
-anchor	anchor	Anchor	center	center
-background	background	Background	SystemButtonFace	SystemButtonFace
-bd	borderWidth			
-bg	background			
-bitmap	bitmap	Bitmap	undef	undef
-borderwidth	borderWidth	BorderWidth	2	2
-command	command	Command	undef	undef
-cursor	cursor	Cursor	undef	undef
-disabledforeground	disabledForeground	DisabledForeground	SystemDisabledText	SystemDisabledText
-fg	foreground			
-font	font	Font	{MS Sans Serif} 8	bless({MS Sans Serif} 8 Tk::font)
-foreground	foreground	Foreground	SystemWindowText	SystemWindowText
-height	height	Height	0	0
-highlightback-ground	highlightBackground	HighlightBackground	SystemButtonFace	SystemButtonFace
-highlightcolor	highlightColor	HighlightColor	SystemWindowFrame	SystemWindowFrame
-highlightthickness	highlightThickness	HighlightThickness	1	1
-image	image	Image	undef	undef
-indicatoron	indicatorOn	IndicatorOn	1	1
-justify	justify	Justify	center	center
-offvalue	offValue	Value	0	0

Checkbutton (continued)

Option name	.Xdefault's name	Class name	Default Value	Current Value
-onvalue	onValue	Value	1	1
-padx	padx	Pad	1	1
-pady	pady	Pad	1	1
-relief	relief	Relief	flat	flat
-selectcolor	selectColor	Background	SystemWindow	SystemWindow
-selectimage	selectImage	SelectImage	undef	undef
-state	state	State	normal	normal
-takefocus	takeFocus	TakeFocus	undef	undef
-text	text	Text	undef	
-textvariable	textVariable	Variable	undef	undef
-underline	underline	Underline	-1	-1
-variable	variable	Variable	undef	undef
-width	width	Width	0	0
-wraplength	wrapLength	WrapLength	0	0

Entry

Option name	.Xdefault's name	Class name	Default Value	Current Value
-background	background	Background	SystemWindow	SystemWindow
-bd	borderWidth			
-bg	background			
-borderwidth	borderWidth	BorderWidth	2	2
-cursor	cursor	Cursor	xterm	xterm
-exportselection	exportSelection	ExportSelection	1	1

Entry *(continued)*

Option name	Xdefault's name	Class name	Default Value	Current Value
-fg	foreground			
-font	font	Font	{MS Sans Serif} 8	bless ({MS Sans Serif} 8 Tk::font)
-foreground	foreground	Foreground	SystemWindowText	SystemWindowText
-highlightback-ground	highlightBackground	HighlightBackground	SystemButtonFace	SystemButtonFace
-highlightcolor	highlightColor	HighlightColor	SystemWindowFrame	SystemWindowFrame
-highlightthickness	highlightThickness	HighlightThickness	0	0
-insertbackground	insertBackground	Foreground	SystemWindowText	SystemWindowText
-insertborderwidth	insertBorderWidth	BorderWidth	0	0
-insertofftime	insertOffTime	OffTime	300	300
-insertontime	insertOnTime	OnTime	600	600
-insertwidth	insertWidth	InsertWidth	2	2
-justify	justify	Justify	left	left
-relief	relief	Relief	sunken	sunken
-selectbackground	selectBackground	Foreground	SystemHighlight	SystemHighlight
-selectborderwidth	selectBorderWidth	BorderWidth	0	0
-selectforeground	selectForeground	Background	SystemHighlightText	SystemHighlightText
-show	show	Show	undef	undef
-state	state	State	normal	normal
-takefocus	takeFocus	TakeFocus	undef	undef
-textvariable	textVariable	Variable	undef	undef
-width	width	Width	20	20
-xscrollcommand	xScrollCommand	ScrollCommand	undef	undef

Frame

Option name	.Xdefault's name	Class name	Default Value	Current Value
-background	background	Background	SystemButtonFace	SystemButtonFace
-bd	borderWidth			
-bg	background			
-borderwidth	borderWidth	BorderWidth	0	0
-class	class	Class	Frame	Frame
-colormap	colormap	Colormap	undef	undef
-container	container	Container	0	0
-cursor	cursor	Cursor	undef	undef
-fg	foreground			
-foreground	foreground	Foreground	Black	Black
-height	height	Height	0	0
-highlightback-ground	highlightBackground	HighlightBackground	SystemButtonFace	SystemButtonFace
-highlightcolor	highlightColor	HighlightColor	SystemWindowFrame	SystemWindowFrame
-highlightthickness	highlightThickness	HighlightThickness	0	0
-label	undef	undef	undef	undef
-labelPack	undef	undef	undef	undef
-labelVariable	undef	undef	undef	undef
-relief	relief	Relief	flat	flat
-takefocus	takeFocus	TakeFocus	0	0
-visual	visual	Visual	undef	undef
-width	width	Width	0	0

Label

Option name	Xdefault's name	Class name	Default Value	Current Value
-anchor	anchor	Anchor	center	center
-background	background	Background	SystemButtonFace	SystemButtonFace
-bd	borderWidth			
-bg	background			
-bitmap	bitmap	Bitmap	undef	undef
-borderwidth	borderWidth	BorderWidth	2	2
-cursor	cursor	Cursor	undef	undef
-fg	foreground			
-font	font	Font	{MS Sans Serif} 8	bless({MS Sans Serif} 8 Tk::font)
-foreground	foreground	Foreground	SystemButtonText	SystemButtonText
-height	height	Height	0	0
-highlightback-ground	highlightBackground	HighlightBackground	SystemButtonFace	SystemButtonFace
-highlightcolor	highlightColor	HighlightColor	SystemWindowFrame	SystemWindowFrame
-highlightthickness	highlightThickness	HighlightThickness	0	0
-image	image	Image	undef	undef
-justify	justify	Justify	center	center
-padx	padx	Pad	1	1
-pady	pady	Pad	1	1
-relief	relief	Relief	flat	flat
-takefocus	takeFocus	TakeFocus	0	0
-text	text	Text	undef	undef
-textvariable	textVariable	Variable	undef	undef

Label (continued)

Option name	Xdefault's name	Class name	Default Value	Current Value
-underline	underline	Underline	-1	-1
-width	width	Width	0	0
-wraplength	wrapLength	WrapLength	0	0

Listbox

Option name	Xdefault's name	Class name	Default Value	Current Value
-background	background	Background	SystemButtonFace	SystemButtonFace
-bd	borderWidth			
-bg	background			
-borderwidth	borderWidth	BorderWidth	2	2
-cursor	cursor	Cursor	undef	undef
-exportselection	exportSelection	ExportSelection	1	1
-fg	foreground			
-font	font	Font	{MS Sans Serif} 8	bless({MS Sans Serif} 8 Tk::font)
-foreground	foreground	Foreground	SystemButtonText	SystemButtonText
-height	height	Height	10	10
-highlightbackground	highlightBackground	HighlightBackground	SystemButtonFace	SystemButtonFace
-highlightcolor	highlightColor	HighlightColor	SystemWindowFrame	SystemWindowFrame
-highlightthickness	highlightThickness	HighlightThickness	1	1
-relief	relief	Relief	sunken	sunken
-selectbackground	selectBackground	Foreground	SystemHighlight	SystemHighlight

Listbox *(continued)*

Option name	.Xdefault's name	Class name	Default Value	Current Value
-selectborderwidth	selectBorderWidth	BorderWidth	1	1
-selectforeground	selectForeground	Background	SystemHighlightText	SystemHighlightText
-selectmode	selectMode	SelectMode	browse	browse
-setgrid	setGrid	SetGrid	0	0
-takefocus	takeFocus	TakeFocus	undef	undef
-width	width	Width	20	20
-xscrollcommand	xScrollCommand	ScrollCommand	undef	undef
-yscrollcommand	yScrollCommand	ScrollCommand	undef	undef

Menu

Option name	.Xdefault's name	Class name	Default Value	Current Value
-activebackground	activeBackground	Foreground	SystemHighlight	SystemHighlight
-activeborderwidth	activeBorderWidth	BorderWidth	1	1
-activeforeground	activeForeground	Background	SystemHighlightText	SystemHighlightText
-background	background	Background	SystemButtonFace	SystemButtonFace
-bd	borderWidth			
-bg	background			
-borderwidth	borderWidth	BorderWidth	1	1
-cursor	cursor	Cursor	arrow	arrow
-disabledforeground	disabledForeground	DisabledForeground	SystemDisabledText	SystemDisabledText
-fg	foreground			
-font	font	Font	Tim 10	bless (Tim 10 Tk::font)

Menu (continued)

Option name	.Xdefault's name	Class name	Default Value	Current Value
-foreground	foreground	Foreground	Black	Black
-overanchor	undef	undef	undef	undef
-popanchor	undef	undef	undef	undef
-popover	undef	undef	undef	undef
-postcommand	postCommand	Command	undef	undef
-relief	relief	Relief	flat	flat
-selectcolor	selectColor	Background	SystemMenuText	SystemMenuText
-takefocus	takeFocus	TakeFocus	0	0
-tearoff	tearOff	TearOff	1	1
-tearoffcommand	tearOffCommand	TearOffCommand	undef	undef
-title	title	Title	undef	undef
-type	type	Type	normal	normal

Radiobutton

Option name	.Xdefault's name	Class name	Default Value	Current Value
-activebackground	activeBackground	Foreground	SystemButtonFace	SystemButtonFace
-activeforeground	activeForeground	Background	SystemWindowText	SystemWindowText
-anchor	anchor	Anchor	center	center
-background	background	Background	SystemButtonFace	SystemButtonFace
-bd	borderWidth			
-bg	background			
-bitmap	bitmap	Bitmap	undef	undef
-borderwidth	borderWidth	BorderWidth	2	2

Radiobutton (continued)

Option name	Xdefault's name	Class name	Default Value	Current Value
-command	command	Command	undef	undef
-cursor	cursor	Cursor	undef	undef
-disabledforeground	disabledForeground	DisabledForeground	SystemDisabledText	SystemDisabledText
-fg	foreground			
-font	font	Font	{MS Sans Serif} 8	bless({MS Sans Serif} 8 Tk::font)
-foreground	foreground	Foreground	SystemWindowText	SystemWindowText
-height	height	Height	0	0
-highlightbackground	highlightBackground	HighlightBackground	SystemButtonFace	SystemButtonFace
-highlightcolor	highlightColor	HighlightColor	SystemWindowFrame	SystemWindowFrame
-highlightthickness	highlightThickness	HighlightThickness	1	1
-image	image	Image	undef	undef
-indicatoron	indicatorOn	IndicatorOn	1	1
-justify	justify	Justify	center	center
-padx	padx	Pad	1	1
-pady	pady	Pad	1	1
-relief	relief	Relief	flat	flat
-selectcolor	selectColor	Background	SystemWindow	SystemWindow
-selectimage	selectImage	SelectImage	undef	undef
-state	state	State	normal	normal
-takefocus	takeFocus	TakeFocus	undef	undef
-text	text	Text	undef	undef
-textvariable	textVariable	Variable	undef	undef

Radiobutton (continued)

Option name	.Xdefault's name	Class name	Default Value	Current Value
-underline	underline	Underline	-1	-1
-value	value	Value	undef	
-variable	variable	Variable	selectedButton	undef
-width	width	Width	0	0
-wraplength	wrapLength	WrapLength	0	0

Scale

Option name	.Xdefault's name	Class name	Default Value	Current Value
-activebackground	activebackground	Foreground	SystemButtonFace	SystemButtonFace
-background	background	Background	SystemButtonFace	SystemButtonFace
-bigincrement	bigIncrement	BigIncrement	0	0
-bd	borderWidth			
-bg	background			
-borderwidth	borderWidth	BorderWidth	2	2
-command	command	Command	undef	undef
-cursor	cursor	Cursor	undef	undef
-digits	digits	Digits	0	0
-fg	foreground			
-font	font	Font	{MS Sans Serif} 8	bless ({MS Sans Serif} 8 Tk::font)
-foreground	foreground	Foreground	SystemButtonText	SystemButtonText
-from	from	From	0	0

Scale (continued)

Option name	.Xdefault's name	Class name	Default Value	Current Value
-highlightback-ground	highlightBackground	HighlightBackground	SystemButtonFace	SystemButtonFace
-highlightcolor	highlightColor	HighlightColor	SystemWindowFrame	SystemWindowFrame
-highlightthickness	highlightThickness	HighlightThickness	2	2
-label	label	Label	undef	undef
-length	length	Length	100	100
-orient	orient	Orient	vertical	vertical
-relief	relief	Relief	flat	flat
-repeatdelay	repeatDelay	RepeatDelay	300	300
-repeatinterval	repeatInterval	RepeatInterval	100	100
-resolution	resolution	Resolution	1	1
-showvalue	showValue	ShowValue	1	1
-sliderlength	sliderLength	SliderLength	10m	38
-sliderrelief	sliderRelief	SliderRelief	raised	raised
-state	state	State	normal	normal
-takefocus	takeFocus	TakeFocus	undef	undef
-tickinterval	tickInterval	TickInterval	0	0
-to	to	To	100	100
-troughcolor	troughColor	Background	SystemScrollbar	SystemScrollbar
-variable	variable	Variable	undef	undef
-width	width	Width	5m	19

Scrollbar

Option name	.Xdefault's name	Class name	Default Value	Current Value
-activebackground	activeBackground	Foreground	SystemButtonFace	SystemButtonFace
-activerelief	activeRelief	Relief	raised	raised
-background	background	Background	SystemButtonFace	SystemButtonFace
-bd	borderwidth			
-bg	background			
-borderwidth	borderWidth	BorderWidth	0	0
-command	command	Command	undef	undef
-cursor	cursor	Cursor	undef	undef
-elementborderwidth	elementBorderWidth	BorderWidth	-1	-1
-highlightback-ground	highlightBackground	HighlightBackground	SystemButtonFace	SystemButtonFace
-highlightcolor	highlightColor	HighlightColor	SystemWindowFrame	SystemWindowFrame
-highlightthickness	highlightThickness	HighlightThickness	0	0
-jump	jump	Jump	0	0
-orient	orient	Orient	vertical	vertical
-relief	relief	Relief	sunken	sunken
-repeatdelay	repeatDelay	RepeatDelay	300	300
-repeatinterval	repeatInterval	RepeatInterval	100	100
-takefocus	takeFocus	TakeFocus	undef	undef
-troughcolor	troughColor	Background	SystemScrollbar	SystemScrollbar
-width	width	Width	13	13

Text

Option name	.Xdefault's name	Class name	Default Value	Current Value
-background	background	Background	SystemWindow	SystemWindow
-bd	borderwidth	BorderWidth		
-bg	background	Background		
-borderwidth	borderwidth	BorderWidth	2	2
-cursor	cursor	Cursor	xterm	xterm
-exportselection	exportSelection	ExportSelection	1	1
-fg	foreground	Foreground		
-font	font	Font	{MS Sans Serif} 8	bless ({MS Sans Serif} 8 Tk::font)
-foreground	foreground	Foreground	SystemWindowText	SystemWindowText
-height	height	Height	24	24
-highlightback-ground	highlightBackground	HighlightBackground	SystemButtonFace	SystemButtonFace
-highlightcolor	highlightColor	HighlightColor	SystemWindowFrame	SystemWindowFrame
-highlightthickness	highlightThickness	HighlightThickness	0	0
-insertbackground	insertBackground	Foreground	SystemWindowText	SystemWindowText
-insertborderwidth	insertBorderWidth	BorderWidth	0	0
-insertofftime	insertOffTime	OffTime	300	300
-insertontime	insertOnTime	OnTime	600	600
-insertwidth	insertWidth	InsertWidth	2	2
-padx	padX	Pad	1	1
-pady	padY	Pad	1	1
-relief	relief	Relief	sunken	sunken
-selectbackground	selectBackground	Foreground	SystemHighlight	SystemHighlight

Text (continued)

Option name	.Xdefault's name	Class name	Default Value	Current Value
-selectborderwidth	selectBorderWidth	BorderWidth	0	0
-selectforeground	selectForeground	Background	SystemHighlightText	SystemHighlightText
-setgrid	setGrid	SetGrid	0	0
-spacing1	spacing1	Spacing	0	0
-spacing2	spacing2	Spacing	0	0
-spacing3	spacing3	Spacing	0	0
-state	state	State	normal	normal
-tabs	tabs	Tabs	undef	undef
-takefocus	takeFocus	TakeFocus	undef	undef
-width	width	Width	80	80
-wrap	wrap	Wrap	char	char
-xscrollcommand	xScrollCommand	ScrollCommand	undef	undef
-yscrollcommand	yScrollCommand	ScrollCommand	undef	undef

Toplevel

Option name	.Xdefault's name	Class name	Default Value	Current Value
-background	background	Background	SystemButtonFace	SystemButtonFace
-bd	borderwidth			
-bg	background			
-borderwidth	borderwidth	BorderWidth	0	0
-class	class	Class	Toplevel	Toplevel
-colormap	colormap	Colormap	undef	undef
-container	container	Container	0	0

Toplevel (continued)

Option name	.Xdefault's name	Class name	Default Value	Current Value
-cursor	cursor	Cursor	undef	undef
-fg	foreground	Foreground		
-foreground	foreground	Foreground	Black	Black
-height	height	Height	0	0
-highlightback-ground	highlightBackground	HighlightBackground	SystemButtonFace	SystemButtonFace
-highlightcolor	highlightColor	HighlightColor	SystemWindowFrame	SystemWindowFrame
-highlightthickness	highlightThickness	HighlightThickness	0	0
-menu	menu	Menu	undef	undef
-overanchor	undef	undef	undef	undef
-popanchor	undef	undef	undef	undef
-popover	undef	undef	undef	undef
-relief	relief	Relief	flat	flat
-screen	screen	Screen	undef	undef
-takefocus	takeFocus	TakeFocus	0	0
-title	undef	undef	Toplevel	Toplevel
-use	use	Use	undef	undef
-visual	visual	Visual	undef	undef
-width	width	Width	0	0

B

Operating System Differences

Perl was originally written for Unix systems. The Tk module was meant for use with the X Window System, which is the graphical user interface associated with Unix. Since then, Perl has been ported for use on many other platforms, including Macintosh and Microsoft Windows (both 95 and NT). The same is true of the Tk module, although the ports for it followed along a bit more slowly. So now we have Perl available on all platforms and Perl/Tk available for both the X Window System (which can be emulated or run on many different platforms) and Microsoft Windows.

There are very few differences between how Perl/Tk operates on the Unix X Window System and how it operates on Microsoft Windows. Most of the differences come about because Microsoft Windows doesn't have all of the different functions that the X Window System has. Throughout this book, you may have seen references to a method that didn't work on Windows 95 or that worked differently on Windows 95. I won't be covering all those minor differences again. One big difference between Unix and Windows is how to specify fonts. Appendix C, *Fonts*, covers font specifications in detail; see that appendix for information for both Unix and Windows.

Unix

All of the methods listed in this book should work well under Unix systems. There might be subtle differences between the different flavors of Unix (such as what type of value you get back on a Solaris machine compared to the values you get back on a Linux machine), but nothing that will cause your program to crash.

All of the screen shots for this book, except where noted, were taken from a Linux system running the X Window System with Motif-style windows. The window manager I used specifically was *fvwm*, but the style of windows is similar to *mwm*. I don't cover the differences between window managers and how they change the style of the window. There are many other books available that discuss the X Window System and the window managers it uses.

Windows NT and 95

When you create a Perl/Tk window for Windows NT or Windows 95, the window comes up looking just like all your other windows do for those operating systems. For instance, it will have a small x in the upper-right corner that will kill the application. Just to the left of that x will be a small button that maximizes the window. To the left of the Maximize button is a small bar that will iconify the application. In the upper-left of the application is a small "Tk" that, if clicked, will display a menu that gives options to minimize, maximize, or close the application. These are all standard features of an MS Windows window. The same functionality is present in the X Window System version of a Tk application; it just looks a little different (see Figure B-1).

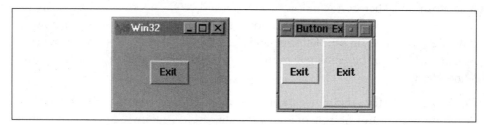

Figure B-1. A Win32 window and an X Windows window

Windows 95 Problems

I used both a Windows 95 machine and a Windows NT 4.0 (Service Pack 3) machine to test the code in this book. I did find some minor problems running applications under Windows 95. Windows NT did not seem to have the same problems, so if I had a choice between 95 and NT, I would develop and run Perl/Tk on Windows NT. Here is a list of some of the problems I ran into while I was testing Perl/Tk applications under Windows 95 (note that these are not necessarily reproducible 100% of the time; I just wanted you to be aware that I did run into some minor problems):

- I created a MainWindow with one button, resized the window, and couldn't click on the Exit button.

- The same scenario as the preceding item; clicking anywhere in the window after it was resized caused the button to be pressed.

- When I tabbed between applications, clicked in another application, and then went back to the Tk app, it didn't recognize the mouse. Clicking on the app icon in the start bar seems to fix this. (There doesn't seem to be any solid reproducible cause and effect for loss of mouse recognition.)

- The -underline option doesn't seem to work properly when I attempted to underline a letter in a menu option, so the corresponding key could be used as a keyboard shortcut.

- Some methods (most of which you wouldn't use because they are obscure) didn't return a reasonable value. These were noted throughout the book as they were discussed.

- When I clicked in a text widget to give it the keyboard focus and then clicked elsewhere, the text widget didn't give up the focus. You can use Shift-Tab to switch between widgets within the window once text has the focus, but it still doesn't seem to want to give up the focus (the cursor stays as an I bar cursor, and won't interact with the button at all).

- When I tried to display a photo as an image in a button (by using the -image option), the photo looked garbled.

Other than these minor problems, most of which probably wouldn't apply to a run-of-the-mill application, everything worked well.

Selections

In the X Window System, the user can select text by simply highlighting it. In Microsoft Windows, you have to highlight the text and put it in the clipboard by typing CTRL-C (for Copy), pasting it back with CTRL-V or the equivalent for the application you're running. Perl/Tk does not interact with the clipboard like this. There are several widgets that have an -exportselection option (such as list-box and text) and still work as indicated; if they are set to zero, however, they won't copy the selected text to the clipboard.

C

Fonts

This appendix describes how to use the new methods in Tk8.0 to create and maintain fonts. In Tk4, you could only pass a font string to `-font` option. You can still pass a font string in Tk8.0, but you can also use some methods to create your own named fonts and perform operations on them. First I'll go over the simple way to use a font string, which works in both versions. Then we'll get into the more complicated methods available with Tk8.0.

The Font String

When there is a `-font` option for a widget, you need to pass a string that indicates which font to use. There are several ways to specify a font string:

- Specify the name of a font with the `fontCreate` method (`fontCreate` is explained later in this chapter in "Font Methods").

- Use a string that describes the font and follows a predefined format (see Appendix B, *Operating System Differences*); for example, "Times 12 Normal."

- Use the name of a font that can be interpreted by the graphics display (typically a Unix system running X Windows). These strings usually have asterisks in them and are very hard for humans to comprehend.

To specify a font in a string, you first have to know which fonts are available on your system.

Determining Available Fonts

In Unix, you must specify fonts by using a long, drawn-out syntax with a lot of asterisks that represent families, size, type, and so on. In the X Window System, you can get a list of Unix fonts by running the command

```
xlsfonts > font_file
```

The file named `font_file` will now contain a huge list of fonts that you can use on your system. Be careful when picking fonts from this huge list. If you are going to be running your application from more than one system, the font you pick might not be available on all systems.

If you use Microsoft Windows, you'll have a different way of seeing what fonts are available. Click on the Start menu and select Settings → Control Panel. Once the Control Panel appears, double-click Fonts and a window similar to the one shown in Figure C-1 appears.

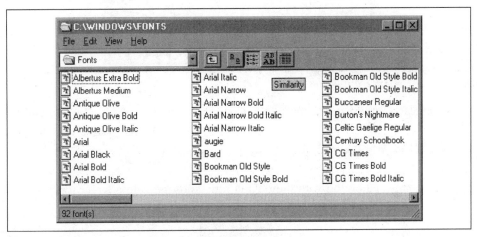

Figure C-1. The Fonts from a Windows 95 System

My system has most of the standard fonts and a few that I've downloaded over the Internet, such as augie and Bard. If I want to use these fonts I have to know how to specify them. If you double-click on a font name, another window appears and displays detailed information about the font (see Figure C-2).

The information about the font includes how much space it takes up on the hard drive (64K in this case), what version it is, and its name. It also lists the available sizes. The Arial font starts at 12 points and goes up to 72 points. To use the `-font` option to specify this font for a widget (for instance, a button), you need to know the name of the font (Arial), the size, and the type (normal, bold, or italic). With these

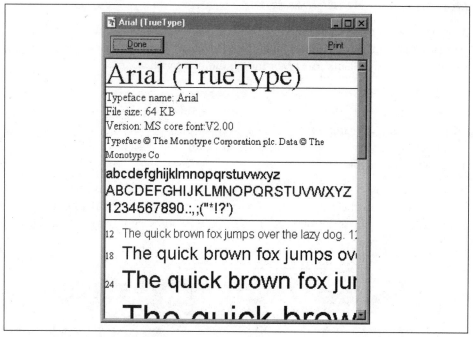

Figure C-2. The Arial font details

three pieces of information, you can build a font string: `"Arial 24 normal"`.*
That's all there is to it. To create a button with this font, use the `-font` option:

```
$mw->Button(-text => "Exit", -command => sub { exit },
            -font => "Arial 24 normal")->pack();
```

Figure C-3 shows a button with the default font, and one with a larger font.

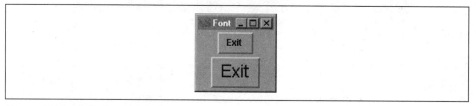

Figure C-3. A default size font button and one with Arial 24

If the name of the font has spaces in it such as Times New Roman, you still build
the string the same way:

```
-font => "Times New Roman 12 normal"
```

---

* You might also see a font specified with curly braces around the name and the style of the font (e.g.,
`"{Arial} 12 {normal}"`). The curly braces are not required.

You might see an error on the console when using this type of font specification:

```
SplitString 'Times New Roman 12 normal' at script line 7
```

You can ignore these errors, and as far as I know, there is no easy way to get rid of them. Hopefully, later versions of the Tk module will deal more gracefully with this (initial tests with Tk 8.0 show that this error no longer appears).

I don't recommend changing the font for the text on any of the standard widgets because you'll have to worry about whether the font is available. The only place you might absolutely have to change font is in the text widget, and then only if you are actually going to format the text.

One more thing: There is a Tk::Fonts module available, but it doesn't work correctly under Microsoft Windows (95 or NT). If you are using X Windows, you should play around with the Tk::Font a bit; it does have some useful features.

Font Methods

The following methods are available only with the newest version of Perl/Tk, which contains Tk8.0.

Create

The `fontCreate` method creates a new font.

```
$name = $widget->fontCreate();
$name = $widget->fontCreate(fontname);
```

You can either specify a font name or one will be generated in the format "font$X$" where X is a number. You can specify options for the font:

```
$name = $widget->fontCreate(-size => 12);
$name = $widget->fontCreate(fontname, -size => 12);
```

The options you can use to create a font are as follows:

`-family => `*name*

> The family name can be `"courier"`, `"times"`, or `"helvetica"`. If you specify one of these, the closest match on your system will be used. You can also specify the name of a font that is specific to your machine (for example, `"Moon Runes"`), but it might not show up on other systems.

`-size => `*amount*

> The amount specified for the font size indicates how big you want the font to be. If the amount is positive, the font will be sized in points. If the amount is negative, the font will be sized by using the absolute value of the amount in pixels.

```
-weight => "normal" | "bold"
```
The -weight option determines the thickness of the font.

```
-slant => "roman" | "italic"
```
The slant of the font is how far it tips over to one side. By default, "roman" means that the font is upright. Specifying "italic" as the value for -slant will tilt the font to the right slightly.

```
-underline => 0 | 1
```
If you want the characters to be underlined, specify 1 for the -underline option.

```
-overstrike => 0 | 1
```
A line is drawn through the text when -overstrike has a value of 1.

Configuring

You can change the options associated with a font by using the fontConfigure method. This method works just like a configure method does on any widget:

```
%optionsNvalues = $widget->fontConfigure(fontname);
$value = $widget->fontConfigure(fontname, -size);
$widget->fontConfigure(fontname, -size => 24); # Change size to 24
```

You can use the same options with fontCreate and fontConfigure.

Actual Information

If a specified font size is not available on the user's system, the system substitutes another font size, or even a different font altogether. You can find out which font is actually displayed by using the fontActual method. To get a list of all options and their values, call fontActual with just a font name:

```
%vals = $widget->fontActual(fontname);
```

To get the actual value for just one option:

```
$value = $widget->fontActual(fontname, -size);
```

Again, all the options used in fontCreate can be used with fontActual.

Deleting

To delete one or more fonts, use the fontDelete method:

```
$widget->fontDelete(fontname);
$widget->fontDelete(font1, font2);
```

If the font is currently being used by a widget, it will not actually be deleted until the widget isn't using it anymore. If you re-create a font by using fontCreate with the name of the original font, the widgets that use the original font will use the new font information.

Text Size

You can find out how much space a text string that uses a particular font would take by calling `fontMeasure`:

```
$pixels = $widget->fontMeasure(fontname, textstring);
```

The value returned into `$pixels` is only an estimate because characters such as `"\t"` or `"\n"` aren't expanded before the measurement is taken.

Font Metrics

Metrics are details about a font: the ascent, descent, space between lines, and whether or not the font is proportional. You can use the `fontMetrics` method to get this information about a named font. Calling `fontMetrics` with only a font name gives you all the metrics and their values for that font:

```
%values = $widget->fontMetrics(fontname);
```

You can also find out the value of a specific metric by passing it in as an option:

```
$value = $widget->fontMetrics("fontname", -ascent);
```

Note that you cannot change a font's metrics. They are calculated when the font is created.

The valid metric options are as follows:

`-ascent`
Measures the highest part of the font above the baseline. Amount returned is in pixels.

`-descent`
Measures the lowest part of the font below the baseline. Amount returned is in pixels.

`-linespace`
Measures the distance between two lines of text that use the same font. Amount returned is in pixels.

`-fixed`
Returns 1 if the font is a fixed width font (all characters take up the same amount of space, such as in Courier). Returns 0 if the font is proportional (each character takes up a different amount of space based on how fat or skinny it is; the letter "I" takes up less space than "M").

Families & Names

To find out all the font families that exist on a particular $widget's display, call
fontFamilies:

```
@families = $widget->fontFamilies();
```

To determine the names of all the fonts that are defined, call fontNames:

```
@names = $widget->fontNames();
```

Index

About the Author

Nancy Walsh is a consultant for Sybase, Inc. She spent too many years at the University of Arizona, changing majors a multitude of times and finally ending up with a B.S. in computer science. Continuing on in life, she has worked mostly with Perl and Java in the last few years.

In the family tradition of not sitting still, Nancy has numerous hobbies, which include quilting (pieced and applique, hand and machine quilting), stained glass (anything that doesn't break yet), martial arts (she is approximately halfway to a black belt in Tae Kwon Do), amateur radio (QRP mostly), and reading (anything with words).

Colophon

Our look is the result of reader comments, our own experimentation, and feedback from distribution channels. Distinctive covers complement our distinctive approach to technical topics, breathing personality and life into potentially dry subjects.

The bird on the cover of *Learning Perl/Tk* is a juvenile emu (*Dromaius novaehollandiae*). This large, flightless bird is found throughout the Australian bush steppes. The emu is one of the largest birds in existence, second only to its cousin the ostrich. Adult emus stand about 5 feet (1.5 m) high and weigh up to 120 pounds (55 kg). The grayish-brown emu's small wings contain only six or seven feathers. They are hidden by the long, hairlike rump plumage. Emus have extremely strong legs, which they use as defensive and offensive weapons when fighting. A human limb can be broken by a kick from an emu. Their powerful legs make emus strong swimmers and fast runners; they can reach speeds of up to 50 km/hour.

Male emus, which are slightly smaller than the females, tend to the incubation of eggs and the raising of the young. An emu nest contains up to fifteen to twenty-five deep green eggs, laid by several hens. Incubation of the eggs takes from twenty-five to sixty days. The large discrepancy in incubation time occurs because the male needs to leave the nest periodically to find food and drink. The length of time he is away affects the time for incubation. Newly hatched emus weigh about 15 pounds (440 g). They are fully grown at two to three years.

The relationship between emus and Australian farmers has always been an adversarial one; three coastal subspecies of emu have been exterminated. Because emus can jump over high fences, it is difficult to keep them out of fields, where they eat and trample crops. In the arid Australian bush, emus also compete with cattle and sheep for grass and water. On the other hand, emus eat many insects that would otherwise eat crops. In 1932 Australian farmers declared war on the emus, making an all-out effort to eradicate them. Fortunately, the effort failed. The battle between emus and farmers continues to this day.

Edie Freedman designed the cover of this book, using a 19th-century engraving from the Dover Pictorial Archive. Kathleen Wilson designed the back cover and produced the cover layout with QuarkXPress 3.32, using the ITC Garamond font.

The interior design was done by Edie Freedman and modified by Nancy Priest, using the ITC Garamond Light and Garamond Book fonts. The text was prepared in FrameMaker 5.5 by Mike Sierra. The illustrations were created by Robert Romano in Adobe Photoshop 5.0 and Macromedia Freehand 8.0. Quality assurance was provided by Ellie Fountain Maden, Jeffrey Liggett, Claire Cloutier LeBlanc, and Sheryl Avruch. This colophon was written by Clairemarie Fisher O'Leary. Editorial and production services were provided by *TIPS* Technical Publishing—copyediting by Judy Flynn, composition and indexing by Karen Brown of Scriptorium Publishing Services, Inc., proofreading by Rachel Anderson of Archer Editorial, and project management by Robert Kern.

Whenever possible, our books use a durable and flexible lay-flat binding, either RepKover[TM] or Otabind[TM]. If the page count exceeds the maximum bulk possible for this type of binding, perfect binding is used.

More Titles from O'Reilly

Perl

Perl in a Nutshell

By Stephen Spainhour, Ellen Siever &
Nathan Patwardhan
1st Edition January 1999
674 pages, ISBN 1-56592-286-7

The perfect companion for working
programmers, *Perl in a Nutshell* is a
comprehensive reference guide to the
world of Perl. It contains everything you
need to know for all but the most obscure
Perl questions. This wealth of information is packed into an
efficient, extraordinarily usable format.

The Perl Cookbook

By Tom Christiansen & Nathan Torkington
1st Edition August 1998
794 pages, ISBN 1-56592-243-3

This collection of problems, solutions,
and examples for anyone programming
in Perl covers everything from beginner
questions to techniques that even the most
experienced Perl programmers might
learn from. It contains hundreds of Perl
"recipes," including recipes for parsing strings, doing matrix
multiplication, working with arrays and hashes, and performing
complex regular expressions.

Learning Perl, 2nd Edition

By Randal L. Schwartz &
Tom Christiansen,
Foreword by Larry Wall
2nd Edition July 1997
302 pages, ISBN 1-56592-284-0

In this update of a bestseller, two leading
Perl trainers teach you to use the most
universal scripting language in the age
of the World Wide Web. Now current for
Perl version 5.004, this hands-on tutorial includes a lengthy new
chapter on CGI programming, while touching also on the use of
library modules, references, and Perl's object-oriented constructs.

Learning Perl on Win32 Systems

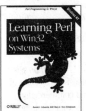

By Randal L. Schwartz, Erik Olson &
Tom Christiansen
1st Edition August 1997
306 pages, ISBN 1-56592-324-3

In this carefully paced course, leading Perl
trainers and a Windows NT practitioner
teach you to program in the language
that promises to emerge as the scripting
language of choice on NT. Based on the
"llama" book, this book features tips for PC users and new,
NT-specific examples, along with a foreword by Larry Wall, the
creator of Perl, and Dick Hardt, the creator of Perl for Win32.

Mastering Regular Expressions

By Jeffrey E. F. Friedl
1st Edition January 1997
368 pages, ISBN 1-56592-257-3

Regular expressions, a powerful tool for
manipulating text and data, are found in
scripting languages, editors, programming
environments, and pecialized tools. In
this book, author Jeffrey Friedl leads you
through the steps of crafting a regular
expression that gets the job done. He examines a variety of tools
and uses them in an extensive array of examples, with a major
focus on Perl.

Mastering Algorithms with Perl

By Jon Orwant, Jarkko Hietaniemi &
John Macdonald
1st Edition August 1999 (est.)
480 pages, ISBN 1-56592-398-7

There have been dozens of books on
programming algorithms, but never
before has there been one that uses Perl.
Whether you are an amateur programmer
or know a wide range of algorithms
in other languages, this book will teach you how to carry out
traditional programming tasks in a high-powered, efficient,
easy-to-maintain manner with Perl. Topics range in complexity
from sorting and searching to statistical algorithms, numerical
analysis, and encryption.

Perl

Perl Resource Kit—UNIX Edition

By Larry Wall, Nate Patwardhan,
Ellen Siever, David Futato &
Brian Jepson
1st Edition November 1997
1812 pages, ISBN 1-56592-370-7

The *Perl Resource Kit—UNIX Edition* gives
you the most comprehensive collection of
Perl documentation and commercially
enhanced software tools available today.
Developed in association with Larry Wall, the creator of Perl,
it's the definitive Perl distribution for webmasters, programmers,
and system administrators.

The *Perl Resource Kit* provides:

- Over 1800 pages of tutorial and in-depth reference
  documentation for Perl utilities and extensions, in 4 volumes.
- A CD-ROM containing the complete Perl distribution,
  plus hundreds of freeware Perl extensions and utilities—
  a complete snapshot of the Comprehensive Perl Archive
  Network (CPAN)—as well as new software written by Larry
  Wall just for the Kit.

Perl Software Tools All on One Convenient CD-ROM

Experienced Perl hackers know when to create their own, and
when they can find what they need on CPAN. Now all the power of
CPAN—and more—is at your fingertips. The *Perl Resource Kit*
includes:

- A complete snapshot of CPAN, with an install program for
  Solaris and Linux that ensures that all necessary modules are
  installed together. Also includes an easy-to-use search tool
  and a web-aware interface that allows you to get the latest
  version of each module.
- A new Java/Perl interface that allows programmers to write
  Java classes with Perl implementations. This new tool was
  written specially for the Kit by Larry Wall.

Experience the power of Perl modules in areas such as CGI,
web spidering, database interfaces, managing mail and USENET
news, user interfaces, security, graphics, math and statistics, and
much more.

Programming Perl, 2nd Edition

By Larry Wall, Tom Christiansen &
Randal L. Schwartz
2nd Edition September 1996
670 pages, ISBN 1-56592-149-6

Coauthored by Larry Wall, the creator of
Perl, the second edition of this authoritative
guide contains a full explanation of Perl
version 5.003 features. It covers Perl
language and syntax, functions, library
modules, references, and object-oriented features, and also explores
invocation options, debugging, common mistakes, and much more.

Perl Resource Kit—Win32 Edition

By Dick Hardt, Erik Olson,
David Futato & Brian Jepson
1st Edition August 1998
1,832 pages, Includes 4 books & CD-ROM
ISBN 1-56592-409-6

The *Perl Resource Kit—Win32 Edition* is
an essential tool for Perl programmers who
are expanding their platform expertise to
include Win32 and for Win32 webmasters
and system administrators who have discovered the power and
flexibility of Perl. The Kit contains some of the latest commercial
Win32 Perl software from Dick Hardt's ActiveState company, along
with a collection of hundreds of Perl modules that run on Win32,
and a definitive documentation set from O'Reilly.

Advanced Perl Programming

By Sriram Srinivasan
1st Edition August 1997
434 pages, ISBN 1-56592-220-4

This book covers complex techniques for
managing production-ready Perl programs
and explains methods for manipulating data
and objects that may have looked like magic
before. It gives you necessary background
for dealing with networks, databases, and
GUIs, and includes a discussion of internals to help you program
more efficiently and embed Perl within C or C within Perl.

Web Programming

CGI Programming on the World Wide Web

By Shishir Gundavaram
1st Edition March 1996
450 pages, ISBN 1-56592-168-2

This book offers a comprehensive explanation of CGI and related techniques for people who hold on to the dream of providing their own information servers on the Web. It starts at the beginning, explaining the value of CGI and how it works, then moves swiftly into the subtle details of programming.

Dynamic HTML: The Definitive Reference

By Danny Goodman
1st Edition July 1998
1088 pages, ISBN 1-56592-494-0

Dynamic HTML: The Definitive Reference is an indispensable compendium for Web content developers. It contains complete reference material for all of the HTML tags, CSS style attributes, browser document objects, and JavaScript objects supported by the various standards and the latest versions of Netscape Navigator and Microsoft Internet Explorer.

Frontier: The Definitive Guide

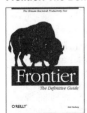

By Matt Neuburg
1st Edition February 1998
618 pages, 1-56592-383-9

This definitive guide is the first book devoted exclusively to teaching and documenting Userland Frontier, a powerful scripting environment for web site management and system level scripting. Packed with examples, advice, tricks, and tips, *Frontier: The Definitive Guide* teaches you Frontier from the ground up. Learn how to automate repetitive processes, control remote computers across a network, beef up your web site by generating hundreds of related web pages automatically, and more. Covers Frontier 4.2.3 for the Macintosh.

JavaScript: The Definitive Guide, 3rd Edition

By David Flanagan & Dan Shafer
3rd Edition June 1998
800 pages, ISBN 1-56592-392-8

This third edition of the definitive reference to JavaScript covers the latest version of the language, JavaScript 1.2, as supported by Netscape Navigator 4.0. JavaScript, which is being standardized under the name ECMAScript, is a scripting language that can be embedded directly in HTML to give web pages programming-language capabilities.

Learning VBScript

By Paul Lomax
1st Edition July 1997
616 pages, includes CD-ROM
ISBN 1-56592-247-6

This definitive guide shows web developers how to take full advantage of client-side scripting with the VBScript language. In addition to basic language features, it covers the Internet Explorer object model and discusses techniques for client-side scripting, like adding ActiveX controls to a web page or validating data before sending to the server. Includes CD-ROM with over 170 code samples.

Web Client Programming with Perl

By Clinton Wong
1st Edition March 1997
228 pages, ISBN 1-56592-214-X

Web Client Programming with Perl shows you how to extend scripting skills to the Web. This book teaches you the basics of how browsers communicate with servers and how to write your own customized web clients to automate common tasks. It is intended for those who are motivated to develop software that offers a more flexible and dynamic response than a standard web browser.

O'REILLY®

TO ORDER: **800-998-9938** • *order@oreilly.com* • *http://www.oreilly.com/*
OUR PRODUCTS ARE AVAILABLE AT A BOOKSTORE OR SOFTWARE STORE NEAR YOU.
FOR INFORMATION: **800-998-9938** • **707-829-0515** • *info@oreilly.com*

System Administration

Essential System Administration

By Æleen Frisch
2nd Edition September 1995
788 pages, ISBN 1-56592-127-5

Thoroughly revised and updated for all major versions of UNIX, this second edition of *Essential System Administration* provides a compact, manageable introduction to the tasks faced by everyone responsible for a UNIX system. Whether you use a stand-alone UNIX system, routinely provide administrative support for a larger shared system, or just want an understanding of basic administrative functions, this book is for you. Offers expanded sections on networking, electronic mail, security, and kernel configuration.

System Performance Tuning

By Mike Loukides
1st Edition November 1990
336 pages, ISBN 0-937175-60-9

System Performance Tuning answers the fundamental question: How can I get my UNIX-based computer to do more work without buying more hardware? Some performance problems do require you to buy a bigger or faster computer, but many can be solved simply by making better use of the resources you already have.

Using Samba

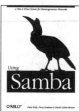

By Peter Kelly, Perry Donham &
David Collier-Brown
1st Edition July 1999 (est.)
300 pages (est.), Includes CD-ROM
ISBN 1-56592-449-5

Samba turns a UNIX or Linux system into a file and print server for Microsoft Windows network clients. This complete guide to Samba administration covers basic 2.0 configuration, security, logging, and troubleshooting. Whether you're playing on one note or a full three-octave range, this book will help you maintain an efficient and secure server. Includes a CD-ROM of sources and ready-to-install binaries.

termcap & terminfo

By John Strang, Linda Mui & Tim O'Reilly
3rd Edition April 1988
270 pages, ISBN 0-937175-22-6

For UNIX system administrators and programmers. This handbook provides information on writing and debugging terminal descriptions, as well as terminal initialization, for the two UNIX terminal databases.

Managing NFS and NIS

By Hal Stern
1st Edition June 1991
436 pages, ISBN 0-937175-75-7

Managing NFS and NIS is for system administrators who need to set up or manage a network filesystem installation. NFS (Network Filesystem) is probably running at any site that has two or more UNIX systems. NIS (Network Information System) is a distributed database used to manage a network of computers. The only practical book devoted entirely to these subjects, this guide is a "must-have" for anyone interested in UNIX networking.

Volume 8: X Window System Administrator's Guide

By Linda Mui & Eric Pearce
1st Edition October 1992
372 pages, ISBN 0-937175-83-8

This book focuses on issues of system administration for X and X-based networks —not just for UNIX system administrators, but for anyone faced with the job of administering X (including those running X on stand-alone workstations).

How to stay in touch with O'Reilly

1. Visit Our Award-Winning Web Site

http://www.oreilly.com/

★ "Top 100 Sites on the Web" —*PC Magazine*
★ "Top 5% Web sites" —*Point Communications*
★ "3-Star site" —*The McKinley Group*

Our web site contains a library of comprehensive product information (including book excerpts and tables of contents), downloadable software, background articles, interviews with technology leaders, links to relevant sites, book cover art, and more. File us in your Bookmarks or Hotlist!

2. Join Our Email Mailing Lists

New Product Releases
To receive automatic email with brief descriptions of all new O'Reilly products as they are released, send email to:
listproc@online.oreilly.com
Put the following information in the first line of your message (*not* in the Subject field):
subscribe oreilly-news

O'Reilly Events
If you'd also like us to send information about trade show events, special promotions, and other O'Reilly events, send email to:
listproc@online.oreilly.com
Put the following information in the first line of your message (*not* in the Subject field):
subscribe oreilly-events

3. Get Examples from Our Books via FTP

There are two ways to access an archive of example files from our books:

Regular FTP
- ftp to:
  ftp.oreilly.com
  (login: anonymous
  password: your email address)
- Point your web browser to:
  ftp://ftp.oreilly.com/

FTPMAIL
- Send an email message to:
  ftpmail@online.oreilly.com
  (Write "help" in the message body)

4. Contact Us via Email

order@oreilly.com
To place a book or software order online. Good for North American and international customers.

subscriptions@oreilly.com
To place an order for any of our newsletters or periodicals.

books@oreilly.com
General questions about any of our books.

software@oreilly.com
For general questions and product information about our software. Check out O'Reilly Software Online at **http://software.oreilly.com/** for software and technical support information. Registered O'Reilly software users send your questions to: **website-support@oreilly.com**

cs@oreilly.com
For answers to problems regarding your order or our products.

booktech@oreilly.com
For book content technical questions or corrections.

proposals@oreilly.com
To submit new book or software proposals to our editors and product managers.

international@oreilly.com
For information about our international distributors or translation queries. For a list of our distributors outside of North America check out:
http://www.oreilly.com/www/order/country.html

O'Reilly & Associates, Inc.
101 Morris Street, Sebastopol, CA 95472 USA
TEL   707-829-0515 or 800-998-9938
           (6am to 5pm PST)
FAX   707-829-0104

International Distributors

UK, EUROPE, MIDDLE EAST AND AFRICA (EXCEPT FRANCE, GERMANY, AUSTRIA, SWITZERLAND, LUXEMBOURG, LIECHTENSTEIN, AND EASTERN EUROPE)

INQUIRIES
O'Reilly UK Limited
4 Castle Street
Farnham
Surrey, GU9 7HS
United Kingdom
Telephone: 44-1252-711776
Fax: 44-1252-734211
Email: josette@oreilly.com

ORDERS
Wiley Distribution Services Ltd.
1 Oldlands Way
Bognor Regis
West Sussex PO22 9SA
United Kingdom
Telephone: 44-1243-779777
Fax: 44-1243-820250
Email: cs-books@wiley.co.uk

FRANCE

ORDERS
GEODIF
61, Bd Saint-Germain
75240 Paris Cedex 05, France
Tel: 33-1-44-41-46-16 (French books)
Tel: 33-1-44-41-11-87 (English books)
Fax: 33-1-44-41-11-44
Email: distribution@eyrolles.com

INQUIRIES
Éditions O'Reilly
18 rue Séguier
75006 Paris, France
Tel: 33-1-40-51-52-30
Fax: 33-1-40-51-52-31
Email: france@editions-oreilly.fr

GERMANY, SWITZERLAND, AUSTRIA, EASTERN EUROPE, LUXEMBOURG, AND LIECHTENSTEIN

INQUIRIES & ORDERS
O'Reilly Verlag
Balthasarstr. 81
D-50670 Köln
Germany
Telephone: 49-221-973160-91
Fax: 49-221-973160-8
Email: anfragen@oreilly.de (inquiries)
Email: order@oreilly.de (orders)

CANADA (FRENCH LANGUAGE BOOKS)

Les Éditions Flammarion ltée
375, Avenue Laurier Ouest
Montréal (Québec) H2V 2K3
Tel: 00-1-514-277-8807
Fax: 00-1-514-278-2085
Email: info@flammarion.qc.ca

HONG KONG

City Discount Subscription Service, Ltd.
Unit D, 3rd Floor, Yan's Tower
27 Wong Chuk Hang Road
Aberdeen, Hong Kong
Tel: 852-2580-3539
Fax: 852-2580-6463
Email: citydis@ppn.com.hk

KOREA

Hanbit Media, Inc.
Sonyoung Bldg. 202
Yeksam-dong 736-36
Kangnam-ku
Seoul, Korea
Tel: 822-554-9610
Fax: 822-556-0363
Email: hant93@chollian.dacom.co.kr

PHILIPPINES

Mutual Books, Inc.
429-D Shaw Boulevard
Mandaluyong City, Metro
Manila, Philippines
Tel: 632-725-7538
Fax: 632-721-3056
Email: mbikikog@mnl.sequel.net

TAIWAN

O'Reilly Taiwan
No. 3, Lane 131
Hang-Chow South Road
Section 1, Taipei, Taiwan
Tel: 886-2-23968990
Fax: 886-2-23968916
Email: benh@oreilly.com

CHINA

O'Reilly Beijing
Room 2410
160, FuXingMenNeiDaJie
XiCheng District
Beijing, China PR 100031
Tel: 86-10-86631006
Fax: 86-10-86631007
Email: frederic@oreilly.com

INDIA

Computer Bookshop (India) Pvt. Ltd.
190 Dr. D.N. Road, Fort
Bombay 400 001 India
Tel: 91-22-207-0989
Fax: 91-22-262-3551
Email: cbsbom@giasbm01.vsnl.net.in

JAPAN

O'Reilly Japan, Inc.
Kiyoshige Building 2F
12-Bancho, Sanei-cho
Shinjuku-ku
Tokyo 160-0008 Japan
Tel: 81-3-3356-5227
Fax: 81-3-3356-5261
Email: japan@oreilly.com

ALL OTHER ASIAN COUNTRIES

O'Reilly & Associates, Inc.
101 Morris Street
Sebastopol, CA 95472 USA
Tel: 707-829-0515
Fax: 707-829-0104
Email: order@oreilly.com

AUSTRALIA

WoodsLane Pty., Ltd.
7/5 Vuko Place
Warriewood NSW 2102
Australia
Tel: 61-2-9970-5111
Fax: 61-2-9970-5002
Email: info@woodslane.com.au

NEW ZEALAND

Woodslane New Zealand, Ltd.
21 Cooks Street (P.O. Box 575)
Waganui, New Zealand
Tel: 64-6-347-6543
Fax: 64-6-345-4840
Email: info@woodslane.com.au

LATIN AMERICA

McGraw-Hill Interamericana
Editores, S.A. de C.V.
Cedro No. 512
Col. Atlampa
06450, Mexico, D.F.
Tel: 52-5-547-6777
Fax: 52-5-547-3336
Email: mcgraw-hill@infosel.net.mx

O'REILLY®

O'REILLY™

O'Reilly & Associates, Inc.
101 Morris Street
Sebastopol, CA 95472-9902
1-800-998-9938

Visit us online at:
http://www.ora.com/
orders@ora.com

O'REILLY WOULD LIKE TO HEAR FROM YOU

Which book did this card come from?

_____

Where did you buy this book?
❏ Bookstore   ❏ Computer Store
❏ Direct from O'Reilly   ❏ Class/seminar
❏ Bundled with hardware/software
❏ Other _____

What operating system do you use?
❏ UNIX   ❏ Macintosh
❏ Windows NT   ❏ PC(Windows/DOS)
❏ Other _____

What is your job description?
❏ System Administrator   ❏ Programmer
❏ Network Administrator   ❏ Educator/Teacher
❏ Web Developer
❏ Other _____

❏ Please send me O'Reilly's catalog, containing
a complete listing of O'Reilly books and
software.

Name _____   Company/Organization _____

Address _____

City _____ State _____ Zip/Postal Code _____ Country _____

Telephone _____   Internet or other email address (specify network) _____

Nineteenth century wood engraving
of a bear from the O'Reilly &
Associates Nutshell Handbook®
Using & Managing UUCP.

POST CARD

BUSINESS REPLY MAIL
FIRST CLASS MAIL   PERMIT NO. 80   SEBASTOPOL, CA

Postage will be paid by addressee

O'Reilly & Associates, Inc.
101 Morris Street
Sebastopol, CA 95472-9902

IIIııııIıIıııIııIıııIııIıIıIIIııIıIıIııIIııııIıIıIIıI